EARLY EDUCATION

EARLY EDUCATION

JANET B. MOTTELY

AND

ANNE R. RANDALL

Editors

Nova Science Publishers, Inc.
New York

For permission to use material from this book please contact us:
Telephone 631-231-7269; Fax 631-231-8175
Web Site: http://www.novapublishers.com

NOTICE TO THE READER

The Publisher has taken reasonable care in the preparation of this book, but makes no expressed or implied warranty of any kind and assumes no responsibility for any errors or omissions. No liability is assumed for incidental or consequential damages in connection with or arising out of information contained in this book. The Publisher shall not be liable for any special, consequential, or exemplary damages resulting, in whole or in part, from the readers' use of, or reliance upon, this material. Any parts of this book based on government reports are so indicated and copyright is claimed for those parts to the extent applicable to compilations of such works.

Independent verification should be sought for any data, advice or recommendations contained in this book. In addition, no responsibility is assumed by the publisher for any injury and/or damage to persons or property arising from any methods, products, instructions, ideas or otherwise contained in this publication.

This publication is designed to provide accurate and authoritative information with regard to the subject matter covered herein. It is sold with the clear understanding that the Publisher is not engaged in rendering legal or any other professional services. If legal or any other expert assistance is required, the services of a competent person should be sought. FROM A DECLARATION OF PARTICIPANTS JOINTLY ADOPTED BY A COMMITTEE OF THE AMERICAN BAR ASSOCIATION AND A COMMITTEE OF PUBLISHERS.

LIBRARY OF CONGRESS CATALOGING-IN-PUBLICATION DATA

Early education / Janet B. Mottely, Anne R. Randall, editors.
    p. cm.
ISBN 978-1-60456-908-7 (hardcover)
1. Early childhood education. I. Mottely, Janet B. II. Randall, Anne R.
LB1139.23.E2746 2009
372.21--dc22
                        2008038159

Published by Nova Science Publishers, Inc. New York

CONTENTS

PREFACE

This new and important book focuses on early childhood education. Infants and toddlers experience life more holistically than any other age group. Social, emotional, cognitive, language, and physical lessons are not learned separately by very young children.Adults who are most helpful to young children interact in ways that understand that the child is learning from the whole experience, not just that part of the experience to which the adult gives attention.

Although early childhood education does not have to occur in the absence of the parent or primary caregiver, this term is sometimes used to denote education by someone other than these the parent or primary caregiver. Both research in the field and early childhood educators view the parents as an integral part of the early childhood education process. Early childhood education takes many forms depending on the theoretical and educational beliefs of the educator or parent.

Chapter 1 - Previous studies suggested that teaching in early childhood settings appeared to be highly structured, highly teacher-directed with a lot of direct instructions, and teacher-initiated questions. With increasing numbers of middle-class parents sending children to kindergartens, the competence of kindergarten teachers has aroused great public concern in Hong Kong. Currently, there is rigorous effort involved in preschool improvement in HK. The present mode of early childhood educational accountability in Hong Kong has been in place since 2000. In the recent educational reforms (www.edb.gov.hk), the focus has been placed on self-evaluation and subsequent evaluation by an external body. A set of performance indicators (www.edb.gov.hk) was developed in 2000 to facilitate the reform process. However, according to the two most recently published reports by the Education Bureau Annual Report, none of the inspected kindergartens met the "excellent" standards set in the Teaching-Learning domain. ECE centres have difficulties in meeting high standards, and this deficiency affects outcomes for children. The 2007 voucher system (www.edb.gov.hk) was introduced and it includes such incentives as a teacher professional development scheme. This investment can potentially be seen as the key to quality assurance in Hong Kong. The focus of the enquiry will be strategic plans and activities undertaken by 10 preschools implementing self-assessment and school improvement. While the present system of school improvement is being implemented, and is in its initial stages, the theorizing of the characteristics and process of practice will inform its future implementation as well as preschool improvement from the cultural perspective.

Chapter 2 - A sociocultural approach to curriculum and pedagogy, promoted by New Zealand's early childhood curriculum Te Whariki emphasizes pedagogical relationships and interactions between learners and knowledgeable others. Dialogue with an adult or peer maximizes children's learning during participation in play. This chapter analyzes an excerpt of dialogue between a four-year-old child and an adult during research that aimed to explore the place of subject knowledge in early childhood curriculum and pedagogy. This interpretive case study in one kindergarten was underpinned by sociocultural theory and used qualitative data gathering techniques such as participant observation. Findings revealed that children's participation in play-based curriculum experiences provided opportunities for them to express, represent, explore, and extend their interests. These interests may be both responsive to the learning and teaching environment and reflect the social and cultural experiences that they participate in with families and communities. The dialogue is analyzed from three perspectives: sociocultural theory, community of practice, and community of inquiry. These perspectives bring to light the child's interests, experiences, knowledge building, inquiry, and emergent citizenship skills. The chapter also describes some challenges that a focus on children's interests presents for teachers in terms of curriculum and pedagogy.

Chapter 3 - Children exposed to community violence are at a greater risk of engaging in violent and aggressive activities than children who do not witness these occurrences. Typically, as antisocial behaviors increase, empathic, prosocial behaviors decrease. The current investigation examines the role of community violence in determining the level of empathy in study participants. Children from fourth, fifth, and sixth grades were given the Index of Empathy for Children and Adolescents (IECA) (Bryan, 1982) to measure levels of empathy. Statistical analyses include univariate analysis of variance and correlation analysis. Three demographic variables, gender, age, and ethnicity, were included in the analyses to determine if these variables mediate the relationship between community violence and levels of empathy. Statistical tests indicate levels of community violence in conjunction with demographic variables significantly influence the amount of empathy present in children and adolescents. Implications for educators and caregivers are examined and suggestions to bolster empathic and decrease antisocial behaviors are discussed.

Although youth violence has long been recognized as a social problem by scholars and social scientists (Whitmer, 1997), youth violence has only been of widespread public concern since the early 1990's (Howard, Flora, & Griffin, 1999). Youth violence in inner-cities, particularly gang violence (Spergel, 1992), has plagued the nation for decades. However, media and political attention were garnered when youth in middle and upper class communities began participating in violent acts (Astor, 1995). Similarly, youth aggression has markedly increased – particularly bullying (Olweus, 1994; Horne, Bartolomucci, & Newman-Carlson, 2003). Bullying is defined as intentional, repetitive negative actions that inflict physical or psychological discomfort upon the recipient (Olweus, 1991). It is estimated that 15% of children are involved in bullying activities (Olweus, 1987). Approximately 2.1 million children and adolescents bully others while 2.7 million children and adolescents are victims of bullying (Astor, 1995). Occasionally, children who are bullied retaliate with violence. In roughly 70% of school shootings since 1974, the attackers report being bullied by one or more peers prior to the incident (Fried & Fried, 2003). Violence and aggression can permeate schools, homes, and the focus of the current investigation, communities.

Children exposed to community violence typically face difficulties uncharacteristic of their counterparts who reside in non-violent areas. For example, children who witness violence in their communities are more likely to experience depression (Lambert, Ialongo, Boyd, & Cooley, 2005; Cooley-Quille, Boyd, Frantz, & Walsh, 2001), anxiety, and fear, as well as engage in violent, aggressive, deviant, and/or other antisocial behaviors (Garbarino, Dubrow, Kostelny, & Pardo, 1992; Gorman-Smith & Tolan, 1998; Herrenkohl, Hawkins, Chung, Hill, & Battin-Pearson, 2001; Patchin, Huebner, McCluskey, Varano, & Bynum, 2006; Salzinger, Ng-Mak, Feldman, Kam, & Rosario, 2006). Research further indicates children from violent neighborhoods have a higher risk of gun possession (Patchin, Huebner, McCluskey, Varano, & Bynum, 2006), suicidal thoughts or gestures, and substance use or abuse (Miller-Johnson, Lochman, Coie, Terry, & Hyman, 1998; Newman, 2000). Despite efforts to 'clean up' neighborhoods through various outreach programs, community violence persists. One major deterrent to antisocial behaviors often lacking in children from these environments is the possession of empathy.

Chapter 4 - This study examines how teachers' affective presentation of children's books influences young children's attention, participation and spontaneous participation during book reading. The hypotheses of the study are based on the premise that children are more motivated to concentrate in books presented with high affect (motivational model of affective information processing) and participate more spontaneously due to the positive affective state of the participants (cognitive model of affective information processing).

Twenty kindergarten teachers read four different types of books, two fiction (familiar/unfamiliar story format) and two information books (expository/narrative text). The language transcripts of each session were transcribed and analyzed at the level of utterance. Teachers' affect was measured by the use of voice intonation, dramatization and personal involvement reactions. From each class, the attentive behavior of eight children (four boys, four girls) was coded.

Children's attention was high, yet it was higher in fiction books compared to the information ones. Teachers' high affective presentation of the unfamiliar fiction book elicited higher concentration, compared to low affective presentation of the same book. In the familiar fiction book, children's spontaneous participation was higher when they interacted with high affect teachers compared to those with low affect. When the constituent parts of affect (intonation, dramatization and personal involvement) were related to children's behavior, we found that dramatization discouraged children's participation whereas teachers' comments of personal involvement prompted their spontaneous participation.

The outcomes are discussed in relation to the motivational and cognitive model of affective information processing while taking into consideration text genre and children's familiarity to the story format.

Chapter 5 - School-wide surveys in five middle schools were used to measure educational aspirations, attitudes toward sexual health risk behaviors and drug use, and perceptions of parental interactions and disapproval of risk behavior at baseline and one year later. Participants were male and female students of Black ($n = 222$), Hispanic ($n = 317$), White ($n = 216$), and Asian or other heritage ($n = 85$), ages 11 to 14. Analyses were performed for three factors with Cronbach's alpha coefficients ≥ 0.65 (youth's attitudes, discourse with parents, and parents' disapproval of risk behavior), and three single items inquiring about use of alcohol, use of marijuana, and sexual behavior. Generalized Linear Model (GLM) with logit link was used to evaluate the contribution of these measures at baseline as predictors of educational aspirations at the one-year follow-up. Results showed race/heritage ($p < .001$), attitudes toward health risk behaviors ($p < .01$), extent to which youth talked with parents about use of drugs and other health risk behaviors ($p < .05$), and perceptions of their parents' disapproval of risk behavior ($p < .05$) each made significant contributions in predicting educational aspirations. Gender did not contribute to the prediction of educational aspiration nor did self-report of actual risk behavior. These results indicate that youth interactions with parents regarding health risk behaviors is worthy of further exploration to develop interventions to reduce adolescent health risks and increase educational aspirations.

Chapter 6 - Educational leadership enables early childhood teachers to advocate for appropriate curriculum and practice but do teachers think they have sufficient skills to enact leadership? This study measured Teacher Leadership of 270 early childhood teachers using self-reports based on a three-aspect model involving General Leadership, Communication, and Influence, with an initial base of 71 stem-items answered in both a real and ideal mode (effectively 142 items). A Rasch measurement model analysis was used to create a 92-item, unidimensional, interval-level scale (50 items didn't fit the model and were discarded) in which the proportion of observed teacher variance considered true was 94%. Findings supported the three-aspect model of Teacher Leadership involving general leadership, communication and influence. The ideal items were 'easier' than the corresponding real items and the ideal items made a stronger contribution to leadership than the real items (54 ideal and 38 real items fitted the model). Most teachers recognised the importance of leadership skills, and were able to enact them at their schools in the three leadership areas, but there are some exceptions.

Chapter 7 - Research has shown that the Greek preschool centers have a satisfactory number of illustrated children's books available, most of which are translations. Most of these books fall in the story/fiction genre while there is a limited number of non-fiction (factual) books. Almost all educators made use of translated children's books, as they proved to be effective for their work purposes since the books deal with a wide range of topics and because they are deemed to be of high quality. Although, a small number of these translations are intentionally applied in order to bring the child into contact with other cultures, a large number of educators question their usefulness. The viewpoint, however, prevails that children all over the world have similar needs and for this reason, when foreign children's books are carefully chosen, not only they do not do any damage whatsoever but on the contrary they may be beneficial.

Chapter 8 - Learning-related skills refer to a set of skills that are necessary for the adequate acquisition of new knowledge in school and include cognitive and behavioral self-regulation. It is assumed that the behavioral regulating skills stem from the domain-general executive functions. Learning-related skills can be seen as the behavioral and social manifestation of these executive functions, such as listening and following directions, but also planning and self-control. The chapter elaborates on the possible relations between executive functions, self-regulation and academic skills.

The topic is illustrated with an empirical study, which was meant to investigate if the learning-related skills can explain part of the individual variance in preparatory mathematics skills of children attending Kindergarten. As individual differences in mathematical development in elementary school often have their origin already before formal schooling starts, this study aims at revealing the skills that are related to later mathematical learning difficulties. A total of 30 5- and 6-year old children participated in the study. Cognitive and behavioral regulation was measured, as well as the counting skills of the children.

The results of this study support our hypothesis that learning-related skills are related to academic outcomes already in Kindergarten. The different learning-related skills were indeed related to children's counting skills. The highest correlations were found between executive functions and counting, whereas behavior regulation was only marginally related to counting. Furthermore, we found that executive functions explained about half of the variance in counting. Behavioral regulation added no further prediction. The results have implications for practice as they give new directions for early screening and possible interventions for young children at-risk for learning disabilities.

Chapter 9 - The common instruction format for students with special educational needs in mathematics education is individually based instruction. We challenge this approach by guided, interactive instruction. The starting point is the student's own informal way of thinking, or in other words, their 'common sense'. This is the basis for construction, and student interaction in the classroom. The confrontation with each other's ways of thinking can stimulate students' reflection, leading to a higher level of semantization and formalization. We translate this theory into school practice by presenting an instruction format in which students are confronted with rich math problems that are embedded in a context. Working in pairs the students discuss, inquire and construct solutions. Through writing down solutions and conjectures, they have a means to communicate their ideas to their classmates and their teacher. The arising interaction, we think, is an essential element for the emergence of reflective thinking in learning mathematics.

Chapter 10 - This study provides some reasoning to support the notion that individuals with mental retardation are less likely to actively inhibit response tendencies to irrelevant information in their visual field. Inherent in this idea is the notion that selective attention processes operate differently for subjects with and without mental retardation. Selection by individuals with mental retardation only involve facilitatory processes directed at the target stimulus, whereas selection by individuals without mental retardation involve both facilitatory processes directed toward the target and inhibitory processes directed against irrelevant information. The aim of the present study was to test the suppression of irrelevant information in a non-laboratory context (testing road crossing abilities of children with and without mental retardation). The sample of the study consisted of 104 young individuals. The participants were further subdivided into four groups (n=26 per group) matched on mean mental age, using the Raven's Colored Progressive Matrices: two groups with children with mental retardation (Group A and Group B) and two groups with children without mental retardation (Group C and Group D). Group A and Group C were matched on mental age at 5.6 yr.; Group B and Group D were matched on mental age at 8.0 yr. Ability to identify safe and dangerous road–crossing sites was assessed using computer presentations. The task featured the image of a child standing at the edge of a road facing towards the road. Two tasks were designed using a number of road-crossing sites in each one: recognition task without irrelevant information (i.e., distracting visual stimuli were removed from the scene, allowing the participant to focus on the road site) and recognition task with irrelevant information (i.e., distracting visual stimuli were included in the scene, obscuring the participant to focus on the road site). Every participant was asked to select the "safe" and "unsafe" (dangerous) road-crossing sites. Results demonstrated statistically significant differences between Groups A and C and Groups B and D in task conditions, especially in those in which irrelevant information was involved. Conclusions were drawn concerning the empirical and theoretical benefits for psychology and education, which arise from the study of safety road education in children with mental retardation.

In: Early Education
Editors: J.B. Mottely and A.R. Randall

ISBN 978-1-60456-908-7
© 2009 Nova Science Publishers, Inc.

Chapter 1

EDUCATIONAL INNOVATIONS IN HONG KONG: ITS IMPLICATIONS OF POLICY CHANGE FOR EARLY CHILDHOOD DEVELOPMENT

Yuen-ling Li[*]

Department of Early Childhood Education, The Hong Kong Institute of Education,
10 LO PING ROAD, TAI PO, NEW TERRITORIES, HONG KONG

Audrey S.E. Lim

National Institute of Education, The Nanyang Technological University,
Singapore 639798

ABSTRACT

Previous studies suggested that teaching in early childhood settings appeared to be highly structured, highly teacher-directed with a lot of direct instructions, and teacher-initiated questions. With increasing numbers of middle-class parents sending children to kindergartens, the competence of kindergarten teachers has aroused great public concern in Hong Kong. Currently, there is rigorous effort involved in preschool improvement in HK. The present mode of early childhood educational accountability in Hong Kong has been in place since 2000. In the recent educational reforms (www.edb.gov.hk), the focus has been placed on self-evaluation and subsequent evaluation by an external body. A set of performance indicators (www.edb.gov.hk) was developed in 2000 to facilitate the reform process. However, according to the two most recently published reports by the Education Bureau Annual Report, none of the inspected kindergartens met the "excellent" standards set in the Teaching-Learning domain. ECE centres have difficulties in meeting high standards, and this deficiency affects outcomes for children. The 2007 voucher system (www.edb.gov.hk) was introduced and it includes such incentives as a teacher professional development scheme. This investment can potentially be seen as the

[*] (ylli@ied.edu.hk)

key to quality assurance in Hong Kong. The focus of the enquiry will be strategic plans and activities undertaken by 10 preschools implementing self-assessment and school improvement. While the present system of school improvement is being implemented, and is in its initial stages, the theorizing of the characteristics and process of practice will inform its future implementation as well as preschool improvement from the cultural perspective.

INTRODUCTION

Questions about quality early childhood education (ECE) have been the subject of international OECD studies but not much related research has been done in Hong Kong (HK). The OECD studies are important as results indicate that the early years of human development affect later learning and behaviour. Findings have led to increased investment in ECE in various countries. Currently, there are generous investments for preschool improvement in HK that have one goal in common-the improvement of instruction and student learning. One underlying assumption of these new schemes is that teachers make significant contributions to school improvement. However, few efforts have been made in HK to connect existing functions of preschool improvement to major conceptions of learning that influence teaching practice.

Education policy makers in Hong Kong have increased their efforts to implement standards-based accountability reform in early childhood education in an attempt to improve the quality of learning of children. The present mode of early childhood educational accountability in Hong Kong has been in place since 2000. In the recent educational reforms (www.edb.gov.hk), the focus has been placed on self-evaluation and subsequent evaluation by an external body. A set of performance indicators (www.edb.gov.hk), providing guidelines and standards for school improvement, was developed in 2000 to facilitate the reform process. According to the two most recently published reports by the Education Bureau Annual Report on Kindergarten Quality Assurance, none of the inspected kindergartens met the "excellent" standards set in the Teaching-Learning domain. ECE centres have difficulties in meeting high standards, and this deficiency affects outcomes for children.

Research suggests that normative structures inside preschools, such as privacy of classroom practice, isolate teachers from one another, and consequently from options for collaboration (Li, 2001b). To improve practice and quality in ECE, formation of social learning networks enables teachers to collectively consider information relevant to teaching and learning, motivate themselves and colleagues to use that information, expend effort to improve practice and build secure knowledge bases for interpreting and applying information about high quality practice (Li, 2007). The process of the interpretation and implementation of supports required to ensure quality teaching and learning is an important component for understanding school support incentives. This project will focus on explaining and identifying the key components/characteristics of development for preschools to achieve school improvement.

Gwyne and Easton (2001), using multilevel analysis of data, have identified several dimensions in the initial capacity of schools which have demonstrated rapid improvement: peer collaboration, teacher-teacher trust, and collective responsibility for student learning. Schools with such patterns of interaction and attention would be more successful at adaptation as these patterns facilitated the dissemination, selection, and interpretation of information relevant to student learning.

Although there are differences among administrative/bureaucratic accountability and legal, professional or market systems in terms of aspects of accountability, current international accountability-based interventions have one goal in common - the improvement of instruction and student learning (Adams & Kirst, 1999; O'Reilly, 1996). New systems of accountability expect schools to produce specific improvements on a self-assessment and evaluation basis (Elmore, Abelmann, & Fuhrman, 1996; Fuhrman, 1999). In addition, a mechanism for school planning, prioritising and reporting is in place to ensure that the focus is on activities directly related to student achievement and improvement strategies (O'Day, 2002). The assumption underpinning new accountability approaches is that external (e.g. government, bureaucratic and social) forces play a determining role in changing the internal workings of schools. Similar guiding values are of relevance to ECE in Hong Kong.

The 2007 voucher system (www.edb.gov.hk) includes such incentives as a professional development scheme. This scheme has the potential to bring out strong and positive interventions to raise quality through its continuing emphasis on professional learning, by which practitioners can acquire support for studying recognized Teacher Education Programmes. In addition to Teacher Education Programmes, principals can acquire support for short courses such as Curriculum Leadership and Principalship.

School incentives, such as external funding for professional learning, have been effective in promoting improvements in UK and US studies. Darling-Hammond (1996) found that a policy based on supporting schools that are 'on probation' to meet the required standards should take into consideration the following: maintaining a balance between internal and external control; providing a programme for assisting schools, including mentoring for principals; helping with school improvement plans; professional and organisational development provided by external partners; and setting improvement targets for all schools and providing rewards for those meeting or exceeding targets.

The proposed research aims to build on this previous work and to uncover the quality of teaching and learning, school support incentives, and teacher knowledge by focusing on current questions about how teachers and principals implement plans, adopt Performance Indicators, and utilize professional learning vouchers.

BACKGROUND

Currently in Hong Kong there is a high demand for quality early childhood education. The long tradition and belief is that the major provisions are privately run and thus liable to vary in quality. In 1981 initial training was introduced on a large scale for in-service kindergarten teachers and in 1998 pre-service training was introduced for a rather small cohort of students. When joining the profession, kindergarten teachers in Hong Kong may not have a strong subject knowledge or academic background. Their training then comprises short, part-time evening courses. When viewed from this perspective, the effectiveness of the preparation of Hong Kong kindergarten teachers appears to be constrained. Parents' expectations sometimes become the major concern in kindergartens' decisions about the curriculum programme. A dilemma arises when the vision of child-centred learning meets the conventional teacher-centred instruction. Staff development opportunities for in-service teachers at schools have been advocated.

Education policy makers in Hong Kong have increased their efforts to implement standards-based accountability reform in early childhood education in an attempt to improve the quality of learning of children. A set of performance indicators (www.edb.gov.hk), providing guidelines and standards for school improvement, was developed in 2000 to facilitate the reform process. According to the three most recently published reports (2004-2005, 2005-2006, 2006-2007) by the Education Bureau Annual Report on Kindergarten Quality Assurance, none of the inspected kindergartens met the "excellent" standards set in the Teaching-Learning domain. ECE centres have difficulties in meeting high standards. The voucher system has been in place in the early childhood sector since April 2007.

In Hong Kong, nearly all children attend kindergartens or nurseries (Li, 2004a) before they start primary education. There are around 9000 early childhood teachers in Hong Kong. In Hong Kong there are two types of regular daily early education and care programmes in existence – kindergartens and day nurseries. Kindergartens (around 700) were regulated by the Education Department, while day nurseries (around 300) were regulated by the Social Welfare Department before the harmonizing exercise in 2004. Up to 95% of children are receiving early childhood education (Education Commission, 1999b). Eighty –five per cent of children attend a half-day programme in kindergartens and the remaining attend day nurseries, which usually offer a full-day programme (L, 2004a; Opper, 1996). The children in Hong Kong start to attend kindergartens when they are two years old. Most kindergartens (70%) in Hong Kong were not subsidised by the Government but were privately run, while all day nurseries were subsidised by the Government before the launch of Voucher Scheme 2007. With the introduction of the Voucher Scheme 2007, kindergartens can receive subsides on the basis of the number of student in-take.

There are around 9,000 early childhood teachers in Hong Kong. In 1981 initial training was introduced for serving kindergarten teachers. However, up until 1998 kindergarten teachers received no pre-service training. New teachers with pre-service training cannot meet the demand of the job market. New teachers without pre-service training are recruited and are more liable to be absorbed into the culture of schools (Kagan, 1992). Moreover, with the launch of a large-scale in-service training programme (the Blister Programme, 1994-99), thousands of teachers received in-service training.

Most kindergarten teachers received their initial training in one of the following modes:

1. A 16-week part-time evening course (Qualified Assistant Kindergarten Teacher Education Course, QAKT) was for kindergarten teachers who did not have two passes in the HKCEE. QAKT is the title of the qualification.
2. A parallel course (Qualified Kindergarten Teacher Education Course, QKT) was conducted for kindergarten teachers with two passes in the HKCEE. QKT is the title of the qualification.
3. The Qualified Kindergarten Teacher Education Course – Conversion (QKT Conversion Course) was introduced for QAKT holders. It included a five-week summer course and a on-year part-time evening course.

The majority (estimated at over 90%) of trained kindergarten teachers are QAKT or QKT holders by 2000 (Li, 2004a).

In 1998 a small cohort of 50 students were enrolled on a pre-service Certificate of Early Childhood Education Course (CE-ECE), which was a three year full-time course. In September 2001, 150 students were enrolled on a pre-service QKT, which was a one-year full-time course. In 1995 a part-time Certificate of Kindergarten Education Course (CE-KG) for kindergarten administrators (principals and head teachers) with QKT qualifications was introduced. In July 2003, only about 10% of the early childhood educators (90% of them are principals, supervisors and head teachers) had gained the CE-KG qualification. By July 2007 about 70% of the teaching force had gained the CE-KG qualification. Starting from 2009, new appointment of kindergarten principals has to meet the requirement of holding an undergraduate degree and the completion of Principalship Training Course. Under the new Voucher Scheme, teachers, head teachers and principals furthering their studies in such courses such as CE-KG, B.Ed Program and Principalship can reimburse the tuition fees.

While undergoing in-service training, head teachers and a large number of teachers (approximately 1000 annually during the Blister Programme, and currently 700) are introduced to the 'child-centered' approach, a prevailing early childhood philosophy (Blenkin & Kelly, 1997). However, a general norm tends to be that teachers quick-fix theories into practice (Li, 2003). This results in the 'implementation gap' identified by Becher (1981).

In fact, kindergartens in Hong Kong were not subsidised by the Government before the Voucher Scheme 2007 and subsides will depend on the number of student in-take after the Voucher Scheme 2007. The success of the kindergartens is reflected to some extent by their popularity and the number of pupils enrolled every year, and therefore a curriculum is expected to be accountable to the parents. Moreover, the only strict regulation of the curricula of kindergartens is the Guide to the Pre-primary Curriculum (Curriculum Development Institute, 1996) which stipulates the ideology of child development and the practice of thematic teaching, and then the Guide to the Pre-primary Curriculum (Curriculum Development Institute, 2006) which highlights the ideas of constructivism, play and a balanced curriuclum. Kindergartens claimed that they organise contexts for children's learning across subject boundaries through themes and topics in a way that reflects the cohesiveness of learning required to meet the demands of the 'curriculum (Li & Li, 2004), and emphasised discipline in daily practice. With the introduction of the new Guide to Pre-primary Curriculum 2006, new methods are sometimes viewed as alternative ways of achieving traditionally defined goals. This is sometimes used to explain why, despite the pervasiveness of educational innovation, most forms of educational experimentation remain tied to achieving established educational objectives.

The construct of quality of instruction complements active learning time, emphasising that the quality of the teaching and learning activities is important for bringing about the desired educational outcomes. When the curriculum is so demanding, whether teachers will undermine or enhance young children's desire to learn depends on their definition of what constitutes their professional role.

Exposure of young children to some form of pre-school education is a worldwide phenomenon, although its application varies considerably across and within countries. Most educators seem to talk the same language of early childhood education (Dahlberg, Moss & Pence, 1999). Observed variations in practice are sometimes justified by claiming that differences are the result of culturally appropriate practice. However, this view does not take into account the intellectual and practical demands of implementing the ideas of early childhood education. An appreciation of the full range of teaching skills required to operate a child-centred approach might not be fully understood by novices and beginning teachers (Berliner, 1992; Galton, 1996).

Kindergarten teachers in Hong Kong are frequently blamed for not putting these early childhood education theories into practice, though they are regularly exposed to them when they go through teacher education course(s) (Li, 2004a). The current educational reform advocated by the latest Education Commission (2000) report, for example, repeatedly emphasises the need to help children with 'learning to learn.' Together with the prevailing expectation from the growing percentage of middle-class parents of giving children a good and early start academically, the competence and the role of kindergarten teachers has aroused great public concern.

Previous studies provided insight into the interactions between the teacher and child (Li, 2004b; Li, 2006c). The account of instances reflected relationships and the climate inside the classroom. Teachers, in general, displayed considerable respect and warmth towards the children by adopting a positive teacher language (Kuykendall, 1993; O'Brien, 1991; Whiren, 1988). Teaching appeared to be highly structured, highly teacher-directed with a lot of direct instructions, and teacher-initiated questions. Teachers mostly tended to ask closed questions. Directions generally involved assigning activities, monitoring students to be on task, directing discussion/teaching sessions to see that students were getting the expected answers, and providing 'corrective' feedback in response to students' errors. The emphasis appeared to be placed on successful task performance and basic skill activities. Non-verbal interactions between pupil and teachers were also observed.

In general, pupils were well informed about and happy to take part in the learning activities, although there were unsuccessful instances of facilitating children's self-expression in art, providing feedback and prompting children to answer questions. The ethos of the classroom was warm and friendly. Teachers smiled a lot. Clapping for encouragement was commonly adopted. Pupils were in a classroom context where risks and costs of failure were not regarded as high. The teacher did not name individual students who made mistakes. Class responsibility, rather than individual responsibility, made no-one feel ashamed. In all these episodes, we can discern the attempt to fashion a harmonious and supportive atmosphere inside the classroom (Li, 2004b).

In general, children helped with ancillary tasks in classrooms. Pupils appeared eager to offer help to teachers. Pupils assisted in ancillary tasks in classrooms. For example, children helped the teacher to set up equipment, helped with the tea break and with tidying up at the end of a teaching session. There were other instances when pupils spontaneously offered help to the teacher without being asked. The spirit of cooperation was enhanced when the teacher asked pupils to remind her when she got things wrong and to give her encouragement when she got things right (Li, 2006a).

Teaching appeared to be structured and directed. Teachers, seemed to be mainly guided by pre-selected activities and outcomes and by less flexible to less unexpected circumstances. In some instances, it was the teacher, not the child who expressed her viewpoint regarding the quality of the work, sometimes verbally and sometimes through actions (Li, 2006a). Some researchers suggest that novices have the tendency of concentrating on discrete events *instead of responding according to context* (Carter, Cushing, Sabers, Stein & Berliner, 1988). A management, not a facilitating, role was generally adopted. Rarely were there opportunities for give-and-take between a challenging teacher and students (Tharp & Gallimore, 1988).

Questions were generally of the closed type and sometimes required straight recall of answers or guesses of expected answers from pupils. An emphasis on adult talk was observed. Pupils in general were ready to be on task and answer questions. However, they were not empowered to own or originate own learning and they seemed to be quite passive in the learning relationship. In general, teachers rarely were able to diagnose errors in pupils' thinking process, instead tending to give hints concerning the required perceived response (Li, 2004b).

The current educational reform requires teachers to combine subject knowledge with the appropriate teaching skills in accordance with the stated objectives of the reforms or, in other words, to develop relevant pedagogical content knowledge (Shulman, 1986). A degree of cognitive dissonance (Kitchener & King, 1981; Reynolds, 1992) is needed to move practitioners in this study to a higher level of competence. If not, any suggested practice that threatens to undermine this ordered structure might be rejected. Therefore, the conceptions held by Hong Kong kindergarten teachers of competence, expertise, learning, teaching and assessment will be challenged and they will need to be reconstructed if children are to be helped in 'learning to learn'.

There is the belief that 'Mentors' working in similar contexts, who exhibit flexibility in their teaching and cope well with the curriculum constraints within the different classroom settings, would help in creating the necessary cognitive dissonance which is an essential step in bringing about changes in concerns of 'mentees' (McIntyre, 1993).

Mentoring courses and BEd Programme (Three-year, Part-time) have been in place since 2001 to address the situation. In 1998, the Pre-service Certificate of Early Childhood Teacher Education Program, a three-year full time program, was introduced in Hong Kong. From then onwards, around 60 students were enrolled annually. The increasing need for schools in which to place students during the practicum led to a new course 'Mentoring in Early Childhood Settings' which was then introduced in 2000. The goal of the course was to provide staff development opportunities for in-service teachers at schools that offered placement to the pre-service student teachers. Since its inception, 200 teachers have been enrolled in the mentoring course on a voluntary basis.

Earlier studies suggested that early childhood teachers were able to spell out the importance about providing learning opportunities for children, catering for individual differences, facilitating children's interactions with the environment and children's learning through play, and providing opportunities for children to talk (Li, 2003). However, in practice, the teachers appeared to be more concerned about their own agenda and eager to tell the children what to do. The culture of the teaching seemed to be characterised by the adoption of pre-selected activities and an emphasis on outcomes. Teachers tended to explain their practice by using time constraint as the justification. (Li, 2004a).

The mentoring course was designed to introduce mentors to ideas of teacher development, pre-lesson conferencing, classroom observation, post-lesson conferencing, and mentoring. During workshop sessions, mentors worked in groups or in peer tutoring situations prior to mentoring student teachers who were placed in their schools. In a previous study, 30 mentors consented to take part in the study, 22 mentors wrote down a record of their experience on a voluntary basis, and 8 students taking it as an elective as part of an in-service certificate program used the record as part of an assignment. All the participants, and the protégés, were female (over 99% of early childhood teachers in Hong Kong are women).

There was a tendency for the protégés to develop conceptions and practices closely resembling those of their mentors. Mentors' guidance of various strategies and techniques tended to follow a linear fashion which left little scope for the protégés' development of flexibility, creativity and initiative of style and approach. The mentor-centred approach used pays scant attention to how learning, motivation and achievement can be encouraged in every protégé as it discourages them from taking risks through experimentation or developing their own theories on the basis of critical reflection (Li, 2006b).

The 2007 voucher system (www.edb.gov.hk) was introduced and it includes such incentives as a teacher professional development scheme. This investment can potentially be seen as the key to quality assurance in Hong Kong. The focus of the enquiry will be strategic plans and activities undertaken by 10 preschools implementing self-assessment and school improvement. While the present system of school improvement is being implemented, and is in its initial stages, the theorizing of the characteristics and process of practice will inform its future implementation as well as preschool improvement from the cultural perspective.

METHOD

The proposed study will examine how early childhood practitioners cope with this new set of standards under incentive systems. The study will also question whether incentive systems promote structural/process changes to raise quality and foster the development of both teachers and children in ten preschools.

A range of qualitative and quantitative techniques (interviews, observations and surveys) were used to tap beliefs of teachers and principals in relations to teaching and learning, school improvement, the effect of performance indicators, and collect data about practice inside classrooms and schools. School's self-assessment reports, annual development plans, inspection reports, inspection annual reports were used for triangulation.

Data will be collected over a 30 month period in 4 cycles.

In the first cycle of the study, 10 preschools each will work out a school-based self-assessment report and evaluation plan. Field/classroom observation and follow-up interviews of principals/teachers will be conducted, video-taped and audio-taped. Teaching and learning activities will be video-taped for analysis of classroom quality. School self-assessment and evaluation reports within the sample preschools will be collected for analysis.

In the second cycle of the study, surveys will be administered to acquire the views of principals and teachers regarding how quality teaching and learning are interpreted and implemented in early childhood settings. Researchers will observe and video-tape discussion sessions on reviewing early childhood educator self-assessment reports and supporting evidence, examining the details of their experiences and factors that may have contributed to their 'success'. Participating schools each will write review reports, revise self-assessment reports and work out an annual improvement plan which will form part of the documentation of the project. Analysis of reports and plans will be undertaken.

In the third cycle of the study, focus group interviews with a sample of principals and teachers in preschool settings will be conducted to investigate the schools' teaching-learning processes and their measures to facilitate quality assurance. The data will be collected via audio-tape and video-tape, and undergo subsequent analysis. Principals and teachers will work out their self-evaluation reports after implementing their improvement plans for one year. Self-evaluation reports will be collected and analysed.

In the fourth cycle of the study, preschools will be visited by the research team to record their discussions on the progress of how they have/have not met the performance standards/criteria. Field/classroom observation will be carried out and recorded via videotape. Details of preschool performance and conditions will inform the researchers regarding the conceptual framework for 'high quality'. This information will be used to develop model(s) for supporting preschools to meet requirements for quality teaching and learning.

The methods outlined will examine three research questions as follows:

1. How do Hong Kong's ECE programmes interpret and implement the current system of school improvement/quality assurance/professional learning?

2. What kind of development is on?

3. What's preschool improvement from the cultural perspective, if any?

Participants (10 principals and 126 teachers) in this study used incentives for teacher development and met regularly: 1) to work out plans to review the 4 domains of Performance Indicators (2001, revised) including the school's management and organization, learning and teaching, support to children and school culture, children's development; 2) to review practice in relation to these 4 domains in the Performance Indicators, 3) to write reports on the review; 4) to revise school self-assessment reports, using the evidence collected; 5) to draft annual improvement plans; 6.) to implement improvement plans; and 7) to evaluate the extent of improvement/achievement.

FINDINGS

The Need for a New Vision

Policy makers tended to focus on relative quality by providing templates for school self-assessment reports and annual development plans (Table 1) for schools' use at the official website. Not much new vision of education has emerged in the ten participating schools (School A-J) as no one mentioned the new vision of the schools. The Education Bureau puts up templates which are to be downloaded, filled in and submitted by preschools. Though the idea of Quality Management is put down as an objective, it is not reflected in the template provided to schools.

All the ten schools put down motto of the school organization or general principles of education like "promoting children's moral, cognitive, physical, social and aesthetic development', "love, respect, diligence, and honesty" under the column of vision. The input asked is very descriptive in nature. Principals of the participating schools admitted that they tended to copy from each other to pay safe that they would not misinterpret the requirement, ensuring "fit for the purpose" and measuring up to the specification and meeting the reform needs. This may explain why school self-assessment reports were very identical and descriptive in nature. The information in the templates may facilitate the collection of evidence for relative quality of which products, services and processes of several organizations at a given time are compared, or when products or services of the same organization over different times are compared.

Table 1. School Development Plan (Template)

ABC School School Development Plan (Template) (2007-2008)
School Vision & Mission Where We Are Now Prior to school development planning, it is advisable for schools to conduct a context analysis such as SWOT analysis to identify external opportunities and threats as well as internal strengths and weaknesses. *Our Strengths* ● ● . *Our Weaknesses* ● ● *Our Opportunities* ● ● *Our Threats* ● ●

Major Concerns for 2007 – 2008 (in order of priority)

1
2
3

School Development Plan (2007 – 2008)

Major Concerns (in order of priority)	Intended Outcomes/ Targets	Strategies	Time Scale		

In interviews, all the principals and teachers touched on ensuring quality as their major concern / new challenge when they were asked about their views of the current development of early childhood education. For instance,

Principal A: "All the preschools have to do school-based self assessment to enhance quality."

Teacher A5: "We have to prepare for the Quality Review conducted by inspectors."

Principal B: "We have to write our School-based Self Assessment Report and Annual Development Plan."

Teacher B3: "We have to maintain quality at a desirable level as stipulated by the Education Bureau."

Principal C: "It's really challenging due to the novelty of report writing and documentation of evidence."

It seems that quality concepts of practitioners are very much related to inspections and quality control. Quality in education tended to be defined as fitness of maintaining quality at a "desirable"/stipulated level and conformance of set goals, specifications and requirements (Gilmore, 1974; Crosby, 1979), instead of designing systems to deliver quality or developing a quality culture. Quality is more about fitness for purpose (satisfying specified intentions) than transformative (captured by the terms like 'qualitative change' or 'continuous improvement' (Harvey and Green, 1993).

Even if the preschools do not need to become competitive and stay in the market, institutions ought to improve on a continuing basis because of explosion of knowledge and changing styles in learning.   Preschools may need to develop long and medium term perspectives for development and move towards that.

Coping Strategies and Implications for Future Development

ECE has been chosen for the Pilot Voucher Scheme Initiative. The 2007 voucher system (www.edb.gov.hk) includes such incentives as a professional development scheme. This scheme has the potential to bring about strong and positive interventions to raise quality through its continuing professional learning emphasis, by which practitioners can acquire support and up-to-date knowledge about high quality programmes and curricula for early years education. This investment can potentially be seen as the key to quality assurance in Hong Kong ECE.

Principals were eager to confront the situation, build up work force, solicit external support and focus on the writing skills of working out the documents. All the ten schools agreed that they would try to work out school improvement when asked about their strategies to cope with the new development in an interview. For instance,

> Principal D: "Unlike some other principals I came across, I will not wait and speculate on whether the Performance Indicators/Quality Review will lift or lower the pass-mark bar. I'll take this as an opportunity to work out improvement in my school."

All the participating schools said core teams (composing the principal, vice principal and head teachers) were formed to work out school self-assessment reports and annual development plans. However, the school principals admitted that only 20%-40% of their teachers were mobilized to take part in the school improvement. Five schools mentioned the involvement of parents in the process. Some commented that

> "The objectives / scale of Performance Indicators has been wide and demanding, with special focus on child development (as outcome indicators)." [Principal E]
> "Teachers and schools had difficulties in relating the work in the three domains with the outcome mentioned in Child Development." [Principal F]

The ten schools tended to develop classroom observation forms, scales for measuring children's learning outcomes. For instance,

> Principal G: "It's very demanding for schools to develop classroom observation forms".
> Principal H: "We found that there was a lack of or the need to update young children's development norm in Hong Kong as well as a set of criteria for observed classroom quality, classroom organization, teacher-pupil interactions, and curriculum."

Teachers and principals were aware of a much more piecemeal manner/ classroom- based manner of school improvement which was in line with current researches on school improvement. Traditionally, school improvement and reform are viewed as a matter of the wholesale replacement of dysfunctional practices with new, 'proven' practices. The current reform era, however, has taught us that improvements occur in a much more classroom-based/piecemeal manner (Darling-Hammond, 2001; Elmore, 2004).Recent research tends to analyze profiles of observed classroom quality to inform teachers' knowledge and practice. Although the assessment of classroom process is a complex task, the increased use of direct observations has pushed the development of reliable and valid tools forward in the ECE sector in Hong Kong.

The ten principals were apt to hire services of academics from universities to assist in drafting their school based self-assessment reports and their annual development plan, carry out mock quality review, and develop observation tools, scales for assessing children's learning. They invited speakers for at least five staff development seminars and workshops within the year, attended seminars/workshops on writing reports and development plans, and enrolled in short courses (Curriculum Leadership and Principalship) commissioned by the Education Bureau.

In order to maximize the money used, the ten school principals tended to organize workshops and seminars together, facilitating meetings among their teachers and themselves and contributing to some kind of professional exchanges between school networks. All these details were put down on either the School-based Self-assessment Reports or School Annual Development Plans.

One out of the ten schools could highlight key evaluation points in her school-based self-assessment report and identify key development areas in the Annual Development Plan though not much effort had been devoted to improve the weak curriculum, of which little focus was put on what the children 'know and can do'. The papers were well written, with key evaluation points and followed by clear elaborations and descriptions of strengths and weakness and then a clear focus for further development. Very good comments were noted in the school's Quality Review/inspection report. It seems that a school may achieve "targets" set by the Quality Review even with a weak curriculum.

Hong Kong must spend more on research on validating the Performance Indicators/norms of children's development, norms of good settings, and re-adjustment of performance indicators. The emphasis should be placed on providing school support for school based assessment to boost up school readiness rather than on monitoring schools through an inspection process. Subsequently, an informed frame of reference for the evaluation of ECE practice in Hong Kong should be developed.

Teacher Knowledge and Leadership

The quality of teachers' knowledge and teaching practice is considered to be an important factor in shaping student growth and learning (Richard & Ingersoll, 2007) and classroom quality. The school administrator cannot be an expert in everything. Individual teachers, of course, have their own particular areas of knowledge, but "a group of teachers can supply the variety of professional knowledge needed for sustained school improvement. School improvement depends more than ever on the active involvement of teacher leaders" (Dozier, 2007).

While school improvement by definition targets the school unit for monitoring, intervention, and change, schools are collections of individuals, and to the extent that the needed change involves the behavior of the members of the organization, it must ultimately occur at the individual level (Li, 2001a, Li, 2007). That is, individual teachers must in some way change what they are doing in the hope that this will change what students do (individually and in interaction with teachers) in such a way as to increase or deepen student learning (Li, 2006b).

All the ten schools tried to introduce peer observation in their schools. The teaching of teachers was video-taped for use at discussion sessions. Teachers were ready to share their opinions. For instance,

[In school E, there are only six teachers in the school. There are thirty children in a class with two teachers.]

Teacher E1: "We do not have time to observe children as we have to take care of two groups of children with seven to eight children in each group."

Teacher E2: "Can we do story telling and theme teaching with a big group of fifteen children?"

Teacher E3: "When we've finished the big group teaching, we can spare ourselves to take care of those children who need more assistance in their learning."

Teacher E4: "We've been constrained by the small group teaching mode. The teacher has to use half an hour doing theme teaching/story telling for two small groups each while supervising children's classwork before the tea break."

Teacher E5: "I agree that we'll need time to observe children."

Teacher E6: "Can we try doing theme teaching with a big group and spare thirty minutes in each session to observe children?"

At sharing sessions, teachers in general were ready to identify some limitations of their teaching. For example,

Teacher C1: "The teacher talked for most of the time. Children were to listen to her. It could be very boring."

Teacher D8: "Questions were not clear / not well structured. (Teacher asked why did the Santa Clause give presents to them? Children responded that they were poor people. Teacher asked how could you know that those people were poor.) Children had difficulty in answering her questions."

Teacher F5: "Children were engaged in their drawing. The teacher kept on talking /asking questions to prompt children 'thinking aloud'. This might not be useful keeping children's interest in work."

Peer collaboration and professional dialogues draw teachers to focus attention on information relevant to teaching and learning, motivate individuals and schools to use that information and expend effort to improve practice, and would help to build the knowledge base necessary for interpreting and applying new information to improve practice. Nevertheless, teachers could not share strategies to change what they are doing or ways to help children to develop learning strategies. From the observation data, teachers in the first ten months were still far from the stage of adapting their practice to enhance children's learning. Not much progress in classroom practice was recorded.

The research suggests that (1) only when teachers share information about instruction as well as student learning, they are better able to adapt their practice to the needs and progress of their students; (2) opportunities for the collective sharing of information and knowledge are useful in facilitating information exchange. When teachers tended to place emphasis on tasks and basic skill rather than on helping children to develop learning strategies and were not putting child-initiated learning theory into practice, teachers showed their inability to extend their thinking beyond their own personal concerns.

Culture and Discourse in Preschools

In the early to mid-80s, the most innovative schools motivated and assisted their staff to work through the reform paradoxes that defined the period (Hargreaves, 1995) by building cultures of collaboration and by twisting and channeling the reforms to advance their schools' own purposes. The school administrator cannot be an expert in everything, but "a group of teachers can supply the variety of professional knowledge needed for sustained school improvement. School improvement depends more than ever on the active involvement of teacher leaders" (Dozier, 2007). As Michael Fullan (2007) writes, "The litmus test of all leadership is whether it mobilizes people's commitment to putting their energy into actions designed to improve things. It is individual commitment, but above all it is collective mobilization."

Sometimes teachers themselves resist taking on leadership roles, or make it difficult for their colleagues to do so. This phenomenon may take the form of teachers' reluctance to announce to their colleagues that they have stepped outside of their traditional practice and adopted new initiatives (Danielson, 2007). Some researchers indicate that quality early childhood provision relies on the consistent collaboration in interrelated areas including staff competence and quality, the development of teachers' incentives, and strengthening of evaluation and accountability (Elliott, 2006; Halász et al, 2004).

There were signs that teachers in this project stepped out to discuss their teaching, share their views among colleagues, though these were sometimes treated as suggestions for titles of staff development workshops by the principals and head teachers. For instance,

[At sharing sessions]Teacher G4: "… We all have the problem of initiating children's thinking, participation and interactions… We'll need to improve our interaction skills with children…"

[At sharing sessions] Teacher H20: "I do not mean to criticize the teacher. In fact, I myself, also find my weakness in questioning skills…"

[At sharing sessions] Teacher I22: "… The child is very engaged in his craft work. The teacher's questions of what he was doing, what was the craft about … cannot serve as a means of assessing the child. We'll need an external consultant to provide the needed input."

[At sharing sessions] Teacher J12: "The activities are very well planned. However, do we need to assess whether children have learnt what's expected? How can we assess children's learning outcomes? We'll need to equip ourselves with the assessment skills"

This explained why all the ten schools organized workshops on Questioning Skills, Assessment of Children's, Learning and Teacher-pupil interactions. Teachers could have advanced their understanding of their practice if they tried to work out strategies to enhance children's participation, dialogues with children and their pedagogy.

On the one hand, institute leadership has to be developed. Schools need to be aware and steer towards decentralized responsibility and authority, and mentoring leadership in staff. On the other hand, the Education Bureau should free up restrictions for teachers' enrollment in the commissioned courses such as Curriculum Leadership and Teacher Leadership (a parallel course equivalent to Principalship Course for principals.)

CONCLUSION

In conclusion, the findings indicate that the quality assurance system in the Hong Kong early childhood sector is still in its early stages of development. Preschools tended to view school effectiveness as an objective referenced mechanism of school assessment. There is a need for schools to involve every staff member in visioning, setting out mission and goals and to involve every one in institutional diagnosis, planning and implementation of individual improvement plans. To a certain extent, schools participating in the study can claim that they are upholding quality in education as they engage in exploring its potentialities, though the quality in school education is characterized by continuous search for improvement through innovative approaches which is not a common characteristic of the participating schools. Schools may need various kinds of school support to enhance readiness as well as leadership.

There are signs of school improvement in aspects such as building up the learning community and placing high priority on the achievement of the objectives of the performance indicators. Schools were able to handle novel situations in practical ways by focusing on aspects that are of immediate concern. All the school principals and teachers in the study were aware of external needs and changes and then focus on internal process monitoring, programme evaluation, development planning, staff development, recording in their school-based assessment reports and annual development plans. The study also suggests that external accountability measures such as professional learning and monetary incentives do influence the development of schools. However, school leaders should be equipped with the implementation of quality management strategies, the data on the target change areas should be collected and compared with the base-line data. The difference will indicate the shift in quality. Then a new base-line is created and all the previous processes will be repeated. This makes an organization continuously searching for the change and moving forward. Further, the need still remains for institute training on the job and school-based on-the-job training for teachers and staff. Schools have to mobilize and encourage teachers to innovate and assure them security to attempt innovations and right to fail.

There are a few implications of the study for the development of early childhood education in Hong Kong. A major change should be effected in the quality assurance mechanism. The present dependence of external inspection should be reviewed and a system of continuous internal quality assurance mechanism should be considered. This 'new' mechanism might bring about a change in the cultural perspective of school principals and teachers towards school improvement. The study reveals that the perspective that accountability leads to quality and change is not challenged, that is, there is a general belief among school principals and teachers in school change in the coming years. There is the prevailing/strong cultural perspective of school improvement: school improvement goes with accountability. Another significant implication for policy change is the fact that there appears to be a lack of consensus among the participating schools in the study regarding the criteria for school quality. There is the need for the development of an informed frame of reference for the evaluation of early childhood practice in Hong Kong. Moreover, all the school principals and teachers were aware of external needs and changes. However, there was a tendency to seek external support to ensure quality – an inclination towards a delivery service model.

The findings of this study have provided indicative information about preschool development in the ten case studies. Although these results are not necessarily generalisable, they will inform the theoretical framework about school improvement practices, strategies and outcomes used in the field of early childhood education in Hong Kong and will the one of the first comprehensive studies of teachers' professional practices in action.

REFERENCES

Adams, J. E., & Kirst, M. (1999). New demands for educational accountability: Striving for results in an era of excellence. In J. Murphey & K. S. Louis (Eds.), *Handbook of research in educational administration* (2nd ed., pp. 463-489). San Francisco: Jossey-Bass.

Becher, T., Eraut, M. & Knight, J. (1981). Policies for Educational Accountability. London: Heinemann.

Berliner, D. (1992), "The Nature of Expertise in Teaching" In Oser, F., Dick, A. and Patry, J. (eds.) Effective and Responsible Teaching: The New Synthesis, pp227-248. San Francisco: Jossey-Bass Press.

Blenkin G. M.& Kelly, A.V. (1997). Principles into Practice in Early Childhood Education. London: Paul Chapman.

Carter, K., Cushing, K., Sabers, D., Stein P. & Berliner, D. (1988). Expert-novice differences in perceiving and processing visual information. Journal of Teacher Education, 39, 25-31.

Chicago Public Schools. (2002). *Iowa test of basic skills: Citywide results over time, 1997, 2002 (Report ITOT-CW-white)*. Chicago.

Crosby, P.B. (1979), Quality Is Free: The Art of Making Quality Certain, *New American Library*, New York, NY .

Curriculum Development Institute (1996). Guide to the pre-primary curriculum. Hong Kong Curriculum Development Council: Education Department.

Curriculum Development Institute (2006). Guide to the pre-primary curriculum. Hong Kong Curriculum Development Council: The Education and Manpower Bureau.

Dahlberg, G., Moss, P. & Pence, A. (1999). Beyond Quality in Early Childhood Education and Care: postmodern perspectives. London: Falmer Press.

Danielson, C. (2007). *Enhancing Professional Practice: A Framework for Teaching (2nd Edition)*. Alexandria: Association for Supervision and Curriculum Development.

Darling-Hammond, L. (1996). Restructuring schools for high performance. In S. Fuhrman & J. A. O'Day (Eds.), *Rewards and reform: Creating educational incentives that work* (pp. 144-192). San Francisco: Jossey-Bass.

Darling-Hammond, L. (2001). *The right to learn: A blueprint for creating schools that work.* San Francisco: Jossey-Bass.

Dozier, T.K. (2007). Turning Good Teachers into Great Leaders. *Educational Leadership*, 65 (1), 54-59.

Education Commission (2000). Learning for Life. Learning through life: Reform proposals for the education system in Hong Kong. Hong Kong Special Administrative Region of the People's Republic of China.

Education Department (2001). Performance Indicators (Pre-primary Institutions). Second Edition.

Elliott, A. (2006). *Early Childhood Education Pathways to quality and equity for all children.* Australian Council for Educational Research.

Elmore R. F., Abelmann, C. H., & Fuhrman, S. H. (1996). The new accountability in state education reform: From process to performance. In H. F. Ladd (Ed.), *Holding schools accountable: Performance-based reform in education* (pp. 65-98). Washington, DC: Brookings Institution.

Elmore, R. (2004). *School reform from the inside out: Policy, practice, and performance.* Cambridge MA: Harvard Education Press.

Fuhrman, S. H. (1999). *The new accountability* (CPRE Policy Brief No. RB-27). Philadelphia: Consortium for Policy Research in Education. Retrieved December 11, 2005.

Fullan, M. (2007). *Leading in a culture of change* (Rev. ed.). San Francisco: Jossey-Bass, p.9.

Galton, M. (1996) "Teaching, learning and the co-ordinator" in O'Niell, J. and Kitson, N. (Eds) Effective curriculum management- co-ordinating learning in the primary school. London: Routledge.

Gilmore, H.L. (1974), "Product conformance cost", *Quality Progress, Vol. 7 No.5*, pp.16-19.

Gwynne, J., & Easton, J. Q. (2001, April). *Probation, organizational capacity, and student achievement in Chicago elementary schools.* Paper presented at the annual meeting of the American Educational Research Association, Seattle.

Harvey, L. and Green, D. (1993) Defining Quality, Assessment and Evaluation *in Higher Education, 18(1)*, pp. 9-34.

Kagan, D. M. (1992) Professional Growth among Pre-service and Beginning Teachers, Review of Educational Research, 62(2), 129-169.

Kitchener K. & King, P. (1981). Reflective judgment concepts of justification and their relationship to age and education. Journal of Applied Developmental Psychology, 2, 89-116.

Kuykendall, J. (1993). "Please", "thank you", "you're welcome": Teacher language can positively impact pro-social development. Day Care and Early Education, 2, 30-32.

Li, Y. L. (2001a). A Model of Teacher Development, Social, Subject Knowledge, Pedagogical and Cognitive. In Y. C. Cheng (eds). *Teaching Effectiveness and Teacher Development.* The Netherlands: Kluwer Academic Publishers (KAP).

Li, Y. L. (2001b). Curriculum Management and Teaching Practice of Kindergarten Teachers. *Education 3-13*, 54-58.

Li, Y. L. (2003). What makes a good kindergarten teacher? A pilot interview study in Hong Kong. *Early Child Development and Care, 173* (1), 19-31.

Li Y.L. & Li, H. (2004). Perceptions of effective pedagogy among teachers in Hong Kong kindergartens, presented at PECERA, Melbourne, Australia.

Li, Y. L. (2004a). The Culture of Teaching in the Midst of Western Influence: The Case of Hong Kong Kindergartens. *Issues in Contemporary Early Childhood Education.*

Li, Y. L. (2004b). Pupil-Teacher Interactions in Hong Kong kindergarten classrooms – Its implications for teachers' professional development. Leaning Environments Research: An International Journal, 7(1), 36-45.

Li, Y. L. (2006a). Classroom Organization: Understanding the context in which children are expected to learn. *Early Childhood Education Journal.*

Li, Y. L. (2006b). *Dialogues between Mentors and Porteges: Understanding Mentoring Practice of Hong Kong Kindergartens.* Paper presented at Asia Pacific Educational Research Association International Conference 2006.

Li, Y. L. (2006c).What makes desirable learning activities? Exploring the rhetoric and practice in Hong Kong kindergartens. In Samuel N. Hogan (Eds). *New Developments in Learning Research.* pp.165-173.Nova Science Publishers, Hauppauge: NY.

Li, Y. L. (2007). Teachers talking about effective practice-Understanding the knowledge and practice of teachers. *Journal of Early Childhood Teacher Education*, 28 (3), 301-310.

McIntyre, D. (1993), "Theory, Theorizing and Reflection in Initial Teacher Education" in Calderhead, J. and Gates, P. (eds.) (1993), Conceptualising Reflection in Teacher Development, 39-52. London: Falmer Press.

O'Brien, S. J. (1991). How do you raise respectful children in a disrespectful world? Childhood Education, 67(3), 183-184.

O'Day, J.A. (2002), Complexity, accountability, and school improvement, *Harvard Educational Review 72 (3) (2002)*, pp. 293–329..

Opper, S (1996). *Hong Kong's Young Children: their early development and learning.* Hong Kong: Hong Kong University Press.

O'Reilly, F. E. (1996). *Educational accountability: Current practices and theories in use.* Cambridge, MA: Harvard University, Consortium for Policy Research in Education.

Reynolds, A. (1992). What is competent beginning teaching?: A review of the literature. Review of Educational Research, 62(1), 1-36.

Richard M. & Ingersoll, R.M. (2007). Short on Power, Long on Responsibility. *Educational Leadership*, 65 (1), 20-25.

Shulman, L. (1986). Those who understand: Knowledge growth in teaching. Educational Researcher,15 (2), 4-14..

Tharp, R. & Gallimore, R. (1988). Rousing minds to life: teaching, learning and schooling in social context. Cambridge, UK: Cambridge University Press.

Westat. (2001). *Report on the final evaluation of the City-State Partnership.* Rockville, MD: Author.

Whiren, A. P. (1988) Children's self-esteem: The Verbal Environment. Childhood Education, 65, 29-32.

In: Early Education
Editors: J.B. Mottely and A.R. Randall

ISBN 978-1-60456-908-7
© 2009 Nova Science Publishers, Inc.

Chapter 2

"YOU DON'T LEAVE BABIES ON THEIR OWN": CHILDREN'S INTERESTS IN EARLY CHILDHOOD EDUCATION

Helen Hedges

University of Auckland, New Zealand

ABSTRACT

A sociocultural approach to curriculum and pedagogy, promoted by New Zealand's early childhood curriculum Te Whariki emphasizes pedagogical relationships and interactions between learners and knowledgeable others. Dialogue with an adult or peer maximizes children's learning during participation in play. This chapter analyzes an excerpt of dialogue between a four-year-old child and an adult during research that aimed to explore the place of subject knowledge in early childhood curriculum and pedagogy. This interpretive case study in one kindergarten was underpinned by sociocultural theory and used qualitative data gathering techniques such as participant observation. Findings revealed that children's participation in play-based curriculum experiences provided opportunities for them to express, represent, explore, and extend their interests. These interests may be both responsive to the learning and teaching environment and reflect the social and cultural experiences that they participate in with families and communities. The dialogue is analyzed from three perspectives: sociocultural theory, community of practice, and community of inquiry. These perspectives bring to light the child's interests, experiences, knowledge building, inquiry, and emergent citizenship skills. The chapter also describes some challenges that a focus on children's interests presents for teachers in terms of curriculum and pedagogy.

INTRODUCTION

New Zealand's early childhood education curriculum, Te Whariki (Ministry of Education, 1996), has two strong theoretical underpinnings: developmental and sociocultural.

Recently, however, it has come to be primarily interpreted as a socioculturally-inclined document. Sociocultural theories of learning have as a fundamental assumption that learning is social in origin and a process of active construction. Much knowledge is gained in social and cultural contexts as a result of interpersonal interactions (Rogoff, 1998, 2003; Valsiner, 1993, 2000; Vygotsky, 1978, 1986). Dahlberg, Moss, and Pence (1999), among others, see relationships and communication as central to children's socially constructed learning. Through meaning-making and dialogue with others and the mediation of cultural tools (e.g., language, books, symbols), children make sense of learning and internalize it in thought. In particular, dialogue in the form of language allows both knowledge construction and the appropriation of complex ideas and cognitive processes. Te Whariki promotes the empowerment of children as learners by viewing them as competent and capable contributors to curriculum co-construction.

Grundy (1994) identifies curriculum as a series of phenomena that are constructed and reconstructed on a moment-by-moment basis during pedagogical relationships. Teachers' curricular decision making is a conscious process that draws on understandings about children, curriculum, pedagogy, theory, philosophy, and context. Pedagogical relationships are therefore likely to be a vital way through which children experience an empowering curriculum. What children learn through these relationships has been investigated and theorized, and linked to outcomes such as literacy and numeracy and implications for teacher knowledge (e.g., see Sammons et al., 2004; Siraj-Blatchford, 2004; Siraj-Blatchford and Sylva, 2004; Siraj-Blatchford, Sylva, Muttock, Gilden, and Bell, 2002). However, while a focus on the teacher's role in listening to children in order to extend their learning has been explicated (Dahlberg and Moss, 2005), the types, nature, and characteristics of pedagogical relationships themselves within early childhood contexts remain largely untheorized. This chapter attempts to theorize children's pedagogical relationships with adults using frameworks and constructs consistent with both the notion of socially constructed learning and the four principles of Te Whariki: relationships, empowerment, family and community, and holistic development. This initial theorising suggests that the advice in Te Whariki for teachers to follow children's interests as a way to weave together planned and evolving curriculum generates significant challenges for teachers.

CHILDREN'S INTERESTS

I undertook a study of teachers', parents', and four-year-old children's beliefs about subject knowledge through the lens of an excursion to Kelly Tarlton's Antarctic Encounter and Underwater World, in Auckland, New Zealand. (Hedges, 2002a; Hedges and Cullen, 2005). This interpretive case study was underpinned by sociocultural theory and used qualitative data-gathering techniques such as focus group interviews with children, teachers, and parents (as separate groups), and daily participant observation each morning for seven weeks in one kindergarten. Innovative approaches to incorporating children's participation in research were used (see Hedges, 2002b). In the study, four pedagogical relationships were evident. These relationships occurred between teachers and children, parents and children, among child peers, and between children and the researcher in a teaching role. These highlighted pedagogical approaches that promoted and supported active, collaborative engagement in meaningful, reciprocal dialogic inquiry.

The excursion was planned to extend one child's interest in sea creatures (Hedges, 2004). Preparation for, participation in, and follow-up from the excursion was the focus for the study. However, data from the participant observation provided other interesting findings, one of which is the focus of this chapter. Interests-based curriculum and pedagogy in early childhood is often participative and spontaneous. Findings revealed that children's participation in play-based curriculum experiences provided opportunities for them to express, represent, explore, and extend a range of interests. The findings support that children's interests do not emerge in a vacuum but emanate from children's participation in social and cultural experiences.

As a working definition for the present theorizing, children's interests are considered to be evidence from children's spontaneous play, discussion, inquiry, or investigation that emanates from their social and cultural experiences. These interests may therefore be both responsive to the learning and teaching environment in an early childhood setting and reflect the experiences that they participate in with families and communities. Field notes made during the participant observation revealed that children had a wide range of interests that they wanted to explore through their play. Through this participation, knowledge is constructed and identities as citizens and learners are developed. This knowledge and identity formation is supported by knowledgeable others who know the child or children well.

To illustrate this point, this chapter now focuses on the analysis of a dialogue that occurred between a four-year-old and me as the researcher, as an example of a pedagogical relationship that developed during the seven weeks of the study's field work observation. In the conversational dialogue that follows in full, Jade initiates an interaction that illustrates her interest in and knowledge about participation in culturally valued activities; in particular, caring for babies' well-being. Woven into the dialogue are other conversations about daffodils and peanut butter that rely on memory of earlier interactions between the child and me. Jade shows that she has knowledge of nutrition and bathing routines for babies based on her experience of having younger cousins, knowledge of the world about daffodils (and inquiry about how long they last if picked or kept in the garden), and that she enjoys participating in activities such as learning to read and learning to dance. The dialogue is analyzed from three perspectives: sociocultural theory, community of practice (Wenger, 1998), and community of inquiry (Wells, 1999, 2001a, 2001b). These perspectives highlight in multiple ways the child's interests, experiences, knowledge building, inquiry, emerging identity as a learner, and emergent citizenship skills.

DIALOGUE WITHIN A PEDAGOGICAL RELATIONSHIP

Jade was aged 4 years and 10 months, and had previously demonstrated interests in literacy and family play. The following field notes record the dialogue analyzed in this chapter.

Jade and another four-year-old continue their play from yesterday with the dolls for about an hour. Firstly they are feeding their babies, using spoons and fruit. Jade says her baby needs to eat this before she can have some chocolate. She shows me some bark she has put in the fridge that she is pretending is chocolate. I suggest this is like the story "Eat up your dinner", and they ask me to find it and read it. I bring it to the family corner and read it to them while they finish feeding their babies. Jade soon recognizes the repeated words "nah" and "eat up your dinner" and reads these with me.

They decide their babies need a bath now. I ask them what they need to give their babies a bath. They tell me new clothes, a towel, soap and warm water—not too hot. Jade tells me you have to be careful not to get soap in the baby's eyes, you need to make sure the baby keeps warm, you must hold the baby safely and not leave them alone in the bath. She is going to dress her baby in a ballet skirt after the bath as she is going to ballet. I put some warm water and detergent in the doll's bath and take it onto the table on the outside deck. I explain that this is special Johnson's [a brand name] baby bath that doesn't make the baby's eyes sting. Jade and Jamie take it in turns to use a wash cloth to bath the doll. Jade is very thorough and knows how to turn the doll over safely to wash its back. She then dries and dresses the doll and goes off to the sandpit.

Soon, she is back. She tells me "She got dirty in the sandpit. I need to give my baby another bath. I rang the ballet teacher and said she didn't want to go today. She goes to ballet and dancing".

Helen: "What's the difference between ballet and dancing?"

Jade: "If you go to dancing you have to dance all time, but I haven't been to ballet so I don't know what you do. When I was about um two and three-quarters, we were going to go to the ballet. But I thought, nah, I thought it would be quite boring. I seen ballet when I was two. I'm holding her head like this to keep her head safe. Can you hold it for me while I come round your side?" I do so and Jade moves to the other side of the bath and turns the doll over. It slips out of the bath.

Helen: "Oh, no!"

Jade: "It's only a doll! Soon she'll get in her ballet clothes again". She notes that on the table beside the bath "Oooh, it's all wet here".

Helen: "Sometimes babies kick and splash water".

Jade: "My friend Anton has a sister Georgia and she just splashes gently. She gets in the big bath now".

Helen: "How old is she?"

Jade: "She's one now and Anton's three".

Jade: "We've got daffodils in our garden. My Mum showed me but I couldn't see them. She said 'Look in the blue pot' and there they were!"

Helen: "Did you recognize they were daffodils because I gave you one a while ago, or because Mum told you?"

Jade: "Mum told me. But we're leaving them in the garden because if you pick them they only last two sleeps".

Helen: "Do they last longer in the garden?"

Jade: "Yes".

Helen: "How long do you think?"

Jade: "I don't know".

Helen: "Will you keep looking at them and let me know?"

Jade: "Haven't you got any in your garden any more?"

Helen: "No".

Jade: "How long did yours last?"

Helen: "I don't know either—that's why I was hoping you could watch yours for me".

I ask her if she remembers the time she made peanut butter for me in the sandpit. She says yes and recalls that some of it dried out quickly in the sun. I ask her if she would like us to make real peanut butter sometime next week. She says yes, but just the Penguins [a small group of girls in the kindergarten] again. Jade notices that the hose is going in the sandpit. She asks me to look after her baby so she can play in the sandpit without her baby getting sandy again. I say that I will and it is responsible of her to leave her baby with someone.

Jade: "Yes, you don't leave babies on their own".

Helen: "Can I feed her for you while you are away?"

Jade: "Yes".

She goes to the sandpit and plays with a group of girls for some time. They all get wet and return for a change of clothes. When I see Jade, I tell her that her baby got tired after I fed her so I put her to bed (I had put the doll in the cot in the family corner). Jade: "Oh, good".

I note that after Jade has changed her clothes, she goes over to the family corner and sees that the doll is in the cot. She then goes away to play elsewhere.

Jade's mother later confirmed that the child had attended a ballet when she was two and that this influenced her decision not to go to ballet classes, and that the children she spoke of were her cousins whom she sees frequently. (Field notes, Oaktree Kindergarten, August 31, 2001)

THEORETICAL ANALYSIS OF THE INTERACTION AND DIALOGUE

Key concepts of sociocultural theory

Vygotsky (1978, 1986) supported that learning should be authentic; that is, it should be relevant to the daily life of a child in a community or culture. As Jordan (2003) notes, "Vygotsky clearly favoured supporting children's learning in the context of their interests" (p. 35). Vygotsky discussed the role of cultural tools in mediating learning and teaching. An example of a cultural tool in the interaction with Jade above is the use of language as the tool of dialogue and thinking, including understanding its written form (the child's recognition of words from the book read to her). This understanding of the written form is important as it supports a positive disposition towards literacy learning. Other key examples of cultural tools in the interaction include: a doll representing and symbolising a baby; sand symbolising peanut butter; and the resources and equipment provided that enabled Jade to demonstrate her expertise in bathing babies.

Another key sociocultural notion is evident: that of intersubjectivity—a shared focus and understanding between people that involves social, emotional, and cognitive interchange. Here the evidence of prior interactions in this pedagogical relationship led to shared understandings about daffodils and representing making peanut butter. In this interaction, the former leads to authentic inquiry and likely future co-construction of knowledge through a genuine question—how long do daffodils stay alive in a garden or in a vase?

Two sociocultural concepts are described as the intended learning outcomes of Te Whariki. Rather than knowledge outcomes, these relate to ways in which "knowledge, skills, and attitudes . . . combine together to form a child's 'working theory' and help the child develop dispositions that encourage learning" (Ministry of Education, 1996. p. 44). A sociocultural perspective of dispositions has been argued recently (Carr and Claxton, 2002; Claxton and Carr, 2004) that has had a major influence on the learning stories assessment practices related to Te Whariki (Carr, 2001a; Ministry of Education, 2004). From this perspective, competent learners are seen to develop positive dispositions for learning linked to the strands of Te Whariki such as curiosity, concentration, persistence, contribution, and communication (Carr, 2001a). Each of these is evident in the interaction analyzed, as are others discussed in the literature such as thinking scientifically (Hedges, 2003), "being nearly five" (Carr, 2001b), or being emergent inquirers (Lindfors, 1999).

The concept of working theories in Te Whariki is most explicit in the strand of "exploration" where the term is used in one of the goals: "[Children] develop working theories for making sense of the natural, social, physical, and material worlds' (Ministry of Education, 1996, p. 82). The concept draws on the work of Claxton (1990) who developed the notion of minitheories based on the idea of implicit theories. Claxton argued that these theories are implicit because much knowledge is tacit; that is, intuitive and intangible. Claxton suggests that implicit theories come largely from three sources: first-hand experience of the physical world, experiences in the social world, and, thirdly, both the explicit and hidden curriculum. Therefore, children's experiences in early childhood settings are likely to inform their working theories as they try to understand the world and reveal themselves in the experiences they choose to participate in. In the interaction described above, Jade reveals a number of working theories about human development and learning and knowledge of the physical and material world.

Another notion consistent with sociocultural theory is that of funds of knowledge. Children's knowledge is based on their unique family and community experiences, encapsulated in the concept of "funds of knowledge" (González, Moll, and Amanti, 2005, Moll, 2000; Moll, Amanti, Neff, and González, 1992). Moll et al. define funds of knowledge as the bodies of knowledge that underlie household functioning, development, and well-being. Examples include economics, such as budgeting, accounting, and loans; repair, such as household appliances, fences, and cars; and arts, such as music, painting, and sculpture (Moll, 2000). Carr (2001a) extended this concept to include broader experiences gained from participation in family and community life, including the occupations of parents. Riojas-Cortez (2001) extended the term to include cultural traits such as parents' language, values, and beliefs; ways of discipline; and the value of education as funds of knowledge sources. My current research extends this analysis to include family members within and beyond the nuclear family and other social and cultural experiences as sources of funds of knowledge (Hedges, forthcoming). Jade's family and community experiences evident in this interaction are, firstly, having younger cousins. This has enabled her to observe and participate in the care of a baby, with consequent understandings about meal and bathing routines, specifically nutrition, safety, care, and well-being. Secondly, Jade has participated in socially and culturally-valued experiences of dancing, attending ballet, and gardening. She draws on these experiences to make sense of her current learning.

A Learning Community

A focus on learning through participation in a community has led to terms such as "community of learners" (Rogoff, Matusov, and White, 1996), "community of practice" (Wenger, 1998) and "community of inquiry" (Wells, 1999, 2001a). Rogoff et al.'s (1996) term emphasizes that learning is commonly a collaborative participation in shared experiences. It highlights the intersubjectivity required for meaningful learning and teaching. This chapter now uses Wenger's and Wells' notions of learning community to analyse the interaction with Jade.

Community Of Practice

Wenger's (1998) notion sites learning as occurring within observation and participation in the contexts of lived experience that are an integral part of daily human life. In this excerpt, Jade reveals that she has watched a baby being bathed, representing and practising this in the kindergarten setting, and participated in gardening activities. Knowledge in a community of practice is viewed as competence in culturally valued activities. In this excerpt, this includes becoming literate, learning parenting skills in order to be a good citizen, and learning to dance.

Four key elements are present in this concept of learning: meaning, practice, community and identity. They can be defined as follows:

- meaning — experiencing the world and engaging with it creates meaning; learning takes place by talking about those experiences
- practice — learning and talking about shared historical and social activities that are meaningful
- community — a recognition that participation in activities is worth pursuing and results in competence
- identity — a social view of learning has an effect on personal identity within the context of communities participated in.

The four elements are "deeply interconnected and mutually defining" (Wenger, 1998, p. 5). Through negotiating meaning, a community member constructs an identity and sense of belonging in relation to the values and goals of the communities. The elements are all clearly present in the dialogue about bathing babies, learning about daffodils, and participating in dancing and ballet activities.

The community of practice conceptual framework can be viewed as an apprenticeship model as established community members induct others into the ways of the community. This is evident in the way that I ask the children about the equipment they need to bath a baby and query the doll's safety when it slips out of the bath. I am focused on their competence in future parenting skills. It is also evident by Jade wanting to practise the bathing again, understanding that this is necessary if a baby gets dirty. However, such an approach could then also be interpreted as adults asking questions to which children already know the answers, thereby not tapping into children's real interests and inquiries.

In relation to the central focus of this chapter, theorizing pedagogical relationships that arise from teachers working with children's interests and inquiries, a flaw therefore emerges with a community of practice interpretation. The model does not clearly describe how knowledge or assumptions are extended on the initiative of the learner, nor how understandings are challenged and new learning and understandings are co-constructed. For example, in this interaction, the child indicates that she knows the doll is a symbol and challenges me about the doll being not real when it is dropped out of the bath, and we share genuine questions about how long daffodils last in the garden. Further, an emphasis on participation rather than a combination of observation and participation may be critical for young children, as evidenced in the child's lack of interest in attending ballet classes as a result of passively viewing a ballet production at the age of two. While this child is a confident and competent communicator, able to challenge an adult's dialogue, other children may not be so self-assured. Adults may therefore need a different approach to draw out and extend children's understandings. This chapter now, therefore, moves to an alternative conceptual framework in an effort to explain pedagogical relationships.

COMMUNITY OF INQUIRY

Human beings appear intrinsically motivated to inquire and to obtain the help of others to go beyond their present understanding. They actively construct and reconstruct knowledge in those pedagogical interactions, intent on understanding the world and their place in it (Lindfors, 1999). Infants, toddlers, and young children observe and talk about things that interest them and try to increase their understanding about them during conversations and interactions with others. This inquiry may be spontaneous and unplanned, and commonly arises out of children taking an interest in everyday experiences and activities in families and communities. Consequently, learning is focused and given meaning by the social and cultural contexts in which it occurs. The disposition to inquire has been linked to the notion of building curriculum on children's interests in learning stories (Carr, 2001a). In learning stories, the notions of inquiry and "taking an interest" are linked to the strand of "well-being" in Te Whariki.

To take a step further and acknowledge the importance of pedagogical relationships in empowering curriculum experiences and children's interests-based learning would be to highlight the integral nature of "learning-and-teaching" (Wells, 2002), a hyphenated term Wells introduces. The term is also consistent with Te Whariki's central metaphor of weaving learning and teaching experiences to form curriculum, and parallels with the Maori term "ako" are also evident, in considering learning and teaching as both a continuum and a concept that operationalizes the knowledge and strengths of teachers and learners. Writing learning-and-teaching stories would also be consistent with the notion of "distributed assessment" (Cowie and Carr, 2004; see also Simmons, Schimanski, McGarva, Cullen, and Haworth, 2005) and acknowledge the centrality of teachers in many of the learning story exemplars (Ministry of Education, 2004).

The concept of a community of inquiry (Wells, 1999, 2001a) arose from researchers observing the importance of children's "real questions" (Wells, 1999, p. 91) and ways in which these questions were responded to by teachers in determining meaningful learning.

Acknowledging the cognitive elements of participation is something that Edwards (2005) suggests requires greater acknowledgement in relation to learning within a community.

In this excerpt, the dialogue that the child initiates and the child's questions are the critical leads to the learning and thinking that occurs. Here, the child has returned to earlier learning, understandings, participation, and experience about feeding and bathing babies, growing daffodils, ballet, and dancing. Her growing understandings occur not only through her participation and engagement, but through the inquiry she demonstrates by building on previous knowledge and experiences. Further, when she returns to give the doll another bath, she indicates a lack of interest in learning ballet. Showing an interest in her understandings, the question I ask about the difference between ballet and dancing leads to dialogue that has several concurrent conversations. These indicate her interest and inquiry in several areas of activities she participates in. Engaging with Wells' ideas appears to be fruitful for a focus on children's interests and inquiry.

Wells (2001b) claims that dialogue is "the discourse of knowledge building" (p. 185). While Wells states that knowledge building also takes place through the written mode, the primacy of dialogue between people is fundamental to the concept of inquiry. This claim is consistent with the notion of socially-constructed learning and the importance of reciprocal and responsive relationships highlighted in Te Whariki. Both need emphasis in order to create and sustain dialogue in a community of inquiry. A relationship approach to pedagogy consistent with a sociocultural perspective supports that inquiry learning and co-constructing knowledge are processes of meaning-making (Dahlberg et al., 1999; Dahlberg and Moss, 2005) or negotiating meaning (Wenger, 1998) through intelligent and informed interactions.

Wells' (1999, 2001a) community of inquiry approach suggests teachers and learners explore together issues to which there are no predetermined answers or outcomes. This resonates with a curriculum that emerges from children's interests, which are likely to be broad and varied as the interaction between Jade and myself illustrates. A further implication might be that co-construction (Valsiner, 1993, 2000) may be a promising pedagogical approach within an early childhood community of inquiry (see also Jordan, 2004).

CHALLENGES FOR TEACHERS

Participation in a community of inquiry

The models of community of learners, community of practice, and community of inquiry acknowledge the sociocultural origins of knowledge and allow for the flexible and changing agency of participants within the learning and teaching processes. Of these models, the community of inquiry is suggested as being most consistent with the sociocultural view of children as capable and competent. It highlights the role of children's interests and inquiry, encourages teachers to build on children's prior knowledge, and emphasizes both the central role of language as a cultural tool in dialogic inquiry and the intersubjective nature of the reciprocal and responsive relationships highlighted in early childhood pedagogy. Such a model, coupled with a multi-faceted and complex interpretation of the principles of Te Whariki, generates challenges to teachers to provide a curriculum that empowers infants, toddlers, and young children. An empowering curriculum involves relationships, holistic development, and family and community.

AN EMPOWERING CURRICULUM

Young children are likely to have a wide range of interests and inquiries but, because of their age, relatively limited experience and cognitive abilities compared to adults. Therefore a sociocultural approach to curriculum places emphasis on the quality of pedagogical relationships that encourage and extend those interests and inquiries. Firstly, spending time in sustained interactions using active listening and wait time (Walsh and Sattes, 2005) with children can establish their prior knowledge and support their interests. A teacher's role becomes that of listening carefully to children, supporting, extending, and challenging their ideas and thoughts. Teachers may need to look at ways to manage their roles and daily routines to enable such pedagogical interactions to occur.

Assessment in a sociocultural paradigm is dynamic and distributed; that is, children are observed in the process of interacting with people, places, and things over time (Carr, 2001a; Cowie and Carr, 2004; Hatherly and Richardson, 2007). It is not about measuring achievement but about processes of learning, development of dispositions for learning, and co-constructed understandings that empower children and enable them to develop and learn in a holistic manner. Assessment therefore occurs within authentic meaningful experiences and leads to purposeful documentation of children's learning.

Te Whariki's advice to teachers to follow children's interests to create planned and evolving curriculum encourages teachers to regard planning as being responsive to the "here and now" of children's interests and experiences, not just as a future-oriented exercise. Moreover, the boundaries between "planned" and "spontaneous" curriculum become blurred and overlapping rather than polarized. To provide an empowering and responsive curriculum requires teachers to relinquish control of curriculum direction and empower children to lead curriculum (Hill, 2001) and negotiate and co-construct curriculum (Dahlberg and Moss, 2005; Fleet and Robertson, 2004).

Furthermore, partnership with families in children's learning is a strong driver in the philosophy and practice of early childhood education. Yet, a body of literature suggests that implementing partnerships with parents can be problematic and requires maturity coupled with specialist skills and knowledge (see Hedges and Gibbs, 2005). In order to genuinely involve families and communities in children's learning, teachers need to develop authentic ways to get to know children and families besides informal dialogue in the education centre setting and sharing assessment portfolios. Other ways include home visits (see Hensley, 2005) or evening events at the centre that teachers use as an opportunity to focus on families. Another suggestion might be children taking photographs of family and community events to bring to the centre (Feiler, Greenhough, Winter, Salway, and Scanlan, 2006; see also Meade, 2006).

CONCLUSION

Transformation. That is the chief purpose of education—that all who are involved should transform their capacities to act, think, and feel in ways that contribute to the common good and enrich their own individual lives (Wells, 2001a, p. 1).

As noted earlier, what children learn during early childhood curriculum experiences has been investigated and theorized and linked to outcomes such as literacy and numeracy. The pedagogical relationships that promote these outcomes, and the outcomes of the pedagogical relationships themselves have been investigated less thoroughly. The importance of dialogue and children's real questions in pedagogical interactions points to the usefulness of a community of inquiry as a theoretical framework that may explain aspects of children's interests, as a framework to theorize pedagogical relationships, and as a way to explore these consistent with other sociocultural notions such as intersubjectivity, funds of knowledge, and working theories.

In relation to outcomes, the process outcomes of learning during pedagogical relationships between teachers and children in early childhood education may also be consistent with sociocultural perspectives including funds of knowledge, working theories, and dispositions. These enable children (and teachers) to become empowered as learners, transform their thinking and actions, constructing identities and a sense of belonging in relation to the values and goals of the communities in which they participate. Such ideas about outcomes, coupled with the spontaneous and intuitive approaches to pedagogy in early childhood education, provoke teachers to think differently about pedagogical techniques and approaches to assessment and planning for young children's interests and inquiry-focused learning.

REFERENCES

Carr, M. (2001a). *Assessment in early childhood settings: Learning stories.* London: Paul Chapman.

Carr, M. (2001b). A sociocultural approach to learning orientation in an early childhood setting. *International Journal of Qualitative Studies,* 14(4), 525–542.

Carr, M., and Claxton, G. (2002). Tracking the development of learning dispositions. *Assessment in Education,* 9(1), 9–37.

Claxton, G. (1990). *Teaching to learn: A direction for education.* London: Cassell Educational.

Claxton, G., and Carr, M. (2004). A framework for teaching learning: The dynamics of disposition. *Early Years,* 24(1), 87–97.

Cowie, B., and Carr, M. (2004). The consequences of socio-cultural assessment. In A. Anning, J. Cullen, and M. Fleer (Eds.), *Early childhood education: Society and culture* (pp. 95–106). London: Sage.

Dahlberg, G., and Moss, P. (2005). *Ethics and politics in early childhood education.* London: RoutledgeFalmer.

Dahlberg, G., Moss, P., and Pence, A. (1999). *Beyond quality in early childhood education and care: Postmodern perspectives.* London: Falmer Press.

Edwards, A. (2005). Let's get beyond community and practice: The many meanings of learning by participating. *The Curriculum Journal*, 16(1), 49–65.

Feiler, A., Greenhough, P., and Winter, J., with Salway, L., and Scanlan, M. (2006). Getting engaged: Possibilities and problems for home-school knowledge exchange. *Educational Review*, 58(4), 451–469.

Fleet, A., and Robertson, J. (2004). *Overlooked curriculum: Seeing everyday possibilities.* Watson, ACT: Goanna Print.

González, N., Moll, L. C., and Amanti, C. (Eds.). (2005). *Funds of knowledge: Theorizing practices in households, communities and classrooms.* Mahwah, NJ: Lawrence Erlbaum.

Grundy, S. (1994). The curriculum and teaching. In E. Hatton (Ed.), *Understanding teaching: Curriculum and the social context of schooling* (pp. 27–39). Marrickville, NSW: Harcourt Brace and Co.

Hatherly, A., and Richardson, C. (2007). Making connections—assessment and evaluation revisited. In L. Keesing-Styles and H. Hedges (Eds.), *Theorising early childhood practice: Emerging dialogues* (pp. 51–70). Castle Hill, NSW: Pademelon Press.

Hedges, H. (forthcoming). *Funds of knowledge in early childhood communities of inquiry.* Unpublished doctoral thesis, Massey University, Palmerston North, New Zealand.

Hedges, H. (2004). A whale of an interest in sea creatures: The learning potential of excursions. *Early Childhood Research and Practice* 6(1). Retrieved June 21, 2004 from http://www.ecrp.uiuc.edu/v6n1/hedges.html

Hedges, H. (2003). Avoiding "magical" thinking in children: The case for teachers' science subject knowledge. *Early Childhood Folio*, 7, 2–7.

Hedges, H. (2002a). *Subject content knowledge in early childhood curriculum and pedagogy.* Unpublished master's thesis, Massey University, Palmerston North, New Zealand.

Hedges, H. (2002b). Beliefs and principles in practice: Ethical research with child participants. *New Zealand Research in Early Childhood Education*, 5, 31–47.

Hedges, H., and Cullen, J. (2005). Subject knowledge in early childhood curriculum and pedagogy: Beliefs and practices. *Contemporary Issues in Early Childhood* 6(1), 66–79.

Hedges, H., and Gibbs, C. J. (2005). Preparation for teacher-parent partnerships: A practical experience with a family. *Journal of Early Childhood Teacher Education*, 26(2), 115–126.

Hensley, M. (2005). Empowering parents of multicultural backgrounds. . In N. González, L. C. Moll, and C. Amanti, (Eds.), *Funds of knowledge: Theorizing practices in households, communities and classrooms* (pp. 143–151). Malwah, NJ: Lawrence Erlbaum.

Hill, D. (2001). Passion, power and planning in the early childhood centre. *The First Years: Nga Tau Tuatahi/New Zealand Journal of Infant and Toddler Education*, 3(2), 10–13.

Jordan, B. (2003). *Professional development making a difference for children: Constructing understandings in early childhood centres.* Unpublished doctoral thesis, Massey University, Palmerston North.

Jordan, B. (2004). Scaffolding learning and co-constructing understandings. In A. Anning, J. Cullen, and M. Fleer (Eds.), *Early childhood education: Society and culture* (pp. 31–42). London: Sage.

Lindfors, J. W. (1999). *Children's inquiry: Using language to make sense of the world.* New York: Teachers College Press.

Meade, A. (Ed.). (2006). *Riding the waves: Innovation in early childhood education.* Wellington: New Zealand Council for Educational Research.

Ministry of Education. (1996). *Te Whariki. He whariki matauranga mo nga mokopuna o Aotearoa: Early childhood curriculum.* Wellington: Learning Media.

Ministry of Education. (2004). *Kei tua o te pae: Assessment for learning exemplars.* Wellington: Learning Media.

Moll, L. (2000). Inspired by Vygotsky: Ethnographic experiments in education. In C. D. Lee and P. Smagorinsky (Eds.), *Vygotskian perspectives on literacy research: Constructing meaning through collaborative inquiry* (pp. 256–268). Cambridge: Cambridge University Press.

Moll, L., Amanti, C., Neff, D., and Gonzalez, N. (1992). Funds of knowledge for teaching: Using a qualitative approach to connect homes and classrooms. *Theory into Practice,* 31(2), 132–141.

Riojas-Cortez, M. (2001). Preschoolers' funds of knowledge displayed through sociodramatic play episodes in a bilingual classroom. *Early Childhood Education Journal,* 29(1), 35–40.

Rogoff, B. (1998). Cognition as a collaborative process. In D. Kuhn and R. Siegler (Eds.), *Handbook of child psychology (5th ed.), Vol. 2, Cognition, perception and language* (pp. 679–744). New York: John Wiley.

Rogoff, B. (2003). *The cultural nature of human development.* New York: Oxford University Press.

Rogoff, B., Matusov, E., and White, C. (1996). Models of teaching and learning: Participation in a community of learners. In D. Olson and N. Torrance (Eds.), *The handbook of education and human development: New models of learning, teaching and schooling* (pp. 388–414). Cambridge, MA: Blackwell Publishers.

Sammons, P., Elliott, K., Sylva, K., Melhuish, E., Siraj-Blatchford, I., and Taggart, B. (2004). The impact of pre-school on young children's cognitive attainments at entry to reception. *British Educational Research Journal,* 30(5), 691–712.

Siraj-Blatchford, I. (2004). Quality teaching in the early years. In A. Anning, J. Cullen, and M. Fleer (Eds.), *Early childhood education: society and culture* (pp. 137–148). London: Sage.

Siraj-Blatchford, I., and Sylva, K. (2004). Researching pedagogy in English pre-schools. *British Educational Research Journal,* 30(5), 713–730.

Siraj-Blatchford, I., Sylva, K., Muttock, S., Gilden, R., and Bell, D. (2002). *Researching effective pedagogy in the early years.* Retrieved June 18, 2003 from http://www.dfes.gov.uk/research/data/uploadfiles/RR356.pdf

Simmons, H., Schimanski, L:, McGarva, P., Cullen, J., and Haworth, P. (2005). Teachers researching young children's working theories. *Early Childhood Folio,* 8, 18–22. Wellington: New Zealand Council for Educational Research.

Valsiner, J. (1993). Culture and human development: A co-constructivist perspective. *Annals of theoretical psychology,* 10, 247–298.

Valsiner, J. (2000). *Culture and human development: An introduction.* London: Sage.

Vygotsky, L. S. (1978). *Mind in society: The development of higher psychological processes.* Cambridge, MA: Harvard University Press.

Vygotsky, L. S. (1986). *Thought and language.* Cambridge, MA: MIT Press.

Walsh, J. A., and Sattes, B. D. (2005). *Quality questioning: Research-based practice to engage every learner.* Thousand Oaks, CA: Corwin Press.

Wells, G. (1999). *Dialogic inquiry: Towards a sociocultural practice and theory of education.* New York : Cambridge University Press.

Wells, G. (2001a). The development of a community of inquirers. In G. Wells (Ed.) *Action talk and text: Learning and teaching through inquiry* (pp. 1–22). New York: Teachers College Press.

Wells, G. (2001b). The case for dialogic inquiry. In G. Wells (Ed.) *Action talk and text: Learning and teaching through inquiry* (pp. 171–194). New York: Teachers College Press.

Wells, G. (2002). Inquiry as an orientation for learning, teaching and teacher education. In G. Wells and G. Claxton (Eds.), *Learning for life in the 21st century* (pp. 197–210). Oxford: Blackwell.

Wenger, E. (1998). *Communities of practice: Learning, meaning, and identity.* Cambridge: Cambridge University Press.

AUTHOR NOTE

Helen Hedges is a Senior Lecturer in the Faculty of Education, University of Auckland, New Zealand. Her research and teaching interests involve early childhood curriculum and pedagogy and teachers' professional learning.

The author wishes to thank the supervisors of the project, Joy Cullen and Jenny Boyack. Acknowledgement is made to Massey University College of Education for providing funding for the field work of the study.

An earlier extended version of this chapter was presented as part of a New Zealand symposium entitled "Young children experiencing an empowering early childhood curriculum" at the European Early Childhood Education Research Association conference, Dublin, September 1, 2005.

Correspondence concerning this chapter should be addressed by email to: h.hedges@auckland.ac.nz

In: Early Education
Editors: J.B. Mottely and A.R. Randall

ISBN 978-1-60456-908-7
© 2009 Nova Science Publishers, Inc.

Chapter 3

COMMUNITY VIOLENCE AND EMPATHY IN CHILDREN: IMPLICATIONS FOR EDUCATORS AND CAREGIVERS

Julie Sprinkle

Appalachian State University, Boone, North Carolina 28607, USA

ABSTRACT

Children exposed to community violence are at a greater risk of engaging in violent and aggressive activities than children who do not witness these occurrences. Typically, as antisocial behaviors increase, empathic, prosocial behaviors decrease. The current investigation examines the role of community violence in determining the level of empathy in study participants. Children from fourth, fifth, and sixth grades were given the Index of Empathy for Children and Adolescents (IECA) (Bryan, 1982) to measure levels of empathy. Statistical analyses include univariate analysis of variance and correlation analysis. Three demographic variables, gender, age, and ethnicity, were included in the analyses to determine if these variables mediate the relationship between community violence and levels of empathy. Statistical tests indicate levels of community violence in conjunction with demographic variables significantly influence the amount of empathy present in children and adolescents. Implications for educators and caregivers are examined and suggestions to bolster empathic and decrease antisocial behaviors are discussed.

Although youth violence has long been recognized as a social problem by scholars and social scientists (Whitmer, 1997), youth violence has only been of widespread public concern since the early 1990's (Howard, Flora, & Griffin, 1999). Youth violence in inner-cities, particularly gang violence (Spergel, 1992), has plagued the nation for decades. However, media and political attention were garnered when youth in middle and upper class communities began participating in violent acts (Astor, 1995). Similarly, youth aggression has markedly increased – particularly bullying (Olweus, 1994; Horne, Bartolomucci, & Newman-Carlson, 2003). Bullying is defined as intentional, repetitive negative actions that inflict physical or psychological discomfort upon the recipient (Olweus, 1991). It is estimated that 15% of children are involved in bullying activities (Olweus, 1987). Approximately 2.1 million children and adolescents bully others while 2.7 million children and adolescents are victims of bullying (Astor, 1995). Occasionally, children who are bullied retaliate with violence. In roughly 70% of school shootings since 1974, the attackers report being bullied by one or more peers prior to the incident (Fried & Fried, 2003). Violence and aggression can permeate schools, homes, and the focus of the current investigation, communities.

Children exposed to community violence typically face difficulties uncharacteristic of their counterparts who reside in non-violent areas. For example, children who witness violence in their communities are more likely to experience depression (Lambert, Ialongo, Boyd, & Cooley, 2005; Cooley-Quille, Boyd, Frantz, & Walsh, 2001), anxiety, and fear, as well as engage in violent, aggressive, deviant, and/or other antisocial behaviors (Garbarino, Dubrow, Kostelny, & Pardo, 1992; Gorman-Smith & Tolan, 1998; Herrenkohl, Hawkins, Chung, Hill, & Battin-Pearson, 2001; Patchin, Huebner, McCluskey, Varano, & Bynum, 2006; Salzinger, Ng-Mak, Feldman, Kam, & Rosario, 2006). Research further indicates children from violent neighborhoods have a higher risk of gun possession (Patchin, Huebner, McCluskey, Varano, & Bynum, 2006), suicidal thoughts or gestures, and substance use or abuse (Miller-Johnson, Lochman, Coie, Terry, & Hyman, 1998; Newman, 2000). Despite efforts to 'clean up' neighborhoods through various outreach programs, community violence persists. One major deterrent to antisocial behaviors often lacking in children from these environments is the possession of empathy.

EMPATHY

Empathy is the cognitive and affective ability to take the point of view of another person, or in essence, to know how another person feels and thinks about a situation (Shantz, 1975). Children who possess empathy are less likely to engage in antisocial behaviors because they know how it will affect the person they are directly or indirectly harming. For instance, if a child teases another child about wearing glasses, the instigator lacks empathy. When a child has empathic abilities, he/she is capable of both feeling the emotional pain and understanding behavioral reactions, such as crying, of the targeted child. The ability to understand the cognitive and affective traits of the victim change attitudes about what is and is not acceptable behavior (Eisenberg-Berg, 1979; Eisenberg, Carlo, Murphy, & Van Court, 1995; Berkowitz & Grych, 2000; Fried & Fried, 2003; Horne, Bartolomucci, & Newman-Carlson, 2003).

Empathy is shaped through a process of modeling behaviors, as well as cognitive and moral developmental phases. Modeling can be incorporated through social learning. Children witness positive, empathic behaviors, enact those behaviors, and are reinforced by praise or rewards from parents or significant others (Bandura, 1968; 1977; 1986). Further, cognitive and moral developmental theorists assert that progression through developmental stages makes prosocial behavior and empathic reasoning possible (Kohlberg, 1969; Eisenberg et al., 1995). Moral behavior is what the dominant society feels individuals should or should not do in a given situation – the "right versus wrong, good versus bad" paradigm. Kohlberg (1969; 1976; 1981) postulated that prior to age nine, children engage in needs oriented or primitive empathic behavior based on rewards and punishments from authority figures.

The first four of Kohlberg's (1969) six stages of moral development are relevant to the current study. Stages one and two comprise the pre-conventional level, spanning from birth to age nine. During stage one, the child is concerned with avoiding punishment. Conversely, during stage two moral reasoning is dictated by obtaining rewards. Between the ages of nine and fifteen, children are in the conventional level of moral development. Stage three of this level is governed by a desire to gain approval while stage four signifies internalization of social rules through conformity to norms. The post-conventional level, including stages five and six, extends from age sixteen until death. Viewed in this light, the ability to make value decisions is a developmental process. After age eight or nine, children develop the ability for complex perspective taking or situational empathy. Children are then capable of ascertaining how others think and feel and incorporating this knowledge into their decision-making and action-oriented schemas. However, some studies have provided evidence that younger children are capable of exhibiting situational empathy. Rosenkoetter (1999) and Hoffman (1979) found that children as young as six can understand moral issues and feel empathy for others.

Unfortunately, exposure to community violence may inhibit or extinguish the development of empathy. Just as children learn prosocial, empathic behaviors from witnessing and enacting those behaviors, children also learn violent and aggressive actions through a process of exposure, reenactment, and reinforcement (Bandura, 1968; Bandura & Walters, 1963). Children witnessing violence in their communities are more likely to imitate these actions, particularly if they do not have prosocial role models.

THE PRESENT STUDY

Goals and Objectives

The goals of the present study are to determine how community violence affects the development of empathy in children and what implications these findings have for educators and caregivers. The objectives are to determine how and to what extent the presence or absence of empathy is mediated by (a) gender, (b) age, and (c) ethnicity. It is hypothesized that (1) children from areas that have high rates of violent crime will have less empathy than children from areas that have low rates of violent crime, (2) female participants will have higher rates of empathy than male participants, and (3) younger children will have higher rates of empathy than older children. Ethnicity is expected to have little to no impact on the presence or absence of empathy (Figure 1).

The Study Population

Children from four middle/elementary schools across three counties were included in the present study. The sample was comprised of 57.1% (n=177) fourth graders, 12.3% (n=38) fifth graders, and 30.6% (n=95) sixth graders. In the present study, grade level is used as a proxy for participant's age. The sample (n=310) was equally divided along gender and ethnic lines with 50.3% of the sample comprised of females, 49.7% males, 43.6% African Americans, and 52.9% Caucasians. Two schools were in a county that has a low crime rate, with zero murders, one rape, five robberies, and only 12 assaults (www.city-data.com) in the past year. The other two schools were in counties with higher crimes rates; with one county having 9 murders, 12 rapes, 35 robberies, and 46 assaults in the past year and the second county having 6 murders, 18 rapes, 48 robberies, and 59 assaults in the past year (www.city-data.com). The low crime rate areas are in a county with a crime index of 240.6, less than the United States average of 327.2, while the high crime rate areas are in counties with crimes indexes of 806.4 and 528.6, respectively.

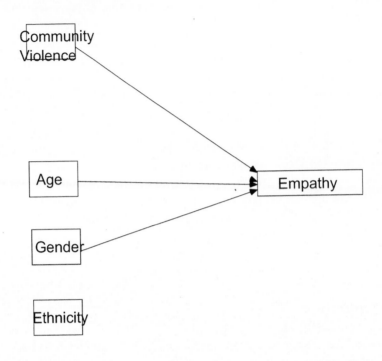

Figure 1. Factors influencing the development of empathy

METHODOLOGY

Data was obtained from selected fourth, fifth, and sixth grade students after written parental/guardian consent had been received. All study participants were given the Index of Empathy for Children and Adolescents (IECA). The IECA is a 22-item instrument designed to measure affective or emotional empathy in children and adolescents (Bryant, 1982). Modeling the IECA after Mehrabian and Epstein's (1972) measure of empathy for adults, Bryant (1982) developed the IECA by simplifying words and concepts and shortening the length of the instrument. The IECA can be used with simple no= 0 or yes= 1 responses, with a nine-point likert-type scale where -4= very strong disagreement and +4= very strong agreement, or with a five-point likert-type scale where 1= strongly disagree and 5= strongly agree (Bryant, 1987). However, it is recommended that children under the age of 12 use the yes/no format. Regardless of the response categories, a higher score is indicative of higher levels of empathy.

RESULTS

IECA

Data was analyzed using the Statistical Package for the Social Sciences version 14.0 (SPSS). Participant scores on the Index of Empathy for Children and Adolescents (IECA) indicated varying empathy levels among the study population. Only .3% (n= 1) of the sample received a score of 22, indicating that they are maximally empathic. Conversely, 1.6% (n=5) of the sample received a score of 0, indicating extremely low empathic traits. The mean score of the IECA was 10.7 (SD= 5.0) while the mode was 13 (Table 1). A frequency distribution for the IECA shows the distribution is almost perfectly symmetrical (skew= .02, kurtosis= -.80).

Table 1. Score on the Index of Empathy for Children and Adolescents (IECA)

Mean	Standard Deviation	Mode	Skew	Kurtosis
10.7	5.0	13	.02	-.80

Correlations

For African American students, the demographic variables gender, grade, and crime rate, were significantly correlated to total scores on the IECA. Grade and crime rate were negatively correlated (r=-.17; r=-.20), while gender was positively correlated (r=.14) with total IECA scores, indicating that as age and neighborhood crime rate increased, scores on the IECA and thus empathy decreased. In addition, empathy levels were also found to be higher in females (Table 2). A similar association was detected in Caucasian study participants. Grade and crime rate were negatively correlated (r=-.36, r=-.35) and gender was positively correlated (r=.20) with IECA scores (Table 3). However, significant correlations were also found between the demographic variables. Older children in the study were African American and from high crime neighborhoods (r=-.95), while younger children were Caucasian and from low crime neighborhoods (r=.95).

Univariate General Linear Model

A univariate general linear model was chosen since the present study has one dependent variable (scores on the IECA) and multiple fixed or independent variables (crime rate, gender, grade level, ethnicity). The test of between subject effects indicated crime rate, gender, grade level, and ethnicity combined significantly impact scores on the IECA (R squared=.203, F=3.661, p=.000) and participant levels of empathy. Individually, each variable barely missed significance at the p=.05 level.

Table 2. Independent and demographic variable correlations with IECA scores

Variables	IECA Score Correlations
Grade	-.17*
Gender	.14*
Crime Rate	-.20*

*p<.0

Table 3. Independent and demographic variable correlations with IECA scores

Variables	IECA Score Correlations
Grade	-.36*
Gender	.20*
Crime Rate	-.35*

*p<.0

DISCUSSION

The study's findings indicate moderate support for the research hypotheses. First, children from areas with high rates of violent crime had significantly less empathy as measured by scores on the IECA than children from low crime areas, supporting the researcher's hypothesis. Children from areas with high crime are less empathic due to chronic exposure to a social environment accepting of and normalizing violence. The converse is also true; children from communities with little violent crime are more empathic due to the absence of displays of aggressive and antisocial behaviors.

Children learn to think, feel, and act based on the world around them. If children are exposed to violence and aggression, they will often react with violence and aggression (Bandura, 1968; 1986), prohibiting or stunting the development of empathy. Second, as hypothesized, younger children had significantly higher levels of empathy than older children, while females had significantly higher levels of empathy than males. In the current study, participant grade level is used as a proxy for age. A review of the literature suggests that violence and aggression increase with age (Eron, 1987; Tremblay, Masse, Vitaro, & Dobkin, 1995), resulting in decreased levels of empathy as participants' age increased. With regard to gender, girls are more likely to exhibit overtly prosocial behaviors than boys (Feshbach, 1969; Eisenberg & Lennon, 1983; Hay, 1994; Hay, Castle, Davies, Demetriou, & Stimson, 1999) due to a socialization process that indoctrinates females to be considerate of the thoughts and feelings of others (Gilligan, 1982).

Finally, it appears that African American students scored lower on the IECA than Caucasian students, indicating less empathy. Ethnicity has received an inordinate amount of attention in violence prevention and prosocial behavior literature, particularly among African American and Latino youths. According to the USDOJ (1996), homicide is the leading cause of death for African American youth. In support of this assertion, Rathus, Wetzler, and Asnis

(1995) studied death and loss in the African American and Latino adolescent population. Over one half of all respondents had lost a close friend or friends to homicide. In conjunction with the high rate of homicide, the risk of becoming a victim of nonfatal violence is also higher among African American and Latino youths than among Caucasians (Hammond & Yung, 1994; Cotton, Resnick, Browne, Martin, McCarraher, & Woods, 1994). Several explanations exist for the high rates of violence among minority populations. First, minorities are more likely than Caucasians to live in poverty or low socioeconomic areas (Garbarino et al., 1992). The lack of adequate financial resources increase risk factors for violence while decreasing protective factors that inhibit violent and aggressive behaviors. Also relevant to minority youth is the victimization they have experienced as a byproduct of discrimination and racism. A past history of victimization is associated with stronger pro-violence attitudes and a greater likelihood of victimizing another (Jenkins & Bell, 1997). However, as the African American students in the current study were older, from low income schools, and were more likely to live in high crime neighborhoods, it is not ethnicity, but the confluence of these three factors that resulted in participant scores.

LIMITATIONS

While the researcher's hypotheses were moderately supported by the study's findings, there are several limitations that must be considered. Not all children living in high crime communities may have witnessed or been exposed to acts of violence or aggression, while not all children living in low crime areas have been fortunate enough to be sheltered from displays of violence and aggression either in their neighborhoods or their own homes. However, it is also feasible that participants have witnessed violence in their communities but are resilient enough to remain empathic. Resiliency in children is typically comprised of protective factors that reduce an individual's likelihood of engaging in antisocial behaviors. Research indicates characteristics commonly perceived as protective are inclusive of community, familial, and individual assets (Howard, Dryden, & Johnson, 1999). The possession of attributes such as a supportive family, prosocial friends, and a sense of self-esteem or worth can increase the strength of protective factors and empathic behaviors while reducing the risk of antisocial behaviors such as violence and aggression. Finally, the sample was geographically limited. A large scale, replicated study would reveal more information about the empathic traits of children in middle and elementary schools.

RECOMMENDATIONS AND CONCLUSIONS

As a significant relationship between community crime rate and empathy was found in the present study, several recommendations for increasing empathy in elementary and middle school students are suggested. First, as age is negatively correlated with empathy, prosocial behavioral programs should begin early in a child's educational career and continue into adolescence to achieve maximum effectiveness. Second, violence prevention and empathy promotion programs are often aimed at children and taught in school settings. However, it is apparent that communities are in need of such programs as well. Perhaps developing empathy promotion programs aimed at the entire community or neighborhood would yield longer lasting, more robust results. Third, schools should offer sanctuary and a safe haven to students, particularly those from violent or high crime neighborhoods. Teachers, administrators, and caregivers must work together to make this protective mechanism a reality for millions of at-risk children by providing before and after school programs where children can complete homework, participate in sports, or join various other social activities designed to positively focus their energies. Caregivers and schools should also increase their efforts in areas where children face daunting risk factors such as poverty, gangs, substance use/abuse, and unstable household compositions in order to bolster protective mechanisms in these most vulnerable youth.

Educators and classroom environments can support or detract from empathic behaviors in children (Alvarez, 2006; Morrison, Robertson, & Harding, 1998). Teachers are in the unique position to strengthen prosocial behaviors and discourage antisocial behaviors by offering positive or negative reinforcement to their students on a daily basis. As teachers are consistently able to observe classroom behaviors, their ratings of empathic and aggressive behaviors may have greater validity than student report and should be utilized when feasible in conjunction with self-report. In addition, children hailing from homes lacking prosocial role models will often formally or informally identify a teacher or other school staff as their mentor. Children are strongly influenced by their teachers, parents, guardians, and/or caregivers, emphasizing the need for these role models to emulate prosocial behaviors. The researcher would advise schools to involve all teachers and consider including caregivers in their antiviolence and prosocial development programs to achieve even greater exposure to empathy in childhood. Finally, children from all neighborhoods, regardless of community violence levels, may need extra attention from caregivers, teachers, counselors, and social workers to discourage antisocial behaviors as a method of gaining attention, status, and recognition. Fostering the development of empathy in children not only provides a buffer against antisocial behaviors, but also creates a generation of kind, compassionate, and caring individuals. Our children, and society as a whole, deserve no less.

REFERENCES

Alvarez, H. K. (2006). The impact of teacher preparation on responses to student aggression in the classroom. *Teaching and Teacher Education, 23(7),* 1113-1126.

Astor, R. (1995). School violence: A blueprint for elementary school interventions. *Social Work in Education, 17(2),* 101-115.

Bandura, A. (1968). *Aggression: A social learning analysis.* Englewood Cliffs, NJ: Prentice-Hall.

Bandura, A. (1977). *A social learning theory.* Englewood Cliffs, NJ: Prentice-Hall.

Bandura, A. (1986). *Social foundations of thought and action: A social cognitive theory.* Englewood Cliffs, NJ: Prentice-Hall.

Bandura, A., & Walters, R. H. (1963). *Social learning and personality development.* New York: Holt, Rinehart, & Winston.

Berkowitz, M. W., & Grych, J. H. (2000). Early character development and education. *Early Education and Development, 11(1),* 55-72.

Bryant, B. (1982). An index of empathy for children and adolescents. *Child Development, 53,* 413-425.

Bryant, B. (1987). Critique of comparable questionnaire methods in use to assess empathy in children and adults. In N. Eisenberg & J. Strayer (Eds.). *Empathy and its development: Cambridge studies in social and emotional development.* (pp. 361-373).

City-data for _____. Retrieved from www.city-data.com September 13, 2007.

Cooley-Quille, M. R., Boyd, R. C., Frantz, E., & Walsh, J. (2001). Emotional and behavioral impact of exposure to community violence in inner-city adolescents. *Journal of Clinical Child Psychology, 30,* 199-206.

Cotten, N. U., Resnick, J., Browne, D. C., Martin, S. L., McCarraher, . R., & Woods, J. (1994). Aggression and fighting behavior among African American adolescents: Individual and family factors. *American Journal of Public Health, 84,* 618-622.

Eisenberg-Berg, N. (1979). Development of children's prosocial moral judgment. *Developmental Psychology, 23(15),* 128-137.

Eisenberg, N., & Lennon, R. (1983). Sex differences in empathy and related capacities. *Psychological Bulletin, 94,* 100-131.

Eisenberg, N., Carlo, G., Murphy, B., & Van Court, P. (1995). Prosocial development in late adolescence: *A longitudinal study. Child Development,* 66, 1179-1197.

Eron, L. D. (1987). Aggression through the ages. *School safety: Special Issue on Bullies* (pp. 12-17). Malibu, CA: Pepperdine University, National School Safety Center.

Feshbach, N. (1969). Sex differences in children's modes of aggressive responses toward outsiders. *Merrill-Palmer Quarterly, 15,* 249-258.

Fried, S., & Fried, P. (2003). *Bullies, targets, and witnesses: Helping children break the pain chain.* New York: M. Evans and Company, Inc.

Garbarino, J., Dubrow, N., Kostelny, K., & Pardo, C. (1992). *Children in danger: Coping with the consequences of community violence.* San Francisco: Jossey-Bass.

Gilligan, C. (1982). *In a different voice: Psychological theory and women's development.* Cambridge, MA: Harvard University Press.

Gorman-Smith, D. & Tolan, P. (1998). The role of exposure to community violence and developmental problems among inner-city youth. *Development and Psychopathology, 10,* 101-116.

Hammond, W. R., & Yung, B. R. (1994). African American's. In L. D. Eron, J. H. Gentry, & P. Schlegel (Eds.), *Reason to hope: A psychosocial perspective on violence and youth* (pp. 105-118). Washington, D.C.: American Psychological Association.

Hay, D. F. (1994). Prosocial development. *Journal of Child Psychology and Psychiatry, 35,* 29-71.

Hay, D., Castle, J., Davies, L., Demetriou, H., & Stimson, C. (1999). Prosocial action in very early childhood. *Journal of Child Psychology and Psychiatry, 40(6),* 905-916.

Herrenkohl, T. I., Hawkins, J. D., Chung, I., Hill, K. G., & Battin-Pearson, S. (2001). School and community risk factors and interventions. In R. Loeber & D. P. Farrington (Eds.), *Child delinquents: Development, intervention, and service needs* (pp. 211-246). Thousand Oaks, CA: Sage.

Hoffman, L. (1979). Maternal employment: 1979. *American Psychologist, 34,* 859-865.

Horne, A., Bartolomucci, C., & Newman-Carlson, D. (2003). *Bully busters: A teacher's manual for helping bullies, victims, and bystanders.* Champaign, IL: Research Press.

Howard, K., Flora, J., & Griffin, M. (1999). Violence-prevention programs in schools: State of the science and implications for future research. *Applied and Preventative Psychology, 8,* 197-215.

Howard, W., Dryden, J., & Johnson, B. (1999). Childhood resilience: Review and critique of literature. *Oxford Review of Education, 25(3),* 307-323.

Jenkins, E. J., & Bell, C. C. (1997). Exposure and response to community violence among children and adolescents. In J. Osofskey (Ed.), *Children in a violent society* (pp. 9-31). New York: Guilford.

Kohlberg, L. (1969). *Stages in the development of moral thought and action.* New York: Holt.

Kohlberg, L. (1976). The cognitive-developmental approach to moral education. In P H. Martorell (Ed.), *Social studies strategies: Theories into practice.* New York: Harper and Row.

Kohlberg, L. (1981). *Essays on moral development (Vol. I). The philosophy of moral development.* San Francisco: Harper & Row.

Lambert, S. F., Ialongo, N. S., Boyd, R. C., & Cooley, M. R. (2005). Risk factors for community violence exposure in adolescence. *American Journal of Community Psychology, 36(1/2),* 29-48.

Mehrabian, A., & Epstein, N. (1972). A measure of emotional empathy. *Journal of Personality*, 40(4), 525-543.

Miller-Johnson, S., Lochman, J. E., Coie, J. D., Terry, R., & Hyman, C. (1998). Comorbidity of conduct and depressive problems at sixth grade: Substance use outcomes across adolescence. *Journal of Abnormal Child Psychology, 26,* 221-232.

Morrison, G. M., Robertson, L., & Harding, M. (1998). Resilience factors that support the classroom functioning of acting out and aggressive students. *Psychology in the Schools, 35(3),* 217-227.

Newman, C. F. (2000). Crisis intervention for depressed adolescents with conduct problems: Two case illustrations. *Crisis Intervention and Time-Limited Treatments, 5,* 213-239.

Olweus, D. (1987). Schoolyard bullying intervention. In *School safety: Special issue on bullies* (pp. 4-11). Malibu, CA: Pepperdine University, National School Safety Center.

Olweus, D. (1991). Bully/victim problems among schoolchildren: Basic facts and effects of a school-based intervention program. In D.J. Pepler & K. H. Rubin (Eds.), *The development and treatment of childhood aggression* (pp. 5-31). Hillsdale, NJ: Lawrence Erlbaum.

Olweus, D. (1994). Annotation: Bullying at school: Basic facts and effects of a school-based intervention program. *Journal of Child Psychology and Psychiatry and Applied Disciplines, 35,* 1171-1190.

Patchin, J. W., Huebner, B. M., McCluskey, J. D., Varan, S. P., & Bynum, T. S. (2006). Exposure to community violence and childhood delinquency. *Crime and Delinquency, 52(2),* 307-332.

Rathus, J., Wetzler, S., & Asnis, G. (1995). Posttraumatic stress disorder and exposure to violence in adolescence. *Journal of the American Medical Association, 273,* 1734.

Rosenkoetter, L. I. (1999). The television situation comedy and children's prosocial behavior. *Journal of Applied Social Psychology, 29(5),* 979-993.

Salzinger, S., Ng-Mak, D. S., Feldman, R. S., Kam, C., & Rosario, M. (2006). Exposure to community violence processes that increase the risk for inner-city middle school children. *Journal of Early Adolescence, 26(2),* 232-266.

Shantz, C. U. (1975). Empathy in relation to social cognitive development. *The Counseling Psychologist, 5(2),* 18-21.

Spergel, I. A. (1992). Youth gangs: An essay review. *Social Services Review,* 120-139.

Tremblay, R. E., Masse, L. ., Vitaro, F., & Dobkin, P. L. (1995). The impact of friends' deviant behavior on early onset of delinquency: Longitudinal data from 6 to 13 years of age. *Development and Psychopathology, 7,* 649-667.

United States Census Data. (2000). Retrieved from www.census2000 September 13, 2007.

Whitmer, B. (1997). *The violence mythos.* Albany, NY: State University of New York Press, Albany.

In: Early Education
Editors: J.B. Mottely and A.R. Randall

Chapter 4

TEACHERS' AFFECTIVE PRESENTATION OF CHILDREN'S BOOKS AND YOUNG CHILDREN'S ATTENTION AND PARTICIPATION DURING CLASSROOM BOOK READING

Eleni Moschovaki

School Adviser, Ministry of Education and Religious Affairs, Greece

ABSTRACT

This study examines how teachers' affective presentation of children's books influences young children's attention, participation and spontaneous participation during book reading. The hypotheses of the study are based on the premise that children are more motivated to concentrate in books presented with high affect (motivational model of affective information processing) and participate more spontaneously due to the positive affective state of the participants (cognitive model of affective information processing).

Twenty kindergarten teachers read four different types of books, two fiction (familiar/unfamiliar story format) and two information books (expository/narrative text). The language transcripts of each session were transcribed and analyzed at the level of utterance. Teachers' affect was measured by the use of voice intonation, dramatization and personal involvement reactions. From each class, the attentive behavior of eight children (four boys, four girls) was coded.

Children's attention was high, yet it was higher in fiction books compared to the information ones. Teachers' high affective presentation of the unfamiliar fiction book elicited higher concentration, compared to low affective presentation of the same book. In the familiar fiction book, children's spontaneous participation was higher when they interacted with high affect teachers compared to those with low affect. When the constituent parts of affect (intonation, dramatization and personal involvement) were related to children's behavior, we found that dramatization discouraged children's participation whereas teachers' comments of personal involvement prompted their spontaneous participation.

The outcomes are discussed in relation to the motivational and cognitive model of affective information processing while taking into consideration text genre and children's familiarity to the story format.

INTRODUCTION

Book reading has been the subject of an enormous amount of psychological and educational research during the last fifteen years. Research on book reading has mainly focused on the development of language skills, early literacy skills and the development of thinking skills (reviews in Scarborough & Dobrich, 1994; Bus, Van Ijzendoorn & Pellegrini, 1995; Blok, 1999). To our knowledge, research has not yet explicitly addressed the issue of how teachers' affective presentation of children's books affects children's behavior. This poses a great contradiction since there is a widespread notion that stories are narratives whose primary function is to entertain by stimulating the affective states of the participants (Brewer & Lichtenstein, 1982; Egan, 1988).

The aim of this study is to examine how teachers' affective presentation of stories affects young children's attention, participation and spontaneous participation during a book session. The available research on the impact of affect across developmental levels is limited. Bugental, Lin & Susskind (1995) suggest, from the little research that is available, that the impact of affect varies according to age, not only due to changes in experience or to increased capacity but also through the emergence of regulation processes in response to affective states.

Schwartz (1990) has proposed that the function of affective states is a bi-directional one. Different situational appraisals elicit different emotions but the experience of a certain emotion also informs the individual about the nature of the current psychological situation. Thus, when book reading becomes a satisfying experience children consider it as a safe and pleasurable experience and they are more motivated to engage in it. According to the motivational model, positive affect directs the subject to maintain and extend the positive state. This indicates that children will be more concentrated on a task they perceive as pleasurable and satisfying in nature (positive affect). Based on the motivational model, it is reasonable to hypothesize that, due to the affective nature of book reading, children will be more motivated to concentrate and pay attention to language alone, in particular in fiction books, in order to satisfy themselves through the story.

Empirical findings suggest that spontaneous thought processes are tuned to meet the requirements signaled by one's affective state. Individuals who are in positive affective states are more likely to foster the use of more simplifying heuristic processing strategies, the exploration of novel procedures and possibilities and the elaboration of unusual creative associations (Fiedler, 1988; Clore, Schwarz & Conway, 1994). Isen (1987), in particular, has argued that positive material is extensive and well interconnected in memory, giving individuals in elated moods access to a wide variety of material. Similar outcomes have been found with young children (Isen, 1990). Children 4-6 years old were more able to sort items into atypical dimensions and to see relations among diverse stimuli under positive affect (by giving a gift). The outcomes from the cognitive model suggest that, in stories with marked positive affect, children are more likely to participate spontaneously, due to the expansion of network associations when listening to the story, thus facilitating the emergence of positive material.

Furthermore, there is evidence that people's subjective emotional experience does seem to be affected by the activation and feedback from facial, vocal, postural and movement mimicry and that people therefore tend to "catch" others' emotions (Hatfield, Cacioppo &

Rapson, 1994). Analysis of classroom interaction has shown that teachers' affective presentation of children's books was effectively transmitted to young children and managed to affectively engage them in both information and fiction books (Moschovaki, Meadows & Pellegrini, 2007). Thus, teachers' affective presentation of books influences young children's affective engagement.

The research questions of the study are as follows:

- -Is teachers' affective presentation of children's books related to young children's attention, participation and spontaneous participation during the book session?
- -How does variation in teachers' affective presentation of the same book affect children's attention, participation and spontaneous participation during the book session?
- -Is the use of affective strategies (intonation, dramatization and personal involvement) by teachers related to young children's attention, participation and spontaneous participation during the book session?

METHODOLOGY

Participants

The data collection took place in Greek kindergarten schools. Twenty teachers participated from two Greek islands and the children in all classes were of mixed ages from 3.5 up to 5.5 years old. Teachers volunteered to participate and the sample consisted mainly of well-experienced teachers (mean teaching experience 12.6 years, range 3-20). Each class had from 10 up to 20 children, all of whom attended the book session. Teachers usually read children's books three times a week.

Materials

Given that the choice of book has considerable impact on the presentation style and the discussion, it was important to give the same books to all teachers. Research on the books Greek children of pre-school age have at home, revealed that they mainly have cheap editions of traditional fairy tales (Kitsaras, 1993). A reason that can account for the lack of children's access to other types of children's literature is the fact that public libraries in Greece are rare and there is no campaign publicizing the impact of book reading on young children's development.

All teachers read the same four books including a variety of book and text genres to the students: "Fire" by Rius and Parramon (1992), "Life under earth" by Rius & Parramon (1994), "Winnie the Witch" by Paul & Thomas (1990) and "The three little wolves" by Trivizas (1993).

"Fire" is an information book with a limited expository text. It describes features of fire such as its color and gives examples of when fire is good or bad, useful or dangerous. The pictures are rather static showing the different uses of fire, e.g. a fireplace, a forest blaze, the candles of a birthday cake, Indians dancing around the fire etc. and complement the text.

"Life under Earth" is an information book with a more extended narrative type of text. A little rabbit describes different events of its life such as how its parents made their burrow, the kind of food it eats etc. The illustrations present life under earth (roots, animals, bulbs) in great detail and either complement or follow the text at each page. "Winnie the Witch" is a contemporary fiction book which presents an eccentric witch who lives in a black house with a black cat. The good witch prefers to change her house to make her cat happy. The text has no dialogues. The illustrations are very impressive and complement the text. The house, the objects and the heroes are presented with great detail and artistry. This particular book is considered as an unfamiliar format since it does not follow the conventions of the fairy tales most children are used to. For example, there are no dialogues or familiar expressions ("once upon a time", "they lived happily ever after"), a lot of information is implicit and is complemented by the book illustrations. "The three little wolves" is a fiction book which follows the traditional style of "The three little pigs" a popular fairy tale well known to children and is considered as a familiar format. All teachers had either read or told this traditional fairy tale in their class. The text in "The three little wolves" has a lot of repetition, dialogues and rhyming all features of traditional fairy tales. The illustrations are also very impressive and either follow or complement the text.

When teachers presented the books, they asked if any child had the specific book at home or if someone had read it to them. During the study, no child from all twenty classes knew the books, apart from one who owned a copy of "The three little wolves".

Procedures

Each session was tape recorded. Books were given to the teachers the day prior to the recording and they were first read during our visit. Teachers were instructed not to read the text to the children in advance, since research has shown that familiarity with the book changes the interaction patterns of book reading, with children participating more actively (Goodsitt, Raitan & Pelmutter, 1988; Beals, DeTemple & Dickinson, 1994). Additionally, we asked teachers to present the book in their usual way and try to ignore the presence of the researcher in the classroom.

Children were sitting on benches opposite to the teacher. Most teachers adopted an interactive style in the presentation of information books (reading each page, showing the picture, discussing it); in fiction books, they adopted a performance-oriented style (read first the whole story and then presented the pictures followed by discussion). The order of presentation of the four books was randomized so that there should be no differences between books due to children's increasing experience of being read to. From each class, we collected four different book readings; each session took place in a different day. In total, 80 sessions were collected. The mean duration of the session for the books was: "Fire" $\underline{M}$=22, $\underline{SD}$= 6.22, "Life under earth" $\underline{M}$=22, $\underline{SD}$= 7.7, "Winnie the Witch" $\underline{M}$=22, $\underline{SD}$= 7.1 and "The three little wolves" $\underline{M}$=33.5, $\underline{SD}$= 12.8. The entire session was transcribed and analyzed.

Measures: Developing a Coding System

The Unit of Analysis

The unit of analysis for the reading of the text by the teacher was the sentence; for the discussion, the utterance. Utterances are defined as phrases that are distinctive in content and include intonation and turn taking between the teacher and the children (Wells, 1975).

During the coding of children's behavior, all their spontaneous comments were counted as separate utterances. More than one reply to a teacher's question, counted if the teacher accepted the child's comment. If the teacher acknowledged more than one reply then all replies counted as separate utterances.

Coding of the Participants' Behavior

To code the data, we adopted three different categories of features used by Wells (1975), Blank, Rose & Berlin (1978) and Dickinson & Smith (1994), adapted for the needs of this study. The first category of feature refers to the speaker (the teacher or child). The second specifies spontaneity or responsiveness. Spontaneous utterances included all questions and statements which initiated discussion. Responsive utterances included all responses to questions and repetitions of questions for a correct answer to be given.

The third category refers to the coding of affect during the book reading interaction. We coded utterances with affect for both the text being read and the discussion. The categories were mutually exclusive and exhaustive (if there was no affect it was coded as 0).

The affect was coded for teacher's utterances and was based on the prosodic and paralinguistic features of book reading. We did not take into consideration non verbal features since video recording was avoided as being too intrusive. However, after each session, notes were kept for particular gestures the teacher used during book presentation and these were taken into consideration during the coding of affect. For example, when the witch was casting her magic spells (abracadabra) some teachers would reenact the scene by waving their hand in the air as if they were holding a magic stick or knock their chair when the bad pig knocked the door. Such gestures were also accompanied by voice reenactment and were coded as dramatization utterances. The recordings, as well the transcription and coding of the data were done by the same person, which facilitated the interpretation of the language transcripts. All paralinguistic cues such as laughter, exclamation etc. that were not accompanied by a verbal comment were counted as separate utterances.

We coded teachers' affective presentations into three main categories:

- Intonation. This category covers features of voice intonation such as pausing with the purpose of stressing a story point; reading slowing in order to emphasize the minimal text in "Fire"; prolonging the end of sentences (storytelling technique), prolonging words to emphasize length, size, duration; whispering or raising the voice in order to stress words or attract children's attention. In addition, all sentences from the original texts with dialogues, rhyming and questions were coded as intonation. Such features create a more fragmented kind of language, similar to strategies used in storytelling, prompting the emotional enchantment of the audience (Chafe, 1982). For example, the author of "The three little wolves" has included questions at particular points of the text with the purpose of exciting children. When the teachers reenacted the dialogues, these utterances were coded as dramatization rather than intonation.

- Dramatization. This category includes re-enactment of the dialogues by voice alterations and re-enactment of scenes.
- Personal involvement. This category refers to all utterances and paralinguistic cues whereby teachers expressed personal interest, pleasure, excitement, empathy and sorrow. Both language content and voice intonation were considered.

Further information on the rational of the coding of affect and related examples can be found elsewhere (Moschovaki, Meadows & Pellegrini, 2007). Eight stories were coded by a second person in order to calculate the interobserver's reliability. Cohen Kappa for the participants ranged from 0.99-1, for spontaneous 0.95-0.99 and for affect 0.75-0.88, reflecting very substantial agreement (Bakeman & Gottman, 1986).

Coding of Children's Attentive Behavior

Eight children, four boys and four girls from each class were randomly selected and their attentive behavior was coded. They were all born on the same year.

During the pilot study, we conducted video recordings of classroom book reading with the purpose of developing a coding system for measuring children's attentive behavior. We originally used Hayward's (1982) coding system but modified it, so as to diminish the mistakes between the two observers and accommodate better the needs of this study.

Attentive behavior includes all cases when the child looks at the book or the teacher, when s/he laughs, speaks at the group, re-enacts or raises his/her hand. Non Attentive Behavior is coded when the child looks elsewhere, when s/he is distracted by outside stimuli, moves in a nervous way, speaks to a nearby child or leaves the group. The coding of children's behavior was done every 10 seconds. Cohen Kappa for the stories of the pilot study ranged from 0.77 to 0.90, reflecting "very substantial" agreement (Bakeman & Gottman, 1986). During data collection, children's attentive behavior was coded apart from three sessions from two different groups. Overall, children's attentive behavior was coded in 77 book sessions. However, it was not possible to code the same children in all four sessions since some children were absent. In such cases, other children of the same age were observed.

Data Analyses

The analysis of the data was done in two ways. First, children's behavior was examined across the four books. The decision was based on findings of a previous set of analyses, which revealed that there were significant differences in both teachers' affective presentation and children's display of affective engagement across the four books –although not in the case of the two information books. In addition, fiction books were presented with more affect than information books (Moschovaki, Meadows & Pellegrini, 2007). Since it was not possible to have exactly the same children during the observation of their attentive behavior across the four books, the data analysis was based on the groups' mean attentive behavior. Secondly, children's behavior was examined separately in relation to teachers' affective presentation of a specific book.

RESULTS

Differences in Children's Behavior among the Four Books

We conducted repeated measures ANOVA for the variables related to children's behavior such as their participation, spontaneous participation and attention. The within subject variable was the four books the teacher read.

The outcomes of the analysis report a book effect on children's behavior. Apart from their spontaneous participation, fiction books seem to prompt more children's participation (with the exception of "Winnie the witch") and more attentive behavior (see Tables 1, 2).

Table 1. Mean and standard deviation of children's behavior across the four books

Variables (N)	Fire		Life		Witch		Wolf	
Children's Behavior	M	SD	M	SD	M	SD	M	SD
Participation (20)	39.6	4.3	39.8	5.1	42.2	3.2	43.6	6.3
Spontaneous Part. (20)	30.2	8.5	29.8	12	31.9	13.6	33.8	16.2
Attentive Behavior (18)*	86.9	9.2	85.9	9	91.7	4.4	92.3	4.8

*Mean group attentive behavior.

Table 2. Repeated measures ANOVA of children's behavior across the four books

Effect	Λ	F	Df	P	η	Tukey
Children's participation	0.57	4.35	3	p<.019	.43	4>1,2
Child. Spont. participation	0.91	.53	3	p<.666	.09	—
Child. Attentive behavior*	0.51	4.74	3	p<.016	.49	3,4>1,2

* Mean group attentive behavior.

Variations in Affective Presentation of Each Book

We decided to examine each book separately and look at how variations in teachers' affective presentation of a particular book is related to young children's attention, participation and spontaneous participation during the book session. Looking closely at the category of affect from the part of the teachers, we identified those whose presentation was highly affective. The cut off line for low and high affective presentation was guided by the mean affect for each book. Teachers with affect above the mean were considered as high while teachers with affect below the mean were considered as low affect (Fire: $\underline{M}$=5.62, $\underline{SD}$=4.4; Life: $\underline{M}$=8.44, $\underline{SD}$=6.5; Witch: $\underline{M}$=13.95, $\underline{SD}$=10.1; Wolf, $\underline{M}$=28, $\underline{SD}$= 11.09).We coded nine teachers as highly affective in their presentation of the two fiction books. In the case of the information book with narrative text, eight teachers were coded as highly affective, as were ten teachers in the presentation of the information book with the expository text. The remaining teachers were coded as low affect.

Table 3 reports the outcomes from Mann Whitney which tests for differences in children's behavior between low / high affect teachers during the reading of each book.

Children who participated in groups with high affect teachers had higher spontaneous participation in "The three little wolves" and were more concentrated in "Winnie the witch". Conversely, in "Fire" children's participation was higher in groups with low affect teachers.

Table 3. Differences in children's behavior between high and low affect teachers in each book

Compared Variables within Books during the Story Session	Mean Rank		Outcomes From Mann-Whitney#
	High	Low	
a. Children's participation			
Fire	7.30	13.70	z= -2.41, p<.01
Life under earth	7.94	12.21	z= -1.58, p<.11
Winnie the witch	10.50	10.50	z= 0 , p<1
The three little wolves	11.78	9.45	z= -.87 , p<.38
b. Children's spontaneous participation			
Fire	9.90	11.10	z= -.45, p<.65
Life under earth	11.88	9.58	z= -.84, p<.39
Winnie the witch	11.72	9.50	z= -.83, p<.40
The three little wolves	13.67	7.91	z= -2.16, p<.03
c. Children's attentive behavior			
Fire	8.56	10.44	z= -.75, p<.45
Life under earth	10.57	9.67	z= -.33, p<.73
Winnie the witch	13.06	8.41	z=-1.74, p<.04*
The three little wolves	9.33	11.45	z= -.79, p<.42

The outcomes from Mann-Whitney test have been estimated in a 2-tailed probability except where otherwise indicated.

* (1-tailed).

Table 4. Spearman correlation between teacher's affect and children's participation, spontaneous participation and attention in information and fiction books [#]

	CP	SP	ATTEN
INFORM	-.41*	.17	.02
FIRE	-.56***	-.07	-.15
LIFE	-.25	.14	.08
FICTION	-.07	.47**	.17
WITCH	-.21	.29	.39*
WOLF	.12	.46**	-.11

[#] 1-tailed,* p<.05, ** p<.01,*** p<.001.

We conducted a correlation analysis with the purpose of relating the whole range of teachers' affect to children's behavior. The outcomes from Spearman Correlation (Table 4) report a negative relationship between teachers' affect and children's participation in information books. In particular, there was a negative correlation between teachers' affect and children's participation in "Fire". In fiction books there is a positive correlation between teachers' affect and children's spontaneous participation. A positive correlation was found between teachers' affect and children's spontaneous participation in "The three little wolves".

Finally, in "Winnie the witch" there was a positive correlation between teacher affect and children's attention.

Different Levels of Affect and their Impact on Young Children's Behavior

Since affect consists of three categories (intonation, dramatization and personal involvement), we were interested to examine how the use of such strategies by the teachers relates to children's behavior during the book session. When all four books were added across each teacher, no relationship was found between children's participation and teachers' intonation (r=-.09, p<.33) and personal involvement (r=-.19, p<.15). We found, however, a negative correlation between children's participation and teachers' dramatization (r=-.36, p<.05). No relationship was found between children's spontaneous participation and teachers' intonation (r=.11, p<.32) and dramatization (r=.006, p<.48). However, children's spontaneous participation was positively related to teachers' use of personal involvement strategies (r=.50, p<.009). Finally, children's attentive behavior was not related to teachers' use of intonation (r=-.34, p<.23), dramatization (r=-.01, p<.40) and personal involvement strategies (r=.05, p<.19).

Table 5. Spearman correlation coefficient between teachers' intonation, dramatization, personal involvement and children's participation, spontaneous participation and attention in "Fire"

	CP	SP	ATTEN
TINT	-.55***	-.30	-.12
TDRA	-.12	.12	-.07
TPER	-.22	.37*	.02

*p<.05, ***p<.001.

Table 6. Spearman correlation coefficient between teachers' intonation, dramatization, personal involvement and children's participation, spontaneous participation and attention in "Life under earth"

	CP	SP	ATTEN
TINT	-.29	-.05	-.03
TDRA	-.09	.007	.20
TPER	-.18	.40*	.21

* p<.05,*** p<.001.

In "Fire" children's participation was negatively correlated to teachers' intonation and their spontaneous participation was significantly related to teachers' personal involvement (see Table 5). In "Life under earth" there was a negative correlation between children's spontaneous participation and teachers' personal involvement (see Table 6). In "Winnie the witch" children's spontaneous behavior and their attentive behavior was positively correlated with teachers' personal involvement (see Table 7). In "The three little wolves" children's participation was positively correlated with teachers' intonation and negatively correlated with theirs' personal involvement and dramatization of the text (see Table 8). In addition, there was a positive correlation between children's spontaneous participation and teachers' intonation.

Table 7. Spearman correlation coefficient between teachers' intonation, dramatization, personal involvement and children's participation, spontaneous participation and attention in "Winnie the witch"

	CP	SP	ATTEN
TINT	-.33	.09	.16
TDRA	-.21	.06	.03
TPER	-.12	.40*	.51**

* p<.05, ** p<.01.

Table 8. Spearman correlation coefficient between teachers' intonation, dramatization, personal involvement and children's participation, spontaneous participation and attention in "The three little wolves"

	CP	SP	ATTEN
TINT	.62***	.47**	-.22
TDRA	-.48**	-.05	.02
TPER	-.40*	-.01	-.11

*p<.05, **p<.01, ***p<.001.

DISCUSSION

The first objective of this study investigates how teachers' affective presentation of different books influences children's behavior. When we studied children's behavior across the four books, we found significant differences. Children's participation in the "The three little wolves" was significantly more than in the two information ones. Since children's spontaneous participation did not vary significantly, the disparity among books must be due to differences in teachers' questioning during the book session. Teachers dominate more the discussion of information books probably because they consider such discussion as a means for transmitting information (in this case about fire and life under earth). In contrast, fiction books are a means for entertainment. Teachers are more concerned if children understood the story, giving them more space to participate during book discussion. Children were also more motivated to concentrate in fiction than in information books due to the affective nature of such books.

Secondly, we examined how variation in teachers' presentation of a particular book influences children's behavior. When each book was examined separately according to high and low affective presentation, we found no differences in children's participation with the exception of "Fire". In that particular book, children's participation was higher in groups with low affect teachers. "Fire" is a minimal expository text which allowed very little expression of affect. Teachers dominated the discussion and discouraged children from participating. Thus, affect per se does not have an impact on children's behavior. No differences were found in children's spontaneous participation in "Fire", "Life under earth" and "Winnie the witch" between high and low affective presentations. In contrast, we found significant differences in children's spontaneous participation in "The three little wolves" with increased participation from children belonging in groups with high affective presentation of the text. This indicates that familiarity with the story format might be a prerequisite for children's spontaneous participation. This complies with findings from research on home and classroom book reading which suggest that, the more familiar with a text children become, the more actively they participate during the book sessions (Goodsitt, Raitan & Pelmutter, 1988; Beals, DeTemple, & Dickinson, 1994). Children's attention was high in all four books and no differences were found in children's attentive behavior in low and high affective groups in "Fire", "Life under earth" and "The three little wolves." This indicates that affect does not have a significant impact on children's attentive behavior in information books and in familiar fiction books. Affect does seem to play a mediator role for fiction books with which children are unfamiliar. This is backed up by the findings in "Winnie the witch". Since our initial hypothesis is that high affect elicits high attentive behavior the result reaches significant levels in a one tail probability ($p<.04$). Thus, in this case the teacher becomes the mediator of children's attention.

The outcomes from the correlation analysis also comply with the outcomes from Mann Whitney. In information books affect does not seem to have any impact and any significant correlations found were negative, indicating that the more the teacher participate the less space is left for children's participation and spontaneous participation. In fiction books the picture is rather different. There is a positive correlation between affect and children's spontaneous participation. In particular, there is a positive correlation between teachers' affect and children's spontaneous participation in the familiar story format and teachers' affect and children's attention in the unfamiliar fiction book. Both correlations comply with the previous findings.

The third objective of the study concerned the relationship between teachers' use of affective strategies and young children's behavior. When investigating the effect of teachers' intonation, dramatization and personal involvement on children's behavior (all four books were added), we found that teachers' personal involvement was related to children's spontaneous participation. This indicates that teachers' personal stance towards the book is one of the best ways to prompt children's spontaneous participation. When teachers show empathy and express their personal thoughts and feelings in front of the group, children become more engaged during the group discussion. The following examples from the data illustrate how such interaction takes place in reality (T: refers to teacher's utterances, C: refers to a child's utterance, Cs: refers to a group of children's simultaneous utterances).

- T- Look how many things they found!
  C- Ants and a big root!
  T- Yes.
  C- Grass.
  C- Carrots.
  T- Let's read it to see what it says.

- T- This big sledgehammer knocked down their...? (Sad voice.)
  Cs- House.
  T- Rouni Rouni the sneaky bad pig. (Sad voice.)
  C- We will make a new one!

Similar outcomes were found in both information books and in the unfamiliar fiction book ("Winnie the witch").

In addition, teachers' re-enactment of the story was negatively correlated with children's participation, suggesting that when children are enchanted by the story they are reluctant to participate to a discussion or to take the initiative to participate with comments and questions. This has mainly to do with how teachers present the book. Some teachers read the text without showing pictures and adopt a performance oriented style of presentation which does not engage children in discussion during the reading of the story; but discussion usually takes place afterwards. Such a style assists children to become engrossed in the story; thus it is very rare for them to interrupt with comments. However, we found no significant relationship between dramatization and children's spontaneous behavior for definite conclusions to be drawn.

In "Fire" we found a negative correlation between teachers' intonation and children's participation therefore, the more the teacher reads or speaks the less children participate. In "The three little wolves" intonation was positively correlated with children's participation and spontaneous participation. Given the fact that the dialogues of the specific book were extensive, repetitive and with lots of rhyming the text elicited a lot of chiming and predictive comments. On the other hand, re-enactment of dialogues was negatively correlated with children's participation, suggesting that when children become enchanted by its storytelling presentation, they tend to participate less. It may also explain the negative correlation between teachers' personal involvement comments and young children's participation that we found in this particular book alone.

In "Winnie the witch" there was a positive correlation between teachers' personal involvement and children's spontaneous participation and their attention. As children were unfamiliar with this type of book, the teacher acted for them as a vicarious form of conscience. Her personal stance made the book attractive and with her personal commenting she managed to capture children's attention and prompt their spontaneous participation. The following examples give a taste of the various strategies teachers use in order to attract children's attention:

- T- Let's see what color she will give him I am excited!
  C- Red (Making predictions).
- T- Look children, poor him (the colorful cat) all the birds are making fun of him! (Sad voice.)
- T- Very nice house. How nice it would have been if we had a similar house! (Comment for the witch's colorful house.)
- T- Oh my goodness me, can you imagine the pain the witch felt when she fell in the roses, the poor witch! (Sad voice.) My god, lets see what happened next!
- T- Aaaa what a funny name she had! Her name was Winnie!

Although great differences were found in children's attention among the four books, there were no such differences for each book separately. Reasons that might account for the lack of replicability in findings between different books and within the same book are as follows:

- Differences in affect between books are greater than within books.
- The draw line for high and low affect was placed at the mean; this might not represent the best cut off line for high and low affect. It is believed that this is not the case mainly because the outcomes from the correlation analysis between affect and children's behavior for each book separately replicated in most cases the findings from Mann Whitney tests. Thus, the selection of teachers according to high and low affective presentation of the book has been validated.
- Children's individual differences may account for the lack of any effect on their behavior. For example, affect may have less impact on children's spontaneous behavior and attention for those children who have been raised in a rich literate environment compared to children who are not familiar with such tasks. For the former the task itself is attractive because they have experienced it as something pleasurable in contrast to the latter who might not be similarly motivated.
- Features of the text itself might play a more important role rather than the teacher's individual style in affective presentation. In this case, the author of the "The three little wolves" used a lot of story telling techniques (rhyming, dialogues, repetitions, sounds) that made the story attractive; thus the teacher had only to follow the story line for the children to become affectively engaged.

CONCLUSION

In summary, the picture that emerged from the analysis is that teachers' affect, in particular their personal involvement comments are positively related to children's spontaneous participation and to their attention in unfamiliar fiction books. Children are motivated to attend an unfamiliar task through teachers' mediation, hence they have the chance to experience the task as something pleasurable and interesting. From the moment children experience the task as being enjoyable the teacher's role diminishes; children no longer need to be motivated to engage in the task. The task has become an attractive one and the teacher's role as a mediator changes considerably. The more children become familiar with the task the more the degree of difficulty diminishes, making it easier to prolong their interest. The wisdom of traditional storytelling lies in the use of rhyming and repetition which facilitate memory and understanding of the task. In addition, the fact that teachers' personal involvement is positively correlated to children's spontaneous participation complies with research findings on emotional contagion. Because children are young and have not yet developed regulatory strategies to handle their emotional states, teachers' personal comments are particularly effective in gripping children's interest during book reading and communicating feelings and attitudes to them. Children catch the feelings and emotions displayed by their teachers which in turn they spontaneously express (Moschovaki, Meadows & Pellegrini, 2007).

Nonetheless, there are certain variations according to story and text genre. Affect does not seem to have the same impact in information books. The unique features of written language in information books as well as teachers' presentation style during the book session can account for this. In information books the sustained organization of written language around a story plot is missing, hence children can follow the discussion at any point; they do not need to be concentrated throughout the whole session to understand and participate successfully. Additionally, the majority of teachers evolve the discussion around the book illustrations and children's personal experiences (Moschovaki & Meadows, 2005). They adopt an interactive style and pace the discussion according to the order of the book illustrations. Children find it easier to concentrate as the beautiful depiction of life under earth and of fire engaged their interest, thus teachers' affective presentation was less important here. In fiction books the picture that emerged is quite different. Affect overall seems to aid children's increased attention and spontaneous participation. Most teachers preferred to adopt a performance oriented style in the presentation of fiction books and read the text without showing the book illustrations. Although the story itself is an appealing experience for the child, yet the task is more demanding since children have to concentrate on language alone without the assistance of pictures for prolonged periods of time. Consequently, teachers' use of paralinguistic cues and their personal involvement comments were particularly useful in sustaining children's interest in the story. However, familiarity with the text is ultimately responsible for the impact affect has on children's behavior. If the text is unfamiliar, variation in teachers' affective presentation of the story has a much stronger impact on children's attention span. Conversely, familiarity with story format has a strong impact on children's spontaneous participation. On the other hand, dramatization discourages children's participation. Children become enchanted with the story, since the story reading becomes for them a strong aesthetic experience.

The outcomes of the statistical analysis comply with the motivational model of affective information processing. According to the motivational model, children are more likely to maintain and extend an experience denoted by positive affect -in this case the satisfaction of listening to a book by being concentrated. The analysis seems to comply with this model since children were significantly more concentrated during the reading and discussion of fiction books. On the other hand, if we want to investigate the impact of positive affect on children's participation, future research will have to control other variables (familiarity with story genre, teachers' participation) during classroom discussion.

This study has certain limitations. First, it has focused only on the verbal demarcations of teachers' and children's affect. The coding of its non verbal manifestations could have been added if a second observer was available during the data collection or if video recording was conducted, thus enhancing the reliability of the measurement of affect. However, such recording could have been intrusive. In addition, the same person did all the classroom observations. Although training was provided beforehand, the observer's fatigue and bias might have influenced data collection. In light of the fact that children's attentive behavior was high in all books, such a criticism should be taken into serious consideration.

The outcomes of this study suggest as one of the qualitative features of book reading, its affective presentation and consequently young children's affective engagement. Since children are more concentrated, future research could examine how young children's affective engagement during the book session is related to text comprehension, recall of information and acquisition of language skills. Hopefully, such questions will become the focus of further educational research which may shed light on how affect mediated by adults can influence young children's literacy development.

REFERENCES

Bakeman, R. & Gottman, J. M. (1986). *Observing interaction: An introduction to sequential analysis.* Cambridge, NY: Cambridge University Press.

Beals, D. E., DeTemple, J. M. & Dickinson, D. K. (1994). Talking and listening that support early literacy development of children from low-income families. In D. K. Dickinson (Ed.), *Bridges to literacy* (pp. 19-40). Cambridge MA, Oxford UK: Blackwell.

Blank, M., Rose, S. A. & Berlin, L. J. (1978). *The language of learning: The preschool years.* N.Y., London: Grune & Stratton.

Blok, H. (1999). Reading to young children in educational settings: A meta-analysis of recent research. *Language Learning, 49,* 343-371.

Brewer, W. F. & Lichtenstein, E. H. (1982). Stories are to entertain: A structural-affect theory of stories. *Journal of Pragmatics, 6,* 473-486.

Bugental, D. B., Lin, E. K. & Susskind, J. E. (1995). Influences of affect on cognitive processes of different ages: Why the change? In N. Eisenberg (Ed.), *Social development* (pp. 159-184). 15th Review of Personality and Social Psychology. London: Sage.

Bus, A. G., Van Ijzendoorn, M. H. & Pellegrini, A. D. (1995). Joint book reading makes for success in learning to read: A meta-analysis on intergenerational transmission of literacy. *Review of Educational Research, 65,* 1-21.

Chafe, W. L. (1982). Integration and involvement in speaking, writing and oral literature. In D. Tannen (Ed.), *Spoken and written language: Exploring orality and literacy.* Advances in Discourse Practices, Vol. 9 (pp.35-53). Norwood, NJ: Ablex.

Clore, G. L., Schwarz, N. & Conway, M. (1994). Affective causes and consequences of social information processing. In R. S Wyer Jr. and T. K. Srull (Eds.), *Handbook of social cognition,* Vol. 1 Basic processes (pp. 323-417). Hillsdale, NJ: Lawrence Erlbaum Associates Publishers.

Dickinson, D. K. & Smith, M. W. (1994). Long-term effects of pre-school teachers' book readings on low-income children's vocabulary and story comprehension. *Reading Research Quarterly, 29,* 104-122.

Egan, K. (1988). *Primary Understanding. Education in early childhood.* NY: Routledge.

Goodsitt, J., Raitan, J. G., & Pelmutter, M. (1988). Interaction between mothers and preschool children when reading a novel and familiar book. *International Journal of Behavioral Development, 11,* 489-505

Hatfield, E., Cacioppo, J. T. & Rapson, R. L. (1994). *Emotional Contagion.* Cambridge: Cambridge University Press.

Hayward, C. (1982). *Literary theme development in the nursery classroom.* Unpublished M.Ed. thesis, University of Bristol.

Fiedler, K. (1988). Emotional mood, cognitive style, and behavior regulation. In K. Fiedler and J. Forgas (Eds.), *Affect, cognition and social behavior* (pp. 100- 119). Toronto: C. J. Hogrefe.

Isen, A. M. (1987). Positive affect, cognitive processes, and social behavior. In L. Berkowitz (Ed.), *Advances in experimental social psychology,* Vol. 20 (pp. 203-253). NY: Academic Press.

Isen, A. M. (1990). The influence of positive and negative affect on cognitive organization: Some implications for development. In N. Stein, B. Leventhal and T. Trabasso (Eds.), *Psychological and biological approaches to emotion* (pp. 75-94). Hillsdale NJ: Erlbaum.

Kitsaras, G. (1993). *Το εικονογραφημένο παιδικό βιβλίο* [Child's picture book]. Αθήνα: Παπαζήσης.

Moschovaki, E & Meadows, S. (2005). Young children's cognitive engagement during classroom book reading: Differences according to book, text genre and story format. *Early Childhood Research & Practice,* [Online], 7 (2), http://ecrp.uiuc.edu/v7n2/moschovaki.html.

Moschovaki, E., Meadows, S. & Pellegrini, A. (2007). Teachers' affective presentation of books and young children's display of affective engagement during classroom book reading. *European Journal of Psychology of Education, XXII,* 405-420.

Paul, K. & Thomas, V. (1990). *Η μάγισσα Παλάβω* [Winnie the witch]. Αθήνα: Μαργαρίτα.

Rius, M. & Parramon, J. M. (1992). *Τα τέσσερα στοιχεία: Φωτιά* [The four elements: Fire]. Αθήνα: Κέδρος.

Rius, M. & Parramon, J. M. (1994). *Η ζωή κάτω από την γη* [Life under earth]. Αθήνα: Κέδρος.

Scarborough, H. S. & Dobrich, W. (1994). On the efficacy of reading to pre-schoolers. *Developmental Review, 14,* 245-302.

Schwartz, N. (1990). Feelings as information. Informational and motivational functions of affective states. In E. T. Higgins and R. Sorrentino (Eds.), *Handbook of motivation and cognition* (pp. 527-561). NY, London: The Guildford Press.

Trivizas, E. (1993). *Τα τρία μικρά λυκάκια* [The three little wolves]. Αθήνα: Μίνωας.

Wells, G. (1975). *Coding manual for the description of child speech in its conversational context.* Unpublished manuscript, University of Bristol, School of Education.

In: Early Education
Editors: J.B. Mottely and A.R. Randall

ISBN 978-1-60456-908-7
© 2009 Nova Science Publishers, Inc.

Chapter 5

PREDICTORS OF MIDDLE SCHOOL YOUTH EDUCATIONAL ASPIRATIONS: HEALTH RISK ATTITUDES, PARENTAL INTERACTIONS, AND PARENTAL DISAPPROVAL OF RISK

Regina P. Lederman[*], Wenyaw Chan[**] and Cynthia Roberts-Gray[***]

[*]University of Texas Medical Branch, Galveston, Texas 77555-1029, USA
[**]University of Texas School of Public Health, Houston, Texas 77225, USA
[***]Resource Network, Harrisonburg, Virginia 22801, USA

ABSTRACT

School-wide surveys in five middle schools were used to measure educational aspirations, attitudes toward sexual health risk behaviors and drug use, and perceptions of parental interactions and disapproval of risk behavior at baseline and one year later. Participants were male and female students of Black ($n = 222$), Hispanic ($n = 317$), White ($n = 216$), and Asian or other heritage ($n = 85$), ages 11 to 14. Analyses were performed for three factors with Cronbach's alpha coefficients ≥ 0.65 (youth's attitudes, discourse with parents, and parents' disapproval of risk behavior), and three single items inquiring about use of alcohol, use of marijuana, and sexual behavior. Generalized Linear Model (GLM) with logit link was used to evaluate the contribution of these measures at baseline as predictors of educational aspirations at the one-year follow-up. Results showed race/heritage ($p < .001$), attitudes toward health risk behaviors ($p < .01$), extent to which youth talked with parents about use of drugs and other health risk behaviors ($p < .05$), and perceptions of their parents' disapproval of risk behavior ($p < .05$) each made significant contributions in predicting educational aspirations. Gender did not contribute to the prediction of educational aspiration nor did self-report of actual risk behavior. These results indicate that youth interactions with parents regarding health risk behaviors

---

[*] Contact Author: Regina P. Lederman, PhD, University of Texas Medical Branch, 301 University Blvd. Galveston, TX 77555-1029. Phone: 713 666 0172. 409 772 6570. email: rlederma@utmb.edu

is worthy of further exploration to develop interventions to reduce adolescent health risks and increase educational aspirations.

INTRODUCTION

Parent-child relations occupy important positions in pathways linking education and health. Parental encouragement for educational attainment is, for example, closely linked to youth educational aspirations (Looker and Thiessen, 2004; Goyette and Xie, 1999). Educational aspirations of youth (Trusty and Harris, 1999) and parental involvement in their children's education (Trusty, 1999) are linked to educational attainment. Lack of educational attainment and low educational aspirations in turn are associated with a variety of health and health behavior problems, including substance abuse (Caetano, 2002) and rates of teenage birth (Pamuk, Makuc, Heck, Reuben, and Lochner, 1998). The association of poor education and poor health is a consistent finding from domestic and international research in economics, epidemiology, and sociology (Blane, 2003; Morowsky and Ross, 2003).

In some formulations of the pathways linking education and health, education is identified as a health-protecting factor (see Hannum and Buchman, 2003). Because of the abundant empirical evidence that better educated people lead longer, healthier lives, those who espouse the health protection formulation recommend investment in programs and practices that promote educational attainment as a means for improving health and reducing health inequalities. At a local program level, such an initiative might include parenting education and supportive services to assist families in encouraging their children to aspire to and achieve higher educational attainments, anticipating that positive health outcomes will accrue.

Other analyses demonstrate that good health in adolescence predicts both higher educational attainment and better adult health (Chandola, Clarke, Blane and Morris, 2003). Recommendations for action from this perspective focus on interventions to help families encourage healthy behaviors in childhood and adolescence with the expectation that better educational and adult health outcomes will follow.

In this chapter we examine a secondary analysis of data from a prevention research project exploring relationships among the educational aspiration of middle school youth, their health risk attitudes and behaviors, and interactions with their parents regarding risk behavior. The data, originally obtained to test the effectiveness of an innovative parent-child program for the prevention of sexual health risk behaviors (see Lederman, Chan, and Roberts-Gray, 2004; Lederman and Mian, 2003), were collected in school-wide surveys at five middle schools during a baseline period and again the next school year. The purpose of this secondary analysis of the data is to explore the possibility that, in addition to putting the health of youth at risk, negative health attitudes and behaviors distract youth from the pursuit of educational goals and thereby constrain educational aspirations, while appropriate parental involvement in discouraging negative health behaviors in youth can contribute to higher educational aspirations. We hypothesized that middle school youth involvement in and attitudes toward health risk behaviors, and their perceptions of interactions with their parents/guardians regarding health risk behaviors would be predictive of educational aspiration measured during the subsequent school year.

RESEARCH DESIGN AND METHODS

This study analyzed data collected in school-wide surveys over two successive school years from students in five middle schools in two school districts in coastal Texas. The written survey questionnaire provided self-report measures of: (1) sexual involvement and the use of alcohol and other drugs; (2) attitudes toward sexual health risk behavior; (3) the frequency and breadth of discourse with parents about sexual health topics; (4) perceptions of parents' disapproval of the youth's involvement in sexual and other health risk behaviors; and (5) educational aspiration. The protocol was approved by the Institutional Review Board of the University of Texas Medical Branch at Galveston. Active assent of students and consent of parents was obtained and documented.

Participant Recruitment

Participants were recruited in four steps. First, we sent invitations through the mail and through presentations at conferences to all urban school districts located in and near Galveston, Texas. Leaders in two school districts indicated willingness to have their schools participate in the prevention intervention research project. The next step was meeting with principals and counselors at middle schools in the consenting districts. Two out of the three middle schools in one district and three of the four middle schools in the second district agreed to participate. The third step was partnership with the consenting schools to invite families to participate. A cover letter, consent form, and informational flyer were sent to parents via the students and through the mail informing them about the program and providing details regarding the research protocol. The school principals at each of the participating schools endorsed the program and signed the letters to parents, which were written in both English and Spanish.

The participating schools represented diversity in school size, ethnic heritage of the student body, and performance characteristics. Two of the schools had approximately 500 students, two had between 700 and 1,000 students, and one had more than 1,200 students. Across the five schools, the percent of students of different heritage ranged from 0.0 to 3.4 Asian, 7.0 to 54.3 African American, 32.8 to 85.8 Hispanic, and 5.2 to 52.1 White. Three of the schools had more than two-thirds of the student body identified as economically disadvantaged. The percent of students with special circumstances ranged from 3.7 to 23.6 with limited English proficiency, 4.5 to 13.6 participating in gifted and talented programs, and 2.2 to 4.3 percent with disciplinary placement. Total enrollment across the five schools was 3,881. Informed consent and actual participation in the survey was obtained for 848 youth.

Demographic Characteristics of The Participating Youth

More than half of the students were in sixth grade at the time they completed the baseline survey. There were approximately equal numbers of females and males. The majority was youth of color with nearly 40% indicating Hispanic/Latino/Mexican ethnicity. These data are displayed in Table 1.

Table 1. Demographic Characteristics of Survey Participants

Youth characteristics	Number of Youth	Percent
GENDER		
Male	383	45%
Female	465	55%
RACE/ETHNICITY		
Hispanic/Latino/Mexican	317	38%
Black/African American	222	26%
White – not Hispanic	216	26%
Asian or Mixed or Other	85	10%
GRADE LEVEL		
Sixth	480	60%
Seventh	249	31%
Eighth	76	9%

Survey Administration

Students completed the survey questionnaire during a special assembly at the school. The survey items originally were selected to be relevant in evaluating outcomes of prevention education interventions to reduce sexual health risk behaviors and prevent teen pregnancy and the spread of HIV and other sexually transmitted infections (STI). Adapted from the National Youth Survey (Elliot, Huizinga, and Ageton, 1985) and a middle school survey developed by ETR Associates (Kirby et al, 1997), the 9-page, 94-item survey questionnaire was divided into sections asking: "What do your parents think?," "What do you think?," "What do you do?," and "Do you talk with your parents?" Students typically completed the survey in 30 to 45 minutes. Unique identifying codes were marked on the survey forms so that records could be matched from year to year without disclosing individual identifying information.

Measures

Survey items addressing a common content domain (e.g., youth attitudes toward risk behaviors) and having similar response options (e.g., strongly agree to strongly disagree) were combined to produce domain scales which then were tested for internal consistency. Those obtaining a Cronbach alpha of 0.65 or greater were retained as scales. The scales and survey items used in the current analyses are described as follows.

- *Educational Aspiration* was measured with a single item asking, "How far do you think you will go in school?" Response options were assigned ordinal codes of 1 = "Won't graduate from high school," 2 = "Will finish high school," 3 = "Will go to trade, vocational, or business school after high school," 4 = "Will attend college."

Youth involvement in and attitudes toward risk behaviors were measured with two sets of survey items, one that counted the number of self-reported risk behaviors and the other a scale measuring perceived acceptability of "someone my age" having sex.

- *Health Risk Behaviors* was measured with three single items: (1) "In the last 30 days, did you drink alcohol such as beer, wine, wine coolers or hard liquor?," (2) "In the last 30 days, did you use marijuana?," and (3) "In the last 6 months, did you try to get someone to have sex with you?" Response options were coded 1 = No and 0 = Yes.

- *Attitude Toward Sexual Health Risk Behavior* was measured with a 14-item domain scale asking about conditions under which it is acceptable to have sex. Sample items are: "I believe it's OK for someone my age to have sex with someone they like, but don't know well," "I believe people my age should always use a condom if they have sex," and "If my boyfriend or girlfriend wanted to have sex and I didn't, it would be OK to say 'no'." Response alternatives were "Strongly agree," "Agree," "Disagree," and "Strongly Disagree," coded 1 through 4 with more desirable responses receiving a higher numerical score. Cronbach's alpha for the baseline sample was 0.76.

Interactions with parents regarding risk behaviors was assessed with two domain scales, one measuring the frequency and breadth of youth discourse with parents about sexual health topics and the other measuring youths' perceptions of whether or not parents or guardians would disapprove of youth engaging in risk behaviors.

- *Discourse with Parents about Sexual Risk Behavior* measured how often in the last three months youth had talked with their parents about five topical items: menstruation, the risk of getting pregnancy or getting someone pregnant, being a teenage parent, different kinds of birth control, and sexually transmitted diseases (STDs) or AIDS. Response options were coded 0 = "Never," 1 = "1-3 times;" and 2 = "More than 3 times." Cronbach's alpha for this domain scale at baseline was 0.73.

- *Parental Disapproval of Risk Behavior* was measured by asking if the parent or guardian would "approve" or "disapprove" if the youth engaged in six types of risk behavior: used alcohol; sniffed paint or glue or used marijuana; used hard drugs such as heroin, cocaine or crack; had sex (made love, went 'all the way'); got pregnant or got someone pregnant; and failed a grade in school. Responses were coded 1 and 0. The Cronbach alpha for this scale at baseline was 0.65.

A study reported elsewhere (Lederman, Chan, and Roberts-Gray, 2004) showed the domain scales selected for the predictive model tested in the current study were independent of one another. The obtained inter-domain correlations were low with Pearson correlation coefficients of $r = 0.10$ for Discourse and youth Attitude, $r = 0.04$ for Discourse and perceived Parental Disapproval, and $r = 0.29$ for youth Attitude and perceived Parental Disapproval.

Data Analyses

Generalized Linear Model with logit link was applied to evaluate the contribution of the baseline measures of interactions with parents and youth involvement in and attitudes toward risk behaviors as predictors of youths' educational aspirations measured in the subsequent school year. Additional variables included in the statistical models were students' age (11 and 12 versus 13 and 14), self-reported ethnic heritage, and gender. A limitation of this study is that all analyses assume the data are taken from random samples. Like many studies reported in the research literature, this study cannot verify this assumption. Generalization of the results should be cautious.

RESULTS

Educational Aspirations. Virtually all (99%) of the middle school students that participated in the survey indicated they plan to finish high school. Ten percent indicated completion of high school is the highest level of education they expect to attain. The vast majority of the students (86%), however, indicated they plan to attend college.

Predictors of Educational Aspirations. Race/heritage ($p < .001$), youth attitudes toward sexual health risk behaviors ($p < .01$), discourse with parents about health risk behavior ($p < .05$), and perception of parental disapproval of youth involvement in risk behavior ($p < .05$) each made significant contributions in predicting educational aspirations. The full model is displayed in Table 2. Neither age nor gender made significant contributions in predicting educational aspirations, nor did actual risk behaviors. Excepting the exclusion of actual risk behavior, the hypothesized model fit the data well (Chi-Square = 735.19, $df = 740$).

Table 2. Generalized Linear Model with PREDICTORS Measured at Baseline and the Criterion Variable EDUCATIONAL ASPIRATION Measured the Subsequent School Year

Predictors	Beta Weight	SE	Chi Square	p-value
Gender	0.1835	0.2376	0.60	NS
Age (11-12 versus 13-14)	0.4917	0.3779	1.69	NS
Race/Ethnicity				
Hispanic / Latino, including Mexican	-1.3867	0.4196	10.92	<.01
Black / African American	0.1924	0.4792	0.16	NS
White – not Hispanic	-0.0617	0.4722	0.02	NS
Asian or Mixed or Other	0		.	
Health Risk Behaviors				
Use alcohol	-0.1672	0.2894	0.33	NS
Use marijuana	0.1890	0.4317	0.19	NS
Try to get someone to have sex	-0.3618	0.4139	0.76	NS
Parental disapproval of risk behaviors	2.0630	1.0186	4.10	<.05
Discourse with parents about risk behaviors	-0.7926	0.3454	5.27	<.05
Attitudes about acceptability of having sex	2.0928	0.6970	9.02	<.05

Lower educational aspiration was predicted by higher levels of discourse with parents about sexual health risk behaviors and with being Hispanic/Latino/Mexican. Higher educational aspiration was predicted by youth holding attitudes less accepting of sexual activity and perceiving that their parents/guardians disapprove of their being involved in risk behaviors.

CONCLUSION

This analysis demonstrates that the attitudes of middle school youth toward health risk behaviors and their perceptions of interactions with their parents/guardians regarding health risk behavior are useful in predicting educational aspiration measured during the subsequent school year. Youth who are at baseline less accepting of involvement in sexual activity and who perceive that their parents disapprove of their involvement in risky behaviors are more likely than those with more tolerant attitudes and perceptions to continue into the next school year with high educational aspirations. The finding that perceived parental disapproval of health risk behavior predicts youths' educational aspiration is consistent with other research indicating that maternal connectedness may facilitate the development of a positive future time perspective by young adolescents (Aronowitz and Morrison-Breedy, 2004).

An unexpected finding in the current analyses was that frequency and breadth of youths' discourse with their parents about sexual health topics showed a negative relationship with youths' educational aspirations. Youth who reported more discourse with parents about sexual health topics were significantly more likely than their peers to report lower educational aspirations. This finding underscores conclusions presented in Healthy People 2010 (U S Department of Health and Human Services, 2000, Chapter 25) regarding the need to give further attention toward helping parents impart information about sexual health risks. The research literature suggests there is no simple, robust relationship between parent-adolescent communication about sexuality and subsequent adolescent sexual health behaviors (Miller, 1998; Dittus and Jaccard, 2000). A hypothesis for exploration in future research is the possibility that young adolescents talk with their parents about risk behavior only when their behavior has created a predicament that forces discussion between parent and child. Another possibility is that more discussion about risks and protection may have a normalizing effect on the youth's perceptions of risk behavior. Yet another possibility is that more discourse about risk behavior occurs in families where parental control experienced as excessive or coercive, and impels the youth toward acting out and/or toward a more negative future time perspective (Tiongson, 1997).

The current study indicates that the interactions of youth with parents regarding health risk behaviors is worthy of further exploration and the development of interventions to improve adolescent health, and educational and adult health outcomes. There is a clear need for additional research to identify ways to marshal, nurture, and work in concert with parental efforts to reduce adolescent health risks and encourage educational attainment.

REFERENCES

Aronowitz, T., and Morrison-Breedy, D. (2004). Comparison of the maternal role in resilience among impoverished and non-impoverished early adolescent African American girls. *Adolescent and Family Health*, 3(4), 155-163.

Blane, D. (2003). Commentary: Explanations of the difference in mortality risk between different educational groups. *International Journal of Epidemiology*, 32, 355-356.

Caetano, R. (2002). *Education, psychiatric diseases and substance use/abuse*. Presentation made at conference on Education and Health: Building a Research Agenda. National Institutes of Health. Available to read online: www.wws.princeton.edu/chw/conferences/conf1002/session/Caetanofiles/frame.html

Chandola, T., Clarke, P., Blane, D., and Morris, J. (2003). *Pathways between education and health: A causal modeling approach*. University College London (UCL). Published online: www.ucl.ac.uk/epidemiology/Chandola/healtheducation.htm

Dittus, P., and Jaccard, J. (2000). The relationship of adolescent perceptions of maternal disapproval of sex and of the mother-adolescent relationship in sexual outcomes. *Journal of Adolescent Health*, 26, 268-278.

Elliot, D., Huizinga, D., and Ageton, S. (1985). *Explaining delinquency and drug use*. Beverly Hills, CA: Sage.

Goyette, K., and Xie, Y. (1999). Educational expectations of Asian-American youth: Determinants and ethnic differences. *Sociology of Education*, 71, 24-38.

Hannum, E., and Buchman, C. (2003). *The consequences of global educational expansion: Social science perspectives*. Cambridge, MA: American Academy of Arts and Sciences. Available to read online: www.amacad.org

Kirby, D., Korpi, M., Adivi, C., and Weissman, J. (1997). An impact evaluation of SNAPP, a pregnancy- and AIDS-prevention middle school curriculum. *AIDS Education Prevention*, 9(Suppl A), 44-67.

Lederman, R., Chan, W., and Roberts-Gray, C. (2004). Sexual risk attitudes and intentions of youth age 12-14 years: Survey comparison of parent-teen prevention and control groups. *Behavioral Medicine*, 29(4), 155-163. Available to read online: www.findarticles.com/p/articles/mi_m0GDQ/is_4_29/ai_n6192603

Lederman, R., and Mian, T., (2003). The Parent-Adolescent Relationship Education (PARE) Program: A curriculum for prevention of STDs and pregnancy in middle school youth. *Behavioral Medicine*, 29, 33-41.

Looker, D., and Thiessen, V. (2004). *Aspirations of Canadian youth for higher education*. Learning Policy Directorate, Strategic Policy and Planning, Canada. Available to read on-line: www.pisa.gc.ca/SP-600-05-04E.pdf

Miller, B. (1998). *Families matter: A research synthesis of family influences on adolescent pregnancy*. Washington, DC: National Campaign to Prevent Teen Pregnancy.

Morowsky, J., and Ross, C. (2003). *Education, Social status, and Health*. New York: Aldine de Gruyter.

Pamuk, E., Makuc, D., Heck, K., Reuben, C., and Lochner, K. (1998). *Socioeconomic Status and Health Chartbook. Health, United States, 1998*. Hyattsville, MD: National Center for Health Statistics, Table 9, page 185 of 464. Available to read online: www.cdc/nchs/data/hus/hus98.pdf

Tiongson, A. (1997). Throwing the baby out with the bathwater: Situating young Filipino mothers and fathers beyond the dominant discourse on adolescent pregnancy. In: M. Root (Ed), *Filipino Americans: Transformation and Identity*, Thousand Oaks, CA: Sage.

Trusty, J. (1999). Effects of eighth-grade parental involvement on late adolescents' educational expectations. *Journal of Research and Development in Education*, 32, 224-233.

Trusty, J., and Harris, M. (1999). Lost talent: Predictors of the stability of educational aspirations across adolescence. *Journal of Adolescent Research*, 14, 359-382.

U S Department of Health and Human Services. (2000). *Healthy People 2010: Understanding and Improving Health* (2nd ed). Washington DC: US Government Printing Office.

In: Early Education
Editors: J.B. Mottely and A.R. Randall

ISBN 978-1-60456-908-7
© 2009 Nova Science Publishers, Inc.

Chapter 6

TEACHER LEADERSHIP IN EARLY CHILDHOOD EDUCATION: A RASCH MEASUREMENT MODEL ANALYSIS

Russell F. Waugh
Edith Cowan University, Joondalup, Western Australia 6027

Glenda S. Boyd and Loraine F. Corrie
Hong Kong Institute of Education, TAI PO, NEW TERRITORIES, HONG KONG

ABSTRACT

Educational leadership enables early childhood teachers to advocate for appropriate curriculum and practice but do teachers think they have sufficient skills to enact leadership? This study measured Teacher Leadership of 270 early childhood teachers using self-reports based on a three-aspect model involving General Leadership, Communication, and Influence, with an initial base of 71 stem-items answered in both a real and ideal mode (effectively 142 items). A Rasch measurement model analysis was used to create a 92-item, unidimensional, interval-level scale (50 items didn't fit the model and were discarded) in which the proportion of observed teacher variance considered true was 94%. Findings supported the three-aspect model of Teacher Leadership involving general leadership, communication and influence. The ideal items were 'easier' than the corresponding real items and the ideal items made a stronger contribution to leadership than the real items (54 ideal and 38 real items fitted the model). Most teachers recognised the importance of leadership skills, and were able to enact them at their schools in the three leadership areas, but there are some exceptions.

INTRODUCTION

Early Childhood Teacher Leadership is important for three reasons. One, teacher leaders model exemplary practice and communicate their professional knowledge to influence others in their schools and communities. Two, they are pro-active change agents who advocate for democratic and inclusive education for young children and families. Three, leadership activities raise the status of the early childhood profession.

Two decades of educational reform have led to calls for teachers to take up leadership roles to enhance their professional development and to help achieve reform goals (Fullan, 1994; Sergiovanni & Starratt, 1998; Lieberman, 1988; Wasley, 1991). School restructuring has replaced traditional hierarchies with collaborative leadership teams to support teachers to be empowered professionals rather than instruments of policy (Fullan, 1994; Wideen, Mayer-Smith & Moon, 1996). The aim is to create teams of colleagues who generate information through interacting, which becomes a feedback spiral that enriches knowledge and relationships (Wheatley, 1992). Accordingly, leadership in restructured schools has moved from being transactional to transformational in style, with a shift from authority, control and rewards to collaboration, team, vision, and values (Morgan, 1997; Pellicer & Anderson,1995).

Work in early childhood leadership has sought to advance theoretical and practical conceptual developments in the field (for example, see Kagan & Bowman, 1997; Rodd, 1994). The present study responded to the call to develop a "durable and perpetuating leadership capacity for the field" (Kagan & Bowman, 1997 p.4), and to criticisms that research in teacher leadership has ignored teachers' voices (Silva, Gimbert, & Nolan, 2000; Smylie & Denny, 1990). The present study investigated 270 early childhood teachers' self-views of leadership. This paper reports the first phase that measured teachers' self-reports of 'How I am' and 'How I would like to be' in terms of leadership. Phase 2 included in-depth interviews with teachers about leadership in their school contexts and will be reported elsewhere.

The Need for Early Childhood Teacher Leadership

Early childhood practitioners are inducted into a profession described as territorial, competitive, defensive and scared (Walker-Duff, 1997 p.83), which are attributes that create difficulties for teacher leaders. The difficulties reflect the genesis of the profession as a low-status, low-paid female occupation (Cannella, 1997; Anning, 1998) that has attracted scant social recognition and respect (Finkelstein, 1988, p.10). Many early childhood practitioners have been reluctant to assert clinical authority or wield political, economic or social power (Finkelstein, 1988, p.10).

Educational reforms have increased the uncertainty and dilemmas that surround teachers' work and Teacher Leadership (Best, 1996, p.98). While Teacher Leadership is subject to varying definitions, it is critical in contexts where systemic reform has included three to five year old children for the first time (Anning, 1998) and where increasing numbers of pre-kindergarten children are enrolled in public schools (Burts, Hart, Charlesworth, DeWolf, Ray, Manuel & Fleege, 1993). Some reform has mandated curriculum and assessment policies more akin to traditional elementary school practice than early childhood pedagogy, and many early childhood teachers now work with elementary school colleagues and administrators who have little understanding of early childhood programs (David, 1993). Increasingly, schools promote formalised instruction and academic skill-based curriculum that undermine young children's opportunities to learn, increase their stress, and potentially damage their well-being (Hart, Burts, Durland, Charlesworth, DeWolf & Fleege, 1998; Burts, Hart, Charlesworth, Fleege, Mosley & Thomasson, 1992). Empirical evidence shows the negative effects of the "push down" curriculum on young children's educational and social outcomes (Burts, et al.1993; Burts, et al.1992; Schweinhart & Weikart (1998). However, some teachers pay little heed to research or feel unable to advocate for programs that facilitate optimum learning and development. These teachers experience tension between their professional knowledge and practice but see complying with the principal as their only course of action (Corrie, 2000; Rothenberg, 1995). The publication of the revised version of the "Developmentally Appropriate Practice" statement (Bredekamp & Copple, 1997) indicates the ongoing need to promote appropriate early childhood programmes, which demands considerable effort from practitioners who have to be leaders to make a difference.

Early Childhood Teacher Leadership

Researchers debate whether leadership is a role, is just knowledge, is composed of competencies or personality characteristics (Morgan, 1997). Post-structuralist theory asserts that individuals do not act just out of what they know, rather they act into the context in terms of the choices that it offers (Davies & Harre, 1990; Shotter, 1986). This view implies that what teachers know and do about leadership is linked inextricably to their experiences in schools (Kolb, 1999), and contextual opportunities and constraints shape individuals' expectations about leadership. However, in addition, actions are shaped by what individuals know and feel about their own competencies (Pajares, 1996).

Research has found that perceptions of leadership are the crucial component of emergent leadership (Kobl, 1999), which reflects the confidence that individuals feel about their leadership abilities (Chemers, Watson & May, 2000; Kolb, 1999; Somech & Drach-Zahavy, 2000). Personality attributes of leaders include: being willing to take risks, make decisions easily, being willing to take a stand, being ambitious and self-sufficient (Kolb, 1999). Teacher leaders must feel confident that they have the requisite skills to answer challenges to their practice (Spodek, 1988). They must feel able to enact models of skilled practice (Berliner, 1994); believe they can influence others (Wasley, 1991); feel able to communicate their knowledge clearly (Berliner, 1994); be confident that they have good interpersonal skills and are able to collaborate with colleagues, professionals and families (Davies & Polinitz, 1994; Pajares, 1996). They must be willing to speak out and make their voices heard (Lubeck, 1994), and most importantly, they need to believe that it is important for them to act as leaders (Duke, 1994).

Difficulties with Teacher Leadership

Enthusiastic support for teacher leadership has not led necessarily to successful outcomes, and strategies to foster leadership have been criticised as being superficial and piecemeal (Fullan, 1994 p.241). Teachers' responses to reform are shaped by their assumptions about what constitutes their work (Cleave & Brown, 1982), which may account for their reluctance to add 'leader' to the job description (Creighton, 1997; Dimmock & O'Donogue, 1997; French & Pena, 1997).

Difficulties in becoming a better leader may be due to a range of contextual and intra-individual factors. These include principals who do not want to relinquish control (Weber,

1996); bureaucratic structures that dis-empower teachers (McLaughlin & Oberman, 1996); egalitarian norms between teachers that are not addressed (Wasley, 1991); not having the required leadership skills (Weber, 1996) and lacking resources to acquire them (Whitebook, 1997); and teachers who adopt leadership roles only because they doubt their power to oppose policy decisions (Woods, 1983).

Teachers' self-knowledge may be a barrier to leadership. One study found that teachers thought that they did not have leadership skills even when they demonstrated them (Silva, Gimbert, & Nolan, 2000). Individuals' knowledge about their own competence embodies self-concept and self-esteem, which are constructed over time by interpreting information, feelings and self-perceptions that guide actions and behaviour (Smith & Mackie, 2000). However self-knowledge may be biased partly because individuals are comprised of a complexity of selves that vary across situations, events and relationships (Smith & Mackie, 2000). For example, teachers may see themselves as leaders in their classrooms but not as leaders in their school.

Difficulties with Teacher Leadership are increased when there is ambiguity about the role (Little, 1989; Smylie & Denny, 1989; Wasley, 1991). Teacher Leadership is new for many early childhood teachers and role clarity is necessary to avoid false expectations (Best, 1996). Similarly, role conflicts must be addressed to avoid tension, low morale and communication difficulties (Best, 1996). Role conflict results from attempting to perform one role that does not fit well with another, for example, being a collaborative team member may conflict with being a teacher leader. Role conflicts can result in resistance to reform efforts with passive dissent, non-involvement and avoidance (Rodd, 1994). Role conflicts must be resolved to enable an individual to experience role congruence and personal integrity, as conflicts reflect serious tensions between the sorts of things teachers think they are expected to do as a teacher leader and the sort of person they think they are (Best, 1996). Lack of role clarity and role conflicts may result in unsatisfying experiences that reinforce the false self-belief in the lack of leadership skills.

Fullan (1994 p.241) has blamed the failure of strategies to promote Teacher Leadership on the lack of "deep, powerful conceptualisation" and Silva, Gimbert & Nolan, (2000) called for teachers' knowledge to be included in the work to promote Teacher Leadership. The present study seeks to contribute to the conceptualisation of Teacher Leadership by investigating what teachers say about what they do as leaders and how they would like to be as leaders. Research studies for over 25 years have investigated individuals' knowledge about their 'real' self and their 'ideal' self by using ideal and real ratings (Waugh, 2001), however, to date, this approach has not been applied to Teacher Leadership. The participants in the current study were early childhood teachers working in a school system that had been subject to the type of reform described earlier, and these changes had highlighted the need for them to take up the challenge of Teacher Leadership.

AIMS

The study had three aims. One was to investigate teachers' self-reports of their leadership qualities by creating an interval level, unidimensional scale for a three-aspect model of Early Childhood Teacher Leadership. The second was to analyse its psychometric properties using a modern measurement model, the Extended Logistic Model of Rasch (Andrich, 1988a, 1988b; Rasch, 1980/1960). The third was to investigate the structure and meaning of the scale in order to draw implications for the professional development of early childhood teachers.

Model of Early Childhood Teacher Leadership for Testing

The elements of leadership found in the literature led to the development of a model of Early Childhood Teacher Leadership consisting of three 1st order aspects and a number of 2nd order aspects, as shown in Figure 1. General Leadership is defined by Classroom Leadership, Self-Leadership, Teacher Preparation Leadership and Program Leadership. Communication Leadership is defined by Communication from me to Parents/Teachers/Principal and Communication from Parents/Teachers/Principal to me. Influence in Leadership is defined by Influence on the School and Influence on the Principal.

1st Order Aspects	2nd Order Aspects (Operational definition of 1st order aspects)
General Leadership	Classroom Leadership (7 stem-items)
	Self-Leadership (9 stem-items)
	Teacher Preparation Leadership (10 stem-items)
	Program Leadership (11 stem-items)
Communication	From me to Parents/Teachers/Principal (11 stems items)
	From parents/Teachers/Principal to me (11 stem-items)
Influences	My Influence on the School (7 stem- items)
	My Influence on the Principal (5 stem- items)

Figure 1. Model of Early Childhood Teacher Leadership tested for Unidimensionality

Note: There are 71 stem-items, each answered in two responses, making 142 items in the model tested. The two response modes are *How I am* (real) and *How I would like to be* (ideal).

PROBLEMS WITH TEACHER LEADERSHIP SCALES

Six general aspects of many Teacher Leadership scales are called into question. One, most of the scales are not based on a multi-aspect model that encompasses a large number of the main aspects of leadership, applicable to early childhood educators. Two, some scales use the well-known Likert response format that contains a discontinuity between the response categories of disagree and agree. That is, the response measurement format is not ordered from low to high and those who are undecided, do not want to answer, are unclear or just neutral, will answer the middle (neutral) category. Participants are forced to answer either agree or disagree if a neutral category is not provided, which means there is a consequent interpretation problem. Three, researchers rarely test the linkage of their Teacher Leadership scales between *How I would like to be* (ideal leadership) and *How I am* (in reality). Both *How I am* (real) and *How I would like to be* (ideal) ought to be measured at the same time and calibrated on the same scale. Four, often the items measuring Teacher Leadership are not separated into their sub-scales on the questionnaires, so that it is not clear to the teachers what is being measured. Five, positively and negatively worded items are mixed often to avoid the fixed response syndrome (a common procedure in traditional measurement), which may cause an interaction effect between items in modern measurement models (see Andrich & van Schoubroeck, 1989). Consequently, it is considered better to word all items in a positive sense when using modern measurement models. Six, the analysis of most Teacher Leadship scales have only been performed with traditional measurement programs and ordinal level scales. Modern measurement programs are now available to create proper interval level measures in which item difficulties and Teacher Leadership measures can be calibrated on the same scale. The programs also test the conceptual structure of Teacher Leadership including its dimensional nature (see Andrich, 1988a, 1988b; Andrich, Lyne, Sheridan & Luo, 1998; Rasch, 1960/1980; Waugh, 2000, 1999, 1998). Rasch measurement model analysis has been shown as appropriate to use in measuring attitude variables (see Andrich, 1985, 1982; Waugh, 2002, 1999; Wright & Masters, 1982, 1981).

A NEW TEACHER LEADERSHIP MODEL

The new model of Teacher Leadership was devised to overcome the six problems. The new model was based on three 1st order aspects and a number of 2nd order aspects. Thirty-seven stem-items (74 items) were based on the four 2nd order aspects of General Leadership. Twenty-two stem-items (44 items) were based on the two 2nd order aspects of Communication and twelve stem-items (24 items) were based on two 2nd order aspects of Influence. The items were ordered under their respective sub-scale headings which makes it clear to the teachers what sub-scale is being measured. They were written in a positive sense, so as to be applicable to the ordered response format. The response format was changed in two ways. First, two columns were added for responses, one for *How I am* (measuring a realistic aspect) and another for *How I would like to be* (measuring an idealistic aspect). Second, the response categories were changed to an ordered format to provide a better measurement structure: (1) none or almost none of the time, (2) some or most of the time, and (3) all or nearly all the time. There are 71 stem-items relating to *How I am* (real self-view) and, in direct correspondence, 71 stem-items relating to *How I would like to be* (ideal self-view). The full scale is given in the Appendix A.

MEASURING TEACHER LEADERSHIP

The model cannot be tested by measuring all the aspects separately and then correlating them to test for any relationships. It is not a test of the model to measure the separate aspects of Teacher Leadership (as shown in Figure 1) and then use various correlation techniques to determine the relationships between them. This model has to be tested by other means. One way is to calibrate all the item difficulties and all the Teacher Leadership scores on the same scale using a Rasch Measurement Model (Andrich, 1988a,b; Rasch, 1980/1960) and the computer program called Rasch Unidimensional Measurement Models (RUMM (Andrich,

Lyne, Sheridan & Luo, 2000). This is done to ensure that the Teacher Leadership scale only includes items that contribute logically and consistently to the measurement of Teacher Leadership and excludes items contributing 'noise'. 'Noise' refers here to items that do not fit on the scale in a consistent pattern with the other items and they are discarded because they may be measuring a trait that is not Teacher Leadership. The RUMM computer program calibrates Teacher Leadership measures and item 'difficulties' on the same scale and checks whether teachers agree on the 'difficulties' of the items along the scale. The program checks whether teachers with high, medium and low Teacher Leadership scores agree to the different 'difficulties' of items along the scale from 'easy' to 'hard'. Items for which there is not agreement are discarded as measuring 'noise'.

The use of the RUMM computer program meant that a new type of questionnaire had to be devised because Teacher Leadership and item 'difficulties' had to be calibrated together on the same scale, in order to form a proper scale. Typically, questionnaires involving, for example, separate measures of ideal and real attitudes analysed with traditional measurement techniques (such as factor analysis, Cronbach Alpha reliability and correlation) do not permit ideal and real attitudes and item 'difficulties' to be calibrated on the same scale.

The RUMM program checks that teachers can discriminate consistently between the ordered response categories. It calculates threshold values where teachers have odds of 1:1 of answering in either of two adjacent categories and, in the present study, there are two thresholds, one between categories 1 and 2, and one between categories 2 and 3. The thresholds have to be ordered in line with the ordering of the response categories for discrimination to be satisfactory.

Measurement Model

Items fitting the measurement model are aligned from 'easy' to 'hard' and Teacher Leadership measures are aligned from low to high, with the item 'difficulties' and teacher measures calibrated on the same scale. Items at the 'easy' end of the scale are answered positively by teachers with higher measures than the item 'difficulty'. Items at the 'hard' end of the scale are answered negatively by teachers with lower measures than the item 'difficulty'. The model allows for probabilities. It calculates the odds of a teacher with a leadership measure of answering a particular item, positively. The odds are related to the difference between the measure and the item 'difficulty' on the scale.

The model, for which the scale is created, postulates a predominate unidimensional trait, in this case, Teacher Leadership, that influence the responses to the items. If other traits influence the responses to the scale items (that is, a multi-dimensional situation is present), then there will be a poor fit to the model for those items predominately influenced by the other trait(s). When a single score is sufficient to describe a measure of Teacher Leadership, then the predominate variable being measured is unidimensional. The mathematical requirement in the Rasch model is that the odds of a teacher answering an item positively are only related to the difference between the Teacher Leadership measure and the 'difficulty' of the item, when both are measured on the same scale. It needs to be pointed out here that the words 'easy' and 'hard' are not usually applied to scale items in Teacher Leadership (they are usually applied to achievement items in tests). However, there is no English word that adequately describes the 'difficulty' of items for attitudes or self-views. Attitude researchers sometimes use 'less reactive' or 'more reactive' and Rasch specialists sometimes use the word 'location' to describe the position of the item on the scale, but these are inadequate too, and they do not convey the meaning needed. The words 'easy' and 'hard' are still the best to use and there is a sense in which the Teacher Leadership items are 'easy' or 'hard' in this study.

The scale is at the interval level and has most of the characteristics of a ruler. In particular, equal differences between measures (scores) on the scale represent equal 'amounts' of Teacher Leadership and the 'noise or other dimensions' in the measure of Teacher Leadership are reduced so that we have close to a unidimensional measure, like length. However, the zero point on the scale does not represent zero Teacher Leadership. It is an artificial point representing the mean of the item 'difficulties', calibrated to be zero. It is possible to calibrate a true zero point if it can be shown that an item represents zero Teacher Leadership. There is no true zero point in the present study. Furthermore, as in a ruler, the odds that a teacher will answer an item positively depends on the difference between the teacher's measure and the item 'difficulty'. If the teacher's measure is the same as the item 'difficulty', then the odds are 1:1. If the teacher's measure is at a much higher position on the scale than the item 'difficulty', the odds are much higher of getting a positive answer. Conversely, if the teacher's measure is much lower than the item 'difficulty', the odds are much lower of getting a positive answer.

The Rasch method produces scale-free teacher measures and sample-free item difficulties (Andrich, 1988b; Wright & Masters, 1982). That is, mathematically, the differences between pairs of teacher measures and pairs of item 'difficulties' are expected to be relatively sample independent, in contrast to classical measurement. Mathematically, for all the items fitting the model, there is a predominant trait. This means that the measure estimated in Rasch modeling should be different from that estimated in classical measurement. There is, however, some conflicting recent practical evidence on this point (see DeMars, 2001; Fan, 1998; Lawson, 1991). Fan (1998) found that person ability estimates using Classical Test Theory gave comparable results to those using a Rasch Measurement Model, implying that there is no need for a Rasch analysis, and that summing individual item scores in a variable is good enough. However, Fan (1998, p.368) also says that the results for the one-parameter Rasch model 'should be viewed with extreme caution' (p.368) because 30% of the items miss-fitted the Rasch model, and DeMars (2001) found similar evidence. The counter argument is that the Rasch analysis is needed to produce a proper scale in which both measures and item 'difficulties' are calibrated together, which classical measurement does not do. Rasch analysis also deletes items that are not influenced by the unidimensional trait and are thus contributing 'noise' and classical measurement does not do this to the same degree.

The RUMM program (2000) parameterises an ordered threshold structure, corresponding with the ordered response categories of the items. The thresholds are boundaries located between the response categories and are related to the change in probability of responses occurring in the two categories separated by the threshold. Teachers with leadership scores at a threshold between two categories have odds of 1:1 of answering either category.

The RUMM program substitutes the parameter estimates back into the model and examines the difference between the expected values predicted from the model and the observed values using two tests of fit: one is the item-trait interaction and the second is the item-teacher interaction. The item-trait test-of-fit (a chi-square) examines the consistency of the item parameters across the Teacher Leadership measures for each item and data are combined across all items to give an overall test-of-fit (see Andrich & van Schoubroeck, 1989, pp479-480 for the equations). This test shows the collective agreement between teachers of different Teacher Leadership measures as to the 'difficulties' of the items. For example, it gives an indication that the calibration of an 'easy' item places it at about the same 'low' location on the scale for teachers of low, medium and high leadership measures. Similarly, it gives an indication that the calibration of a 'difficult' item places it at about the same 'high' location on the scale for teachers of low, medium and high leadership measures.

The item-teacher test-of-fit examines both the response patterns for teachers across items and for items across teachers. It examines the residual between the expected estimate and the actual values for each teacher-item summed over all items for each teacher and summed over all teachers for each item (see Styles & Andrich, 1993, p914 or Andrich & van Schoubroeck, 1989, p482 for the equations). The fit statistics approximate a distribution with a mean near zero and a standard deviation near one, when the data fit the measurement model. Negative values indicate a response pattern that fits the model too closely (the further from zero negatively, the closer the fit, probably because response dependencies are present, see Andrich, 1985) and positive values indicate a poorer fit to the model (the further from zero positively, the poorer the fit, probably because other dimensions ('noise') affect the measures).

ADMINISTRATION, SAMPLE AND DATA ANALYSIS

The item-sample consisted of 71 stem-items based on a model of Teacher Leadership, making a total of 142 items. The questionnaire was pretested with 33 Early Childhood teachers and discussed with them before being used in the study. Some changes were made to the wording, as considered appropriate. The teacher-sample consisted of 270 (267 female and 3 male) teachers of Early Childhood Education in one state in Australia and is basically a convenience sample. The mean experience was 12.5 years (and the median 11 years) with a range from several months teaching to 39 years teaching. The teachers came from the metropolitan area of a medium sized city (214 from a city of about 2 million) and rural areas (54) with 4 unspecified. Most of the Early Childhood Teachers taught in an Early Childhood Centre on-site with the main school (238) and 31 in an off-site Centre.

Permission was obtained from the University Ethics Committee and from the State Government's Education Department to administer the questionnaire. The 142 items were analysed as a whole group. Forty-six items were discarded as not fitting the measurement model, leaving 96 items in the final scale. There are at least two reasons for the non-fit of items to the scale. First, some response categories were not answered consistently and logically for some items, which shows up as disordered thresholds. Second, teachers did not agree on the 'difficulty' of an item on the scale. For example, some of the teachers with high leadership measures found some items 'easy' and others with high leadership scores found the same item 'hard', which shows up as an inconsistent response pattern and poor fit to the measurement model.

RESULTS

The results are set out in Appendices A, B, C, and D, Tables 1 and 2, and Figures 2, 3, 4, and 5. Appendix A shows the questionnaire and the 'difficulties' of the items that fit the Rasch Measurement Model. Appendix B shows the item thresholds. Appendix C shows item 'difficulties', standard errors and residuals, and chi-squares and fit tot he measurement model. Table 1 shows a summary of the psychometric characteristics of the Teacher Leadership scale and the statistics for fit to the model. Table 2 shows the mean item 'difficulties' by sub-group by Real/Ideal mode. Figures 2, 3 , 4 and 5 show the graphs of the item threshold 'difficulties' ordered from 'easy' to 'hard' along the scale with the Teacher Leadership measures calibrated on the same scale from low to high, for each of four aspects of Teacher Leadership: general leadership (classroom and self), general leadership (teacher preparation and program), communication, and influences.

Table 1. Summary statistics for 92 item Teacher Leadership scale

	Items	Teachers
Number	92	270
Location mean	0.00	2.80
Standard deviation	1.76	1.14
Fit statistic mean	-0.25	-0.51
Standard deviation	0.91	1.43
Item-trait interaction chi square = 295.82.27, df=276, p=0.20		
Teacher Separation Index = 0.94		
Power of tests-of-fit are excellent		

Notes:
1. The item means are constrained to zero by the Rasch Measurement Model program.
2. The fit statistic approximates a distribution with a mean near zero and a SD near one, when the data fit the model (in this case, a good fit).
3. The item-trait interaction indicates the agreement displayed for the item 'difficulties' across all teachers with different measures of Teacher Leadership (in this case, good).
4. The Teacher Separation Index is the proportion of observed Teacher Leadership variance considered true (in this case 94% and high).
5. Location for items means 'difficulty' and location for teachers means measures.
6. The Ses of measurement are about 0.14. All results are reported to 2 decimal places in line with the errors.

PSYCHOMETRIC CHARACTERISTICS OF THE TEACHER LEADERSHIP SCALE

The final 92 items relating to the Teacher Leadership Scale have a good fit to the measurement model. The item-teacher tests-of-fit indicate that there is good consistency of teacher and item response patterns in line with the ordering of the Teacher Leadership measures from low to high and the item 'difficulties' from 'easy' to 'hard' along the scale (see Table 1). The fit statistics have a mean near zero and a SD near 1, as required for a good fit to the measurement model.

There is good agreement between all 270 teachers as to each of the 'difficulties' of the items on the scale. The item-trait interaction chi-square is 295.82, df=276, and the significance p= 0.20 (see Table 1). The item-trait fit means that the teachers with different measures of Teacher Leadership agree that the 'easy' and the 'hard' items are in their 'right' positions on the scale.

Teacher Leadership, for all the teachers, can be represented by a single score on the scale and this means that there is a predominate trait, Teacher Leadership, that has influenced the scores. In turn, this means that teachers' responses to all 92 leadership items, involving Classroom Leadership, Self-Leadership, Teacher Preparation Leadership, Program Leadership, Communication to Me, Influence on the School and Influence on the Principal, are influenced by the same trait.

Table 2. Mean Item Difficulties by Sub-Group from 'easiest' to 'hardest'

Teacher Leadership Sub-Group	Mean score	
Teacher Preparation Leadership	-1.88	Ideal mode
Self-Leadership	-1.66	Ideal mode
Communications from me to parents/teachers/principal	-1.49	Ideal mode
Classroom Leadership	-1.37	Ideal mode
Program Leadership	-1.19	Ideal mode
My Influence on the School	-0.49	Ideal mode
Self-Leadership	-0.03	**Real mode**
Communications from parents/teachers/principal to me	+0.17	Ideal mode
My Influence on the Principal	+0.64	Ideal mode
Teacher Preparation Leadership	+0.92	**Real mode**
Communications from me to parents/teachers/principal	+1.00	**Real mode**
Program Leadership	+1.02	**Real mode**
Classroom Leadership	+1.22	**Real mode**
My Influence on the School	+1.76	**Real mode**
My Influence on the Principal	+2.35	**Real mode**
Communications from parents/teachers/principal to me	+3.06	**Real mode**

Notes:

1. The scores are the mean of the item 'difficulties' in logits for the items that fit the model and belong to the sub-group named.
2. Negative values indicate the means are low on the scale (or 'easier'). Positive values indicate that the means are high on the scale (or 'harder').
3. The mean of the item 'difficulties' in the real mode is 'harder' than the mean of the corresponding item 'difficulties' in the ideal mode, as conceptualised.

The 'difficulties' of the items are well targeted against the teachers (except that there are too many easy items) and match the range of Teacher Leadership measures (see Appendix D and Figures 2, 3 and 4), although some improvements should be made in a future version of the scale. The item threshold 'difficulties' range from about –5 to +6 logits and the Teacher Leadership measures range from about zero to +6 logits. Thus, there are too many 'easy items' (with no matching teachers with low Teacher Leadership measures). This means that the 'easiest' items (from –0.5 to –5 logits) could be discarded for the teachers in this study (or other teachers with low measures could be added).

Location	Teacher Scores	Item Difficulties
	High Leadership	Hard items
6.0	X	
	X	
	XXX	
5.0	XXXX	
	XX	
	X	
	XXXX	
	XXXX	
4.0	XXXX	
	XXX	
	XXXXXXX	
	XXXXXX	
	XXXXXXX	
3.0	XXXXXXXXXXXX	
	XXXXXXXXXX	
	XXXXXXXXXX	
	XXXXXXXXXXX	
	XXXXXXXXXX	
2.0	XXXXXXX	
	XXXXXXXXXX	
	XXXX	**item13(cl)**
	XXXXXXX	
	XXXXXX	
1.0·	XXX	
	X	**item9(cl)**
	X	
	XX	**item17(sl)**
	X	**item31(sl)**
0.0	X	item6(cl)
		item21(sl)
		item15(sl)
		item14(cl)
-1.0		
		item30(sl)
		item12(cl),
		item10(cl), item20(sl), item22(sl)
		item24(sl), item26(sl), item28(sl), item32(sl)
-2.0		item4(cl)
		item2(cl)
-3.0	Low Leadership	Easy items

Figure 2. Teacher Leadership measures and item difficulties for classroom leadership (cl) and self-leadership (sl) (Real perspectives are in bold, each X represent two teacher leadership measures)

Location	Teacher Scores	Item Difficulties
	High Leadership	Hard items
6.0	X	
	X	
	XXX	
5.0	XXXX	
	XX	
	X	
	XXXX	
	XXXX	
4.0	XXXX	
	XXX	
	XXXXXX	
	XXXXX	**item73(pl)**
	XXXXXX	
3.0	XXXXXXXXXXXX	
	XXXXXXXXXX	
	XXXXXXXXXX	
	XXXXXXXXXX	
	XXXXXXXXXX	item74(pl)
2.0	XXXXXXX	
	XXXXXXXXXX	**item37(tpl), item41(tpl)**
	XXXX	
	XXXXXXX	
	XXXXXX	
1.0	XXX	
	X	**item47(tpl)**
	X	**item59(pl)**
	XX	
	X	
0.0	X	
		item62(pl)
		item33(tpl)
		item63(pl)
-1.0		
		item42(tpl)
		item60(pl)
		item64(pl),item68(pl)
		item46(tpl),item48(tpl),item66(pl)
-2.0		item34(tpl),item44(tpl),item52(tpl),
		item54(pl), item56(pl)
		item50(tpl),item58(pl)
		item40(tpl)
-3.0	Low Leadership	Easy items

Figure 3. Teacher Leadership measures and item difficulties for teacher preparation leadership (tpl) and program leadership (pl) (real perspectives are in bold, each X represents two teacher leadership measures).

Location	Teacher Scores	Item Difficulties
	High Leadership	Hard items
6.0	X	
	X	
	XXX	
5.0	XXXX	
	XX	
	X	
	XXXX	item115(tome)
	XXXX	item117(tome)
4.0	XXXX	
	XXX	
	XXXXXXX	
	XXXXXX	item113(tome)
	XXXXXXX	
3.0	XXXXXXXXXXXX	
	XXXXXXXXXX	
	XXXXXXXXXX	item99(tome),item103(tome),item109(tome)
	XXXXXXXXXX	
	XXXXXXXXXX	item77(frome)
2.0	XXXXXXX	
	XXXXXXXXXX	item79(frome)
	XXXX	item83(frome),item107(tome),item116(tome)
	XXXXXXX	item118(tome)
	XXXXXX	
1.0	XXX	item 75(frome),item91(frome)
	X	item89(frome)
	X	item95(frome)
	XX	item81(frome)
	X	item112(tome)
0.0	X	
		item78(frome),item87(frome)
		item100(tome)
		item82(frome),item84(frome),item110(tome)
-1.0		
		item98(tome)
		item76(frome)
-2.0		item90(frome),item96(frome)
		item88(frome),item92(frome)
-3.0	Low Leadership	Easy items

Figure 4. Teacher Leadership measures and item difficulties for communicatiom from me (frome) and communication to me (tome) (real perspectives are in bold, and each X represents two teacher measures).

Location	Teacher Scores	Item Difficulties
	High Leadership	Hard items
6.0	X	
	X	
	XXX	
5.0	XXXX	
	XX	
	X	
	XXXX	
	XXXX	
4.0	XXXX	
	XXX	
	XXXXXXX	
	XXXXXX	
	XXXXXX	
3.0	XXXXXXXXXXXX	**item141(prin)**
	XXXXXXXXXX	
	XXXXXXXXXX	**item133(prin)**
	XXXXXXXXXX	
	XXXXXXXXXX	**item131(schl),item135(prin),item139(prin)**
2.0	XXXXXXX	**item119(schl),item129(schl)**
	XXXXXXXXXX	**item137(prin)**
	XXXX	
	XXXXXXX	
	XXXXXX	
1.0	XXX	**item127(schl)**,item142(prin)
	X	item130(schl),item134(prin)
	X	item132(schl)
	XX	item136(prin)
	X	
0.0	X	
		item140(prin)
		item128(schl)
-1.0		
		item124(schl),item126(schl)
-2.0		
-3.0	Low Leadership	Easy items

Figure 5. Teacher Leadership measures and item difficulties formy influence on school (schl) and my influence on the principal (prin) (real perspective in bold) .

The threshold values (see Appendix B) are ordered from low to high for each item fitting the Rasch model, indicating that the teachers answered the response categories consistently and logically for the 92 items. As the response categories increase, teachers need correspondingly higher Leadership scores in order to answer them positively. The Index of Teacher Separability (akin to traditional reliability) for the 92 item scale with four response categories is 0.94. This means that the proportion of observed variance considered true is 94%. Taken together, these data indicate that a good unidimensional scale of Teacher Leadership has been constructed in which the errors are small, the internal reliability is high, the power of the tests-of-fit are excellent, and the items conform both to the measurement model and to the three-aspects of the conceptual model.

GENERAL MEANING OF THE TEACHER LEADERSHIP SCALE

The 92 items that fit the model of Teacher Leadership are conceptualised as involving *General Leadership* (Classroom Leadership, Self-Leadership, Teacher Preparation Leadership and Program Leadership), *Communication* (from Parents /Teachers /Principal to me) and *Influences* (My Influence on the School and My Influence on the Principal). Fifty-four items identify teachers' self-views about *How I would like to be* (an ideal self-concept for leadership) and 38 items identify self-views about *How I am* (a real self-concept for leadership). Teachers found it 'easier' to have high ideal leadership self-views than to have high real self-views for the corresponding item, as conceptualised. This is reflected by the lower ideal item 'difficulties' on the scale in comparison to the 'difficulties' for the same item real self-views (see Appendix A, and Figures 2-5). The mean item 'difficulty' for each of the three-factors of Teacher Leadership is set out in Table 2. As expected, all the ideal perspectives are 'easier' than their corresponding real perspectives.

The item 'difficulties' and the Teacher Leadership measures are calibrated on the same scale at the interval level. Equal differences on the scale between measures of Teacher Leadership represent equal differences in item difficulty. However, there is no true zero point of item difficulty or Teacher Leadership. The 92 items are ordered from 'easy' to 'hard' (see Figure 2) along the scale. They all fit the measurement model and are linked together on the scale. The 'very easy' items are all those with difficulties less than zero logits, that is, lower than the lowest Teacher Leadership measure. Nearly all the teachers answered the 'very easy' items positively (for example, items 40, 2, 58, 50, 92, 56, 4, 54). As the items become progressively harder on the scale, the teachers need a higher Teacher Leadership measure to answer them positively. The 'medium hard' items are all those with difficulties between zero and +2.00 logits (for example, items 112, 47, 9, 89, 91, 107). The 'very hard' items are those with difficulties over +4.00 logits (for example, 115, 117, 73, 113 and 141) and they are only answered positively by teachers who have high Teacher Leadership measures (for example, measures of +4 or more logits). Teachers with low measures of Teacher Leadership cannot answer the 'very hard' items positively.

DISCUSSION

Three-Aspect Model

The analysis supported the three-aspect model of Teacher Leadership involving (1) General Leadership, (2) Communication and (3) Influence, for early childhood teachers. General Leadership was conceptualised as consisting of Classroom Leadership, Self-leadership, Teacher Preparation Leadership, and Program Leadership and this was supported. Communication was conceptualised as being directed from the early childhood teacher to parents, other teachers and the principal, and as being directed from parents, other teachers and the principal to the early childhood teacher, because of the early childhood teacher's leadership example, and this was supported. Influence was conceptualised as being directed from the early childhood teacher to the school and as being directed from the early childhood teacher to the principal, both as a result of the teacher's leadership example, and this also was supported. So Leadership involves early childhood teachers in General Leadership, Communication and Influence. The implication is that early childhood teachers have to be trained in each of these three aspects, if they are going to lead (or advocate) for early childhood education in their schools. Early childhood teacher training groups at universities (and elsewhere) should take note.

Unidimensional Trait

In order to fit the measurement model so well, the mathematics of the Rasch model requires that the items be aligned from 'easy' to 'hard' along the scale and that teachers with low, medium and high leadership measures agree with the placement of the items along the scale. This means that a single score measuring leadership for each teacher can be used in the Rasch equations. This in turn means that a unidimensional trait, Teacher Leadership, has been measured. The implication is that all of the items that fit the model are influenced by a focus on Leadership by advocating for early childhood teaching.

Easy and Hard Items

One can examine the 'difficulties' of the items on the scale to see what early childhood teachers report as 'easy' and what they report as 'hard'. Communications from parents, other teachers and the principal, as a result of the teacher's leadership example, is ' hard'. Being able to influence the principal is ' hard', as is being able to influence other teachers in the school about early childhood education. The implication is that administrators in primary and secondary education need to be educated about early childhood education to some extent so that they don't think of it as just 'baby sitting', for example. An implication for early childhood educators at universities is that early childhood teachers need to be trained in strategies to influence parents, primary and secondary teachers, and the principal.

The analysis supports the view that early childhood teachers recognise the importance of the 'hard' leadership skills but have trouble putting them into practice. This is reflected in the measurement where more items measuring the ideal mode fit the model than items measuring the real mode (54 v. 38) and, where corresponding ideal and real items fit the model, the real self-views are 'harder' than the ideal self-views. For example, in Communication, teachers reported that it was 'very easy' ideally to want to explain the early childhood way of teaching to other staff (item 90) and to the principal (item 92), but 'harder' to actually do this (items 89 and 91). As another example, teachers reported that it was 'very easy' ideally to argue their point of view with other staff (item 84) and with parents (item 82), but 'harder' to actually do this (items 83 and 81).

Advocating for ECE

The teachers who participated in this study worked in schools that had been part of recent educational reforms and many worked with school colleagues and administrators with little experience in early childhood education. This suggests that it was necessary for them to enact leadership to ensure that appropriate early childhood practices were maintained. While the findings suggest that the teachers were more comfortable with enacting teacher leadership within the classrooms rather than in the school and community, there was some reluctance to embrace some aspects of classroom leadership for a minority of teachers. Some early childhood teachers said that they found it difficult to take a leadership role in classrooms (item 13), although it is part of what they have to do in their work. One issue concerns the close link in conceptualisation between classroom leadership and "good teaching" and some findings may indicate that refinements are necessary to this aspect of the questionnaire. For example, it was 'hard' for some early childhood teachers to say that they were satisfied with their record keeping (item 37), felt involved with their school life (item 41), conveyed clear role responsibilities to other staff (item 9), and take a leadership role in the wider community (item 73), when these activities are accepted widely as part of teachers' work. Leadership means taking it a step further so teacher leaders would be willing to talk about their programming and record keeping techniques at staff meetings, and to share ideas informally with other teachers or the principal, which would enable others to learn more about early childhood programs, and it was these activities that teachers found hard to say that they do. Jorde-Bloom (1997 p.35) discusses the difference between competent practitioners and leaders who demonstrate excellence, noting that in child care settings, this is the difference between management and leadership. Part of the work of conceptualising early childhood teacher leadership means distinguishing 'good teaching' from leadership.

The so-called "third wave" of teacher leaders (Silva, Gimbert, & Nolan, 2000) places high priority on collaborative interactions between teaching colleagues that result in knowledge generation to move the work of teaching forward (Wheatley, 1992). The findings suggest that many of these teachers have found it 'easy' to come out of the 'secret garden of the early childhood classroom' and it is inferred that these teachers could collaborate with colleagues and share expertise, to mentor beginning teachers, model skilled teaching to student-teachers or share part of their knowledge with the children's parents.

Aspects of leadership that were problematic for many teachers in their real perspective involved the principal, other teachers and parents asking the early childhood teacher questions about their philosopohy. Ideally, many teachers wanted these aspects to happen. The implication is that many parents and principals, either didn't want to communicate with the early childhood teacher about philosophy, or couldn't do so. Some teachers found it a liitle hard to say that they wanted principals to be involved in the classroom or that they wanted to help principals to gain more knowledge of early childhood, which may relate to being either territorial, defensive or scared (Walker Duff, 1997, p. 83). Some teachers may keep the early childhood classroom door closed because they feel unable to stop the flow of elementary school practice into their program, or they may feel unable to explain, justify and argue the case for developmentally appropriate programs. The results indicated that many early childhood teachers are reasonably well-placed to assert clinical authority or wield power in their schools and communities. This does not support the views of Finkelstein (1988). There teachers recognised the competencies they held and identified areas of teacher leadership they found problematic in themselves. However, it seemed that their competencies did not include the range of activities being promoted in restructured schools. However, in the present study, it is suggested that the findings reflect a view of many early childhood teachers as professional who lead and control their classrooms, and want to bring early childhood philosophies to the schools and wider community.

Relationships between Items

Part of the reason for making an interval-level scale of Teacher Leadership is to develop some relationships between aspects that may be useful (in the same way that laws are developed and used in physics). This view is supported by Wright (1999) who suggests that raw scores are not measures, that the Rasch measurement model is making a minor revolution in the social sciences, and that useful relationships in social science are possible, if proper measures are made. It would be easier to develop some relationships if the Teacher Leadership scale had a true zero point and, because it doesn't, the relationships are a little complicated and involve differences between item difficulties. Nevertheless, it has been possible to create some relationships for Influence on the Principal, for Communication from the ECE Teachers, for Program Leadership, and for relationships between real and ideal aspects. It should be noted that, while other relationships can be created from the data, the following ones seem interesting.

The difference between ECE teachers really helping the principal acquire more knowledge about ECE and really encouraging the principal to support ECE is about 3 times as 'hard' as the difference between really encouraging the principal to be involved in an ECE classroom and really encouraging the principal to support ECE [(3.03- 1.87)/(2.22-1.87) = 3.3]. The difference between really speaking confidently about ECE and really explaining ECE to parents is about 2 times as 'hard' as the difference between really communicating effectively with the principal and really explaining ECE to parents [(2.22- -0.28)/(0.88- -0.28) = 2.1]. The difference between ECE teachers really taking a leadership role in the wider community and really looking for ways to improve their teaching practice is about 3 times as 'hard' as the difference between really keeping up-to-date with the latest developments in ECE and really initiating their own professional development [(3.36- -0.78)/(0.49- -0.78) = 3.2].

The difference between ECE teachers really helping the principal to acquire more knowledge about ECE and ideally encouraging the principal to be involved in what happens in the classroom is about 1.5 times as 'hard' as really encouraging the principal to be involved in what happens in the classroom and ideally encouraging the principal to be involved in what happens in the classroom [(3.03 –0.46)/(2.22-0.46) = 1.5]. The difference between ECE teachers really speaking confidently about ECE and ideally communicating effectively with the principal is about 1.5 times as 'hard' as the difference between ECE teachers really communicating effectively with the principal and ideally communicating effectively with the principal [(2.22- -1.77)/(0.88- -1.77) = 1.5]. The difference between ECE teachers really taking a leadership role in the wider community and ideally keeping up-to-date with the latest developments in ECE is about 2 times as 'hard' as the difference between ECE teachers looking for ways to improve their teaching practice and ideally keeping up-to-date with the latest developments in ECE [(3.67- -1.49)/(0.78- -1.49) =2.2].

Some Further Implications

The Teacher Leadership model needs further testing and refinement. Some of the 'very easy' items can be deleted. Some 'much harder' items need to be devised and added. The model has only been tested with early childhood teachers from Perth and rural Western Australia. The model needs to be tested in other countries. The model can be expanded to give more explanatory power. In the present study, the responses were limited to ideal views and real views. A revised model could incorporate ideal self-views, capability self-views and real self-views, for example. These would expect to be ordered from high (ideal self-views), through medium (capability self-views) to low (real self-views) and this can, of course, be tested. Each stem-item could be re-worded to reflect a series of ordered Guttman patterns (as an example see Waugh 2002a, 2002b). For example, in Self-leadership, the stem-item 'I know my own weaknesses' could be replaced by:

1. I think about my own weaknesses
2. I do something about trying to overcome my own weaknesses
3. I evaluate my progress in overcoming my own weaknesses

It is suggested that the conceptualisation of durable and perpetuating leadership capacities (Kagan & Bowman, 1997) must be based on a broad definition of teachers' work, and that the difference between being a skilled teacher and a teacher leader may need to be explored further. Teachers need a wide range of communication, collaboration and advocacy skills for leadership in today's schools, and they need help to develop them. It is suggested that early childhood teacher education courses should foster the knowledge and skills that teachers need and they must support the growth of teachers' self-confidence and self-knowledge to empower them to enact these skills. The present study suggests that ECE teachers must develop their ideal self-views in order to implement the various aspects of Leadership and thus advocate for early childhood education. This has, in turn, implications for the training of early childhood teachers at universities.

CONCLUSIONS

Educational reform has brought the need for Early Childhood Teacher Leadership into sharp focus. Teachers' self-views recognise the importance of leadership and teachers consider that they would like more skills to enact it. The Rasch model was very useful in creating a scale of Early Childhood Teacher Leadership based on a model of leadership involving an ideal self-view and a real self-view. The teachers found it easy to say that they would like to have high self-views for General Leadership, Communication and Influence, but found it harder to say that they think of themselves as having high real self-views for these skills. The teachers in this study found it easy to enact their leadership skills in ECE in regard to general leadership, communication and influence. It seems reasonable to infer that these teachers found it easy to advocate for appropriate and effective curriculum, pedagogy and practices for young children. Reform in early childhood has enabled teachers to develop the leadership skills they need, and the findings of this study have implications for pre-service and in-service teachers' professional development. The main areas where ECE teachers found it very hard was in getting parents and principals to question them about their ECE philosophy and in trying to get the principals to acquire more knowledge about ECE.

REFERENCES

Andrich, D. (1988a). A General Form of Rasch's Extended Logistic Model for Partial Credit Scoring. Applied Measurement in Education, 1 (4), 363-378.

Andrich, D. (1988b). Rasch models for measurement. Sage university paper on quantitative applications in the social sciences, series number 07/068. Newbury Park, California: Sage Publications.

Andrich, D. (1985). A latent trait model for items with response dependencies: Implications for test construction and analysis. In S.E. Embretson (Ed.), Test design: developments in psychology and psychometrics (pp. 245-275).Orlando: Academic Press.

Andrich, D. (1982). Using latent trait measurement to analyse attitudinal data: a synthesis of viewpoints. In D. Spearitt (Ed.), The improvement of measurement in education and psychology (pp. 89-126). Melbourne: ACER

Andrich, D., Sheridan, B., Lyne, A. & Luo, G. (1998). RUMM: A windows-based item analysis program Employing Rasch unidimensional measurement models. Perth: Murdoch University.

Andrich, D. & van Schoubroeck, L. (1989). The General Health Questionnaire: a psychometric analysis using latent trait theory. Psychological Medicine, 19, 469-485.

Anning, A. (1998). Appropriateness of effectiveness in the early childhood curriculum in the UK: Some research evidence. International Journal of Early Years Education, 6(3) 299-314.

Berliner, D.C. (1994). Teacher expertise. In T. Husen & T.N. Postlethwaite (Eds.), International encyclopedia of education (2nd ed., pp. 6020-6026). NY: Pergamon.

Best, R. (1996). Role Clarity. In V.A. McClelland & V. Varma (Eds.), The needs of teachers pp. 98-112. London: Cassell.

Bredekamp, S., & Copple, C. (Eds.) (1997). Developmentally appropriate practice in early childhood programs. Washington, DC: National Association for the Education of Young Children.

Burts, D.C., Hart, C.H., Charlesworth, R., Fleege, P.O., Mosley, J., & Thomasson, R.H. (1992). A comparison of frequencies of stress behaviours observed in kindergarten children in classrooms with developmentally appropriate versus developmentally inappropriate instructional practices. Early Childhood Research Quarterly, 5, 407-423.

Burts, D.C., Hart, C.H., Charlesworth, R., DeWolf, D.M., Ray, J., Manuel, K. & Fleege, P.O. (1993). Developmental appropriateness of kindergarten programs and academic outcomes in first grade. Journal of Research in Childhood Education,8(1) 23-31.

Cannella, G.S. (1997). Deconstructing early childhood education: Social justice and revolution. New York: Peter Lang Publishing.

Chemers, M.M., Watson, C.B., & May, S.T. (2000). Dispositional affect and leadership effectiveness: A comparison of self-esteem, optimism, and efficacy. Personality and Social Psychology Bulletin, 26(3) 267-277.

Cleave, S. & Brown, S. (1982). Early to school: Four year olds in infant classes. London: Routledge

Corrie, L. (2000). The politics of restructuring and professional accountability: A case study of curriculum choice for early childhood programs. In J. Hayden (Ed.) Landscapes in Early Childhood services: Cross national perspectives on empowerment and restraint, (291-306). New York: Peter Lang.

Creighton, T.B. (1997). Teachers as leaders: Is the principal really needed? Paper presented at the 6th Annual National Conference on Creating the Quality School, Oklahoma City, OK, 1997. ED411117.

David, T. (Ed.). (1993). Educational provision for our youngest children: European perspectives. London: Paul Chapman.

Davies, B. & Harre, R. (1990). Positioning: Conversation and the production of selves. Journal for the Theory of Social Behaviour 20, 43-63.

Davies, M. & Pollnitz, L. (1994). Internship: An innovation in early childhood education. Australian Journal of Early Childhood, 19 (3), 20-27.

DeMars, C. (2001). Group differences based on IRT scores: Does the model matter? Educational and Psychological Measurement, 61 (1), 60-70.

Dimmock, C. & O'Donoghue, T. (1997). The edited topical life history approach: A new methodology to inform the study of school leadership. Leading and Managing, 3(1), 48-70.

Duke, D.L. (1994). Drift, detachment and the need for teacher leadership. In D.R. Walling (Ed.), Teachers as leaders. Perspectives on the professional development of teachers pp.255-273. Bloomington IN: Phi Delta Kappa Educational Foundation.

Fan, X. (1998). Item response theory and classical test theory: An empirical comparison of their item/person statistics. Educational and Psychological Measurement, 58, 357-381.

Finkelstein, B. (1988). The revolt against selfishness: Women and the dilemmas of professionalism in early childhood education. In In B. Spodek, O.N. Saracho, & D.L. Peters (Eds.), Professionalism and the early childhood practitioner pp.10-28. New York: Teachers College.

French, J. & Pena, S. (1997). Principals' ability to implement "Best Practices" in early childhood. ERIC Document Reproduction Service No: ED 413 149.

Fullan, M. (1994). Teacher leadership: A failure to conceptualise. In D.R. Walling (Ed.) Teachers as leaders. Perspectives on the professional development of teachers pp.241-253.Bloomington, IN: Phi Delta Kappa Educational Foundation.

Hart, C.H., Burts, D.C, Durland, M.A., Charlesworth, R., DeWolf, M. Fleege, P.O. (1998). Stress behaviours and activity type participation of preschoolers in more and less developmentally appropriate classrooms: SES and sex difference. Journal of Research in Childhood Education, 12(2) 176-196.

Jorde-Bloom (1997). Commentary. In S.L. Kagan & B.T. Bowman (Eds.) Leadership in early care and education (pp.3-8). Washington, D.C. National Association for the Education of Young Children.

Kagan, S.L. & Bowman, B.T. (Eds.) (1997). Leadership in early care and education. Washington, D.C. National Association for the Education of Young Children.

Kolb, J. (1999). The effect of gender role, attitude toward leadership and self-confidence on leader emergence: Implications for leadership development. Human Resource Development Quarterly, 10(4) 305-320.

Lawson, S. (1991). One parameter latent trait measurement: Do the results justify the effort? In B. Thompson (Ed.), Advances in educational research: Substantive findings, methodological developments (vol.1, pp. 159-168). Greenwich, CT: JAI Press.

Lieberman, A. (1988). Expanding the leadership team. Educational Leadership, 45(5) 4-8.

Little (1998). The persistence of privacy: Autonomy and initiative in teachers' professional relations. Paper presented at the annual meeting of the American Educational Research Association, San Francisco, March, 1989.

Lubeck, S. (1994). The politics of developmentally appropriate practice: Exploring issues of culture, class and curriculum. In B.L. Malory & R.S. New (Eds.), Diversity and developmentally appropriate practices. Challenges for early childhood education pp. 17-43. NY: Teachers College.

McLaughlin, M.W. & Oberman, I. (1996). Teacher learning: New policies, new practices. NY: Teachers College.

Morgan (1997). Historical views of leadership. In S.L. Kagan & B.T. Bowman (Eds.), Leadership in early care and education pp.9-14. Washington, D.C.: National Association for the Education of young children.

Pajares, F. (1996). Self-efficacy beliefs in academic settings. Review of Educational Research, 66 (4), 543-578.

Pellicer, L.O. & Anderson, L.W. (1995). A handbook for teacher leaders. Thousand Oaks, Ca: Corwin.

Rasch, G. (1980/1960). Probabilistic models for intelligence and attainment tests (expanded edition). Chicago: The University of Chicago Press (original work published in 1960).

Rodd, J. (1994). Leadership in early childhood: The pathway to professionalism. New York: Teachers College Press.

Rotherberg, D. (1995). Full-day kindergarten programs. ERIC Clearinghouse on Elementary and Early Childhood Education. EDD00036.

Schweinhart, L.J. & Weikart, D.P. (1998). Why curriculum matters in early childhood education. Educational Leadership, 55, 57-60.

Sergiovanni, T.J. & Starratt, R.J. (1998). Supervision: A redefinition. Boston: McGraw-Hill.

Shotter, J. (1986). A sense of place: Vico and the social production of social identities. British Journal of Social Psychology, 25, 199-211.

Silva, D.Y., Gimbert, B., Nolan, J.F. (2000). Sliding the doors: locking and unlocking possibilities for teacher leadership. Teachers College Record, 102(4), 779-804.

Smith, E.R., & Mackie, D.M. (2000). Social Psychology. Philadelphia: Psychology Press.

Smylie, M., & Denny, J. (1990). Teacher leadership: Tensions and ambiguities in organisational perspective. Educational Administration Quarterly, 26(3), 235-259.

Somech, A., & Drach-Zahavy, A. (2000). Understanding extra-role behavior in schools: The relationships between job satisfaction, sense of efficacy, and teachers' extra-role behavior. Teaching and Teacher Education 16, 649-659.

Spodek, B. (1996). The professional development of early childhood teachers. Early Child Development and Care, 115, 115-124.

Spodek, B. (1988). Implicit theories of early childhood teachers: Foundations for professional behavior. In B. Spodek, O.N. Saracho, & D.L. Peters (Eds.), Professionalism and the early childhood practitioner pp. 161-172. New York: Teachers College Press.

Styles, I. & Andrich, D. (1993). Linking the standard and advanced forms of the Raven's Progressive Matrices in both the pencil-and-paper and computing-adaptive-testing-formats. Educational and Psychological Measurement, 53 (4), 905-925.

Walker-Duff, A. (1997). Commentary In S.L. Kagan & B.T. Bowman (Eds,) Leadership in early care and education. Washington, D.C.: National Association for the Education of Young Children.

Wasley, P.A. (1991). Teachers who lead. The rhetoric of reform and the realitites of practice. New York: Teachers College Press.

Waugh, R. F. (2002a). Creating a scale to measure motivation to achieve academically for university students: Linking attitudes and behaviours using Rasch measurement. British Journal of Educational Psychology, 72 (1), 65-86.

Waugh, R. F. (2002b). Measuring self-reported studying and learning for university students: Linking attitudes and behaviours on the same scale. British Journal of Educational Psychology, 72 (4), 573-604.

Waugh, R.F. (2001). Measuring ideal and real self-concept on the same scale, based on a multifaceted, hierarchical model of self-concept. Educational and Psychological Measurement, 61 (1), 85-101.

Waugh, R.F. (2000). Measuring attitudes and behaviours to studying and learning for university students: A Rasch measurement model analysis. Paper presented at the Australian Association for Research in Education, 4-7 December 2000, at the University of Sydney, Sydney, Australia.

Waugh, R. F. (1999). Approaches to Studying Inventory for students in higher education: A Rasch measurement model analysis. British Journal of Educational Psychology, 69, 63-79

Waugh, R. F. (1998). A Rasch measurement model analysis of an Approaches to Studying Inventory for students in higher education. Paper presented at the Latent Trait Theory Conference: Rasch measurement, held at the University of Western Australia from January 22-24, 1998.

Weber, J. (1996). Leading the instructional program. In: S.C. Smith & P.K. Piele (Eds.), School leadership: Handbook for excellence. University of Oregon: ERIC Clearinghouse on Educational Management.

Wheatley, M.J. (1992). Leadership and the new science. San Francisco: Berrett-Koehler.

Whitebook, M. (1997). Who's missing at the table? Leadership opportunities and barriers for teachers and providers. In S.L. Kagan & B.T. Bowman, (Eds.), Leadership in early care and education (pp.77-82). Washington, D.C.: National Association for the Education of Young Children.

Wideen, M.F., Mayer-Smith, J.A. & Moon, B.J. (1996). Knowledge, teacher development and change. In I.F. Goodson & A. Hargreaves (Eds.), Teachers' professional lives (pp. 187-204). London: Falmer Press.

Woods, P. (1983). Sociology and the school: An interactionist viewpoint. London: Routledge & Kegan Paul.

Wright, B. D. (1999). Fundamental measurement for psychology. In: The new rules of measurement, S. E. Ebretson & S. L. Hershberger (Eds.), pp.65-104. Mahwah, NJ: Lawrence Erlbaum Associates.

Wright, B. & Masters, G. (1982). Rating scale analysis: Rasch measurement. Chicago, IL: MESA Press

Wright, B. & Masters, G. (1981). The measurement of knowledge and attitude (Research memorandum No. 30). Chicago, IL: University of Chicago, Department of Education, Statistical Laboratory.

APPENDIX A.
QUESTIONNAIRE: TEACHER LEADERSHIP FOR EARLY CHILDHOOD EDUCATORS

Please rate the 142 stem-items according to the following response format and place a number corresponding to *How I am* and *How I would like to be* on the appropriate line opposite each statement:

All the time or nearly all the time	put 3
Some or most of the time	put 2
None of the time or almost none of the time	put 1

Example
If you handle a classroom crisis well some of the time, put 2 and if you would like to be able to handle a classroom crisis well all of the time, put 3.

Item 1/2 Handle a classroom crisis well 2 3

Item no.	Item wording	How I am (real view)	How I would like to be (ideal)
General Leadership			
	Classroom leadership		
1/2	I handle a classroom crisis well.	No fit	**-2.19**
3/4	I set clear standards.	No fit	**-2.06**
5/6	I am willing to take calculated risks.	No fit	**-0.04**
7/8	I share decision-making.	No fit	No fit
9/10	I convey clear role responsibilities to other staff.	**+0.85**	**-1.60**
11/12	I motivate and inspire other staff to do their best.	No fit	**-1.42**
13/14	I take a leadership role.	**+1.58**	**-0.89**
	Self-leadership		
15/16	I set clear goals.	**-0.44**	No fit
17/18	I am proactive rather than reactive (initiating rather than responding).	**+0.49**	No fit
19/20	I stand up for what I believe in.	No fit	**-1.62**
21/22	I achieve what I set out to achieve.	**-0.33**	**-1.60**
23/24	I know my own strengths.	No fit	**-1.78**
25/26	I know my own weaknesses.	No fit	**-1.72**
27/28	I am a confident person.	No fit	**-1.83**
29/30	I am an assertive person.	No fit	**-1.29**
31/32	I am an optimistic person.	**+0.17**	**-1.79**

Item no.	Item wording	How I am (real view)	How I would like to be (ideal)
	Teacher Preparation Leadership		
33/34	I am proud of my achievements at school.	-0.73	-1.91
35/36	I am satisfied with my programming.	No fit	No fit
37/38	I am satisfied with my record keeping.	+1.77	-1.92
39/40	I feel good about the work I do at school.	No fit	-2.29
41/42	I feel involved in school life.	+1.84	-1.16
43/44	I have a good rapport with other ECE staff I work with.	No fit	-1.97
45/46	I have a good rapport with other staff at my school.	No fit	-1.74
47/48	I am sure of myself at school.	+0.79	-1.85
49/50	I feel I am viewed as an equal by colleagues of my sex.	No fit	-2.17
51/52	I feel I am viewed as an equal by colleagues of the opposite sex.	No fit	-1.92
	Program Leadership		
53/54	I implement a developmentally appropriate program.	No fit	-2.05
55/56	I reflect my own teaching practice.	No fit	-2.08
57/58	I advocate for early childhood teaching philosophy.	No fit	-2.19
59/60	I initiate my own professional development.	+0.49	-1.34
61/62	I am willing to be involved in extra curricula activities.	No fit	-0.18
63/64	I look for ways to improve my teaching practice.	-0.78	-1.61
65/66	I feel in control of what happens in the classroom.	No fit	-1.78
67/68	I keep up-to-date with the latest developments in ECE.	No fit	-1.49
69/70	I implement a child-initiated program.	No fit	No fit
71/72	I take a leadership role in the classroom.	No fit	No fit
73/74	I take a leadership role in the wider education community.	+3.36	+2.02
	Communication		
	From me to Parents/Teachers/Principal		
75/76	I communicate effectively with the Principal.	+0.88	-1.77
77/78	I am a confident speaker about ECE.	+2.22	-0.26
79/80	I can argue my point of view strongly with the Principal.	+1.77	No fit
81/82	I can argue my point of view strongly with children's parents.	+0.41	-0.76
83/84	I can argue my point of view strongly with other school staff.	+1.54	-0.74
85/86	I can argue my point of view easier with same sex persons than with opposite sex persons.	No fit	No fit
87/88	I am confident in explaining to children's parents about the early childhood way of teaching.	-0.28	-2.19
89/90	I am confident in explaining to other school staff about the Early Childhood way of teaching.	+0.86	-2.05
91/92	I am confident in explaining to the Principal about the Early Childhood way of teaching.	+0.94	-2.10
93/94	I feel more comfortable talking to persons of my sex than persons of the opposite sex.	No fit	No fit
95/96	I have good communication skills.	+0.68	-2.07

Item no.	Item wording	How I am (real view)	How I would like to be (ideal)
	From Parents/Teachers/Principal to me		
97/98	I am given positive feedback for my program by the children's parents.	No fit	-1.27
99/100	I am given positive feedback for my program by other teachers.	+2.63	-0.30
101/02	I am given positive feedback for my program by my Principal.	No fit	No fit
103/04	Preprimary staff look to me for leadership in ECE.	+2.61	No fit
105/06	My Principal looks to me for leadership in ECE.	No fit	No fit
107/08	I am praised for particular projects by children's parents.	+1.61	No fit
109/10	I am praised for particular projects by other teachers.	+2.67	-0.75
111/12	I am praised for particular projects by my Principal.	No fit	+0.21
113/14	I am asked questions about my philosophy by the children's parents.	+3.30	No fit
115/16	I am asked questions about my philosophy by other teachers.	+4.42	+1.56
117/18	I am asked questions about my philosophy by my Principal.	+4.18	+1.59
	Influences		
	My Influence on the School		
119/20	I make sure I am included in school decision-making.	+2.01	No fit
121/22	If necessary, I would push for male and female staff to have equal say in school decision-making.	No fit	No fit
123/24	I feel comfortable in the school staff room.	No fit	-1.52
125/26	I feel I am a valued member of school staff.	No fit	-1.62
127/28	If necessary, I would push for preprimary staff to share equal status with primary staff in my school.	+0.96	-0.85
129/30	I encourage others to do things consistent with my Early Childhood philosophy.	+1.94	+0.83
131/32	I would try to change school policy, if it conflicts with my philosophy.	+2.12	+0.70
	My Influence on the Principal		
133/34	I tell the Principal of my Early Childhood philosophy.	+2.47	+0.77
135/36	I encourage the Principal to be involved in what happens in my classroom.	+2.22	+0.46
137/38	I encourage the Principal to support my Early Childhood philosophy.	+1.87	No fit
139/40	I would try to change my Principal's attitude about ECE, where it conflicts with mine.	+2.14	+0.35
141/42	I try to help Principal acquire more knowledge about ECE.	+3.03	+1.00

Notes on Appendix A:
1. The item 'difficulties' are in logits (the log odds of answering the response categories positively). The item 'difficulties' range from –2.29 (item 40 which is 'very easy') to +4.42 (item 115 which is 'very hard').
2. 92 of the 142 items fit the measurement model to produce a proper interval-level scale (item 'difficulties' in bold) with a predominant unidimensional influence.
3. 54 real and 38 ideal items fit the measurement model to form the scale of Teacher Leadership.
4. All the real items are 'harder' than their corresponding 'ideal' items, as conceptualised.

APPENDIX B. ITEM THRESHOLDS FOR TEACHER LEADERSHIP

Item Code	Mean	Thresholds	
		1	2
General Leadership			
Classroom Leadership			
Item 2	-2.190	-3.200	-1.180
Item 4	-2.056	-2.978	-1.135
Item 6	-.043	-1.814	1.729
Item 9	.851	-2.383	4.086
Item 10	-1.601	-3.029	-.174
Item 12	-1.423	-3.329	.484
Item 13	1.581	-.666	3.827
Item 14	-.892	-3.927	2.143
Self-leadership			
Item 15	-.437	-4.457	3.583
Item 17	.493	-3.219	4.205
Item 20	-1.621	-3.591	.350
Item 21	-.329	-4.858	4.201
Item 22	-1.602	-3.351	.148
Item 24	-1.785	-3.152	-.419
Item 26	-1.723	-3.294	-.152
Item 28	-1.835	-3.457	-.213
Item 30	-1.288	-3.605	1.029
Item 31	.166	-2.807	3.140
Item 32	-1.787	-3.591	.018
Teacher preparation			
Item 33	-.733	-4.078	2.612
Item 34	-1.910	-3.473	-.347
Item 37	1.771	-1.567	5.109
Item 38	-1.923	-3.268	-.579
Item 40	-2.294	-3.215	-1.374
Item 41	1.841	-.216	3.899
Item 42	-1.161	-3.668	1.346
Item 44	-1.967	-3.278	-.657
Item 46	-1.736	-3.411	-.062
Item 47	.794	-1.967	3.554

Item Code	Mean	Thresholds	
		1	2
Item 48	-1.853	-3.552	-.155
Item 50	-2.171	-3.440	-.902
Item 52	-1.923	-3.446	-.401
Program leadership			
Item 54	-2.046	-2.819	-1.273
Item 56	-2.082	-3.279	-.884
Item 58	-2.186	-3.471	-.901
Item 59	.489	-1.678	2.656
Item 60	-1.343	-3.365	.678
Item 62	-.181	-2.522	2.159
Item 63	-.779	-3.932	2.373
Item 64	-1.611	-3.469	.248
Item 66	-1.781	-3.295	-.267
Item 68	-1.495	-3.515	.526
Item 73	3.361	1.247	5.476
Item 74	2.017	.570	3.463
Communication			
From me to parents/teachers/principal			
Item 75	.881	-1.443	3.205
Item 76	-1.767	-3.275	-.258
Item 77	2.220	.042	4.398
Item 78	-.260	-1.497	.976
Item 79	1.773	-.358	3.903
Item 81	.413	-2.256	3.083
Item 82	-.759	-1.714	.197
Item 83	1.541	-.823	3.905
Item 84	-.741	-1.992	.510
Item 87	-.278	-2.656	2.100
Item 88	-2.188	-3.436	-.940
Item 89	.858	-1.399	3.115
Item 90	-2.055	-3.493	-.618
Item 91	.942	-1.199	3.082
Item 92	-2.099	-3.462	-.736
Item 95	.684	-2.573	3.942
Item 96	-2.074	-3.490	-.658
From parents/teachers/principal to me			
Item 98	-1.272	-3.461	.917
Item 99	2.634	.843	4.425
Item 10	-.302	-2.372	1.768
Item 10	2.614	.622	4.605
Item 10	1.611	-.388	3.610
Item 10	2.674	.721	4.628
Item 11	-.747	-4.176	2.682

Item Code	Mean	Thresholds	
		1	2
Item 11	.207	-1.994	2.407
Item 11	3.297	1.303	5.290
Item 11	4.421	2.268	6.574
Item 11	1.558	-.385	3.501
Item 11	4.178	2.174	6.182
Item 11	1.588	-.232	3.407
Influences			
My influence on the school			
Item 11	2.006	-.003	4.015
Item 12	-1.524	-3.536	.488
Item 12	-1.621	-3.634	.391
Item 12	.956	-.286	2.198
Item 12	-.852	-1.851	.147
Item 12	1.945	.080	3.810
Item 13	.835	-.402	2.071
Item 13	2.117	.316	3.918
My influence on the principal			
Item 13	.702	-.456	1.860
Item 13	2.470	.866	4.073
Item 13	.766	-.604	2.137
Item 13	2.224	.272	4.177
Item 13	.456	-1.492	2.405
Item 13	1.871	.082	3.660
Item 13	2.137	.415	3.858
Item 14	.347	-1.290	1.985
Item 14	3.035	1.406	4.663
Item 14	1.004	-.431	2.439

APPENDIX C.
ITEM DIFFICULTIES, STANDARD ERRORS AND RESIDUALS

Item	Location	SE	Residual	DegFree	DatPts	Chi Sq	Probability
General Leadership							
Classroom leadership							
Item 2	-2.190	0.35	0.025	265.06	270	6.120	0.078
Item 4	-2.056	0.34	0.250	265.06	270	6.247	0.073
Item 6	-0.043	0.14	1.397	263.09	268	1.887	0.584
Item 9	0.851	0.15	1.032	264.07	269	7.339	0.033
Item 10	-1.601	0.24	0.110	264.07	269	4.533	0.185
Item 12	-1.423	0.19	-0.408	263.09	268	1.331	0.713
Item 13	1.581	0.13	0.507	264.07	269	1.678	0.631
Item 14	-0.892	0.14	-0.711	264.07	269	2.667	0.429

Item	Location	SE	Residual	DegFree	DatPts	Chi Sq	Probability
Self-leadership							
Item 15	-0.437	0.14	1.450	264.07	269	5.556	0.109
Item 17	0.493	0.16	0.373	265.06	270	1.998	0.560
Item 20	-1.621	0.20	-0.711	265.06	270	0.669	0.877
Item 21	-0.329	0.16	1.022	265.06	270	6.116	0.079
Item 22	-1.602	0.21	0.864	265.06	270	0.794	0.846
Item 24	-1.785	0.26	0.457	265.06	270	1.977	0.564
Item 26	-1.723	0.23	1.344	265.06	270	7.845	0.020
Item 28	-1.835	0.24	-1.112	265.06	270	2.344	0.489
Item 30	-1.288	0.17	0.805	265.06	270	1.803	0.602
Item 31	0.166	0.14	1.246	264.07	269	4.251	0.212
Item 32	-1.787	0.22	-1.391	264.07	269	1.952	0.570
Teacher preparation leadership							
Item 33	-0.733	0.14	-0.063	265.06	270	0.888	0.823
Item 34	-1.910	0.25	-1.127	265.06	270	2.606	0.440
Item 37	1.771	0.18	0.208	265.06	270	7.425	0.031
Item 38	-1.923	0.27	1.075	265.06	270	4.643	0.175
Item 40	-2.294	0.38	-0.388	265.06	270	0.512	0.914
Item 41	1.841	0.13	0.141	265.06	270	3.443	0.307
Item 42	-1.161	0.16	-0.749	265.06	270	1.151	0.758
Item 44	-1.967	0.28	-0.746	264.07	269	1.400	0.697
Item 46	-1.736	0.23	-0.590	263.09	268	0.232	0.971
Item 47	0.794	0.14	-0.789	265.06	270	1.646	0.638
Item 48	-1.853	0.24	-1.540	265.06	270	2.983	0.376
Item 50	-2.171	0.31	-1.026	265.06	270	4.254	0.212
Item 52	-1.923	0.26	0.999	260.15	265	3.384	0.316
Program leadership							
Item 54	-2.046	0.36	0.321	265.06	270	8.109	0.014
Item 56	-2.082	0.31	-0.747	265.06	270	0.700	0.869
Item 58	-2.186	0.31	-1.060	264.07	269	2.054	0.548
Item 59	0.489	0.13	1.666	265.06	270	2.673	0.428
Item 60	-1.343	0.18	-0.695	265.06	270	1.378	0.702
Item 62	-0.181	0.14	-0.721	265.06	270	6.463	0.063
Item 63	-0.779	0.14	0.514	265.06	270	0.194	0.978
Item 64	-1.611	0.21	-1.316	265.06	270	3.314	0.326
Item 66	-1.781	0.24	-0.859	265.06	270	1.846	0.593
Item 68	-1.495	0.19	-1.092	265.06	270	1.764	0.611
Item 73	3.361	0.13	-0.778	265.06	270	2.274	0.503
Item 74	2.017	0.11	-0.361	265.06	270	2.336	0.490
Communication							
From me to parents/teachers/principal							
Item 75	0.881	0.13	1.270	265.06	270	4.398	0.198
Item 76	-1.767	0.24	0.059	265.06	270	1.021	0.790
Item 77	2.220	0.13	-0.361	265.06	270	0.589	0.896
Item 78	-0.260	0.16	-0.998	265.06	270	1.837	0.595
Item 79	1.773	0.13	-0.962	264.07	269	1.843	0.594
Item 81	0.413	0.13	0.014	264.07	269	4.401	0.197

Item	Location	SE	Residual	DegFree	DatPts	Chi Sq	Probability
Item 82	-0.759	0.20	-0.511	264.07	269	4.360	0.201
Item 83	1.541	0.13	0.160	265.06	270	5.647	0.103
Item 84	-0.741	0.18	-0.453	265.06	270	5.405	0.118
Item 87	-0.278	0.14	-0.348	265.06	270	3.604	0.286
Item 88	-2.188	0.32	-1.565	265.06	270	4.201	0.217
Item 89	0.858	0.13	-1.101	264.07	269	4.123	0.225
Item 90	-2.055	0.28	-1.085	264.07	269	1.880	0.585
Item 91	0.942	0.13	-1.730	263.09	268	1.611	0.646
Item 92	-2.099	0.29	-1.351	263.09	268	2.441	0.470
Item 95	0.684	0.15	-0.634	265.06	270	5.151	0.135
Item 96	-2.074	0.28	-1.438	265.06	270	2.530	0.454
From parents/teachers/princiapl to me							
Item 98	-1.272	0.17	-1.051	265.06	270	3.186	0.344
Item 99	2.634	0.12	1.392	265.06	270	6.910	0.046
Item 100	-0.302	0.14	0.331	265.06	270	2.909	0.388
Item 103	2.614	0.13	-0.093	259.17	264	1.367	0.704
Item 107	1.611	0.13	0.806	265.06	270	6.789	0.051
Item 109	2.674	0.12	0.697	264.07	269	5.706	0.100
Item 110	-0.747	0.14	-1.721	264.07	269	1.202	0.745
Item 112	0.207	0.13	-1.473	264.07	269	0.906	0.819
Item 113	3.297	0.13	0.322	263.09	268	1.456	0.683
Item 115	4.421	0.13	0.757	263.09	268	1.873	0.587
Item 116	1.558	0.12	-0.995	263.09	268	6.281	0.071
Item 117	4.178	0.13	1.563	261.13	266	7.112	0.040
Item 118	1.588	0.12	-0.356	261.13	266	4.397	0.198
Influences							
My influence on the school							
Item 119	2.006	0.13	-0.212	265.06	270	3.055	0.364
Item 124	-1.524	0.19	1.225	265.06	270	5.428	0.117
Item 126	-1.621	0.20	-1.386	265.06	270	1.516	0.669
Item 127	0.956	0.12	0.973	260.15	265	3.786	0.264
Item 128	-0.852	0.20	-0.884	260.15	265	3.078	0.361
Item 129	1.945	0.12	-0.160	263.09	268	1.933	0.574
Item 130	0.835	0.12	-1.057	263.09	268	1.609	0.647
Item 131	2.117	0.12	-0.726	261.13	266	0.888	0.823
Item 132	0.702	0.13	-0.919	261.13	266	1.695	0.627
Item 133	2.470	0.11	-1.348	262.11	267	5.156	0.135
My influence on the principal							
Item 134	0.766	0.13	-0.363	262.11	267	5.124	0.137
Item 135	2.224	0.12	-0.716	264.07	269	2.836	0.400
Item 136	0.456	0.13	-1.629	264.07	269	4.051	0.233
Item 137	1.871	0.12	-0.840	261.13	266	4.766	0.165
Item 139	2.137	0.12	0.351	260.15	265	2.423	0.474
Item 140	0.347	0.13	-0.555	260.15	265	4.477	0.190
Item 141	3.035	0.12	0.261	261.13	266	2.847	0.398
Item 142	1.004	0.12	-0.865	261.13	266	1.229	0.738

Notes on Appendic C:
1. Location is the item difficulty in logits.
2. SE is the standard error of the difficulty estimate.
3. The residual is the difference between the actual response and the estimated response according to the model paramters.
4. Chi Sq is the chi-square for the item-trait interaction statistic for the item, for the degrees of freedom given.
5. The last column gives the probability of fit to the measurement model for the chi-square value.

APPENDIX D. TEACHER LEADERSHIP VERSUS ITEM THRESHOLD MAP

Location	Teacher Scores	Item Thresholds (uncentralised)
7.0	High Leadership	Hard items
		115.2
6.0	X	117.2
	X	73.2
	XXX	113.2
5.0	XXXX	37.2
	XX	
	X	103.2 109.2 141.2
	XXXX	99.2
	XXXX	21.2 17.2 77.2
4.0	XXXX	119.2, 133.2, 9.2, 135.2
	XXX	129.2, 13.2, 139.2, 41.2, 79.2, 83.2, 131.2, 95.2
	XXXXXXX	107.2 137.2
	XXXXXX	118.2 74.2 116.2 47.2 15.2
	XXXXXXX	75.2
3.0	XXXXXXXXXXXXX	91.2 81.2 89.2 31.2
	XXXXXXXXXX	
	XXXXXXXXXX	33.2 59.2 110.2
	XXXXXXXXXX	136.2 112.2 142.2
	XXXXXXXXXX	115.1 63.2
2.0	XXXXXXX	130.2, 87.2, 134.2, 14.2, 62.2, 117.1, 127.2
	XXXXXXXXXX	132.2 140.2
	XXXX	6.2 100.2
	XXXXXXX	141.1
	XXXXXX	73.1 113.1 42.2
1.0	XXX	30.2
	X	99.1 133.1 98.2 78.2
	X	103.1 60.2 109.1

Location	Teacher Scores	Item Thresholds (uncentralised)
	XX	139.1, 12.2, 124.2, 84.2, 68.2, 74.1
	X	64.2 135.1 131.1 20.2 126.2
0.0	X	32.2, 77.1, 129.1, 137.1, 128.2, 22.2, 82.2
		10.2 48.2 26.2 46.2 119.1
		107.1, 116.1, 79.1, 34.2, 127.1, 66.2, 76.2, 118.1
		41.1 28.2
		38.2, 132.1, 142.1, 24.2, 130.1, 52.2
		92.2, 13.1, 96.2, 44.2, 90.2, 134.1
-1.0		88.2 50.2 58.2 56.2 83.1
		91.1 2.2 4.2
		89.1 40.2 140.1 54.2
		37.1 78.1 136.1 75.1
		82.1 59.1
-2.0		112.1 84.1 47.1 128.1 6.1
		9.1 100.1 81.1
		95.1 62.1
		87.1
-3.0		4.1 54.1 31.1
		24.1 10.1
		60.1 22.1 12.1 66.1 26.1 56.1 44.1
		76.1 38.1 17.1 40.1 12.1
		20.1 32.1 48.1 124.1 68.1 90.1 96.1
		58.1 64.1 92.1 98.1 28.1 52.1
		50.1 88.1 46.1
		42.1 126.1 30.1
-4.0		63.1 14.1
		110.1 33.1
		15.1
		21.1
-5.0	Low Leadership	Easy Items

Notes on Appendix D:

1. The scale is in logits, the log odds of answering the response categories.

2. Teacher Leadership measures are placed on the LHS of the scale from Low Leadership (bottom) to High Leadership (top). Each X represents 2 teachers.

3. Item thresholds are placed on the RHS of the scale from 'easy' (bottom) to 'hard' (top). Item thresholds relating to the real perspective(How I am) are odd numbered and item thresholds relating the ideal perspective (How I would like to be) are even numbered.

4. The thresholds for items in the real mode are more or less evenly distributed along the scale, whereas the thresholds for the ideal mode are mostly at the 'easy' end of the scale (as expected).

5. 21.2 refers to the threshold between the response categories 2 and 3 for item 21. 21.1 refers to the threshold between the response categories 1 and 2 for item 21. These thresholds are ordered in line with the ordering of the response categories. 115.1 is 'easier' ('difficulty' is –4.8 logits) and 21.2 is 'harder' ('difficulty' is -3.4 logits). Other item thresholds are labeled similarly.

In: Early Education
Editors: J.B. Mottely and A.R. Randall

ISBN 978-1-60456-908-7
© 2009 Nova Science Publishers, Inc.

Chapter 7

Translated Children's Books in Greek Preschool Centers: How They Are Applied as Educators' Implements

Triantafillia Natsiopoulou[1] and Chrisoula Melissa-Halikiopoulou[2]

[1]Department of Baby/Infant Care, Alexandrio Technological Educational Institution of
Thessaloniki, Greece
[2]Department of Nursing, Alexandrio Technological Educational Institution of
Thessaloniki, Greece

ABSTRACT

Research has shown that the Greek preschool centers have a satisfactory number of illustrated children's books available, most of which are translations. Most of these books fall in the story/fiction genre while there is a limited number of non-fiction (factual) books. Almost all educators made use of translated children's books, as they proved to be effective for their work purposes since the books deal with a wide range of topics and because they are deemed to be of high quality. Although, a small number of these translations are intentionally applied in order to bring the child into contact with other cultures, a large number of educators question their usefulness. The viewpoint, however, prevails that children all over the world have similar needs and for this reason, when foreign children's books are carefully chosen, not only they do not do any damage whatsoever but on the contrary they may be beneficial.

DEFINITIONS

In Greek, the term children's book is used in both the wider and narrower sense. In the broader context a children's book is any book that has been designed and written to be read by/to children (Patakis, 1994) whereas, in the narrower context it refers to any book written for children and which has become accepted by them, in other words those books that entertain kids (Karpozilou, 1994; Sakellariou, 1991). In this study, the term children's book is used with the latter meaning.

TRANSLATED CHILDREN'S BOOKS IN GREECE

The writing of books specifically for children that are not textbooks, began in modern times as the notion of "childhood" developed (Escarpit, 1993). Non-textbook publications for children first appeared in Europe in the 18th century. In Greece such books were available in the last decades of that century by Greek publishing houses in Vienna and Venice. These books were translations of Aesop's Tales as well as other well-known non-Greek writers of that period.

In the 19th century, 956 children's books were published, initially by Greek publishing houses abroad followed by local ones. The majority of these translations were Aesop's Tales and popular foreign literature. These works were loosely translated or adapted into purer Greek forms of writing often without any mention whatsoever of the original author. Most of the books available in Greek at that time were translations from the French, many of which were not original works in that language but had been translated into French. This was followed by a smaller number of translations of German, English and Italian works. Throughout the 19th century there was such an admiration for the foreign literature that the majority of Greek writers overlooked their quest for an authentic writing style and thematic subject matter preferring instead to imitate their foreign fellow writers (Delopoulos, 1995). Only at the end of that century did some notable original Greek works appear.

Translated works continued to dominate the Greek market throughout the 20th century. Until the end of the 1960's there was a ratio of three or four translated children's books to one Greek. Most of the books translated were French, English, German or Italian, with a small number from the rest of the international output for children. In the following decades Greek children's books predominated. From the decade of the 1970's the publication ratio of Greek children's books to foreign were four to one, declining to three to one in the 80's (Anagnostopoulos, 1999).

In the 1990's a remarkable increase in translations was noted. In 1990 translated children's books were 40%; this figure rose significantly to 66.7% by 1999. More specifically, during this decade 57% of children's publications were translations. Thus, despite the increase of works by Greek writers, the dramatic rise overall in children's books (128%) in Greece during the years 1990 to 1999 was due to translations (Ichneftis, 2000). The majority of the books translated in this decade were from west European countries and the United States, most of which (61%) were works by English writers (Ichneftis, 2000). This is in accordance with other research studies conducted in other European countries (e.g. the Netherlands 40.7%, Finland 70%). However, in the USA translations comprise only up to 2% and in Great Britain 2.7%-5% (Ghesquiere, 2007).

In the 21st century translated children's books continue to dominate the Greek market. During the period 2000 – 2006 children's books made one quarter of the total Greek book market, of which two thirds were translations. For this same period, books for preschoolers made up the largest share (51-62%) of children's books (National Book Center, 2007).

CHILDREN'S BOOKS IN GREEK PRESCHOOL CENTERS

According to the laws of the market where demand determines supply, there is a large number of children's books published for preschoolers which confirms that people in Greece show a great interest in this type of book. Research has shown that Greek parents buy and read books to their kids throughout the preschool age (Natsiopoulou, Souliotis, Kyridis, & Hatzisavvides, 2006; Natsiopoulou, Souliotis, & Kyridis, 2006). Furthermore, all institutions of early education in Greece (preschool centers: 2.5 – 6 years of age, and kindergartens: 5 – 6 years of age) implement books as an important pedagogical tool applied in numerous activities. The education provided by these institutions aims at a holistic development of the child.

The Greek Ministry of Education (2003) has designated, that all kindergartens have a well-organized children's library where illustrated books with fairytales, fables, poems, short stories, magazines and encyclopedias as well as any other printed matter of .educational interest for children in this age group are available. In accordance with the Ministry's specified Kindergarten Program (Greek Ministry of Education, 1989) the main objective of reading literary children's books is to entertain as well as to cultivate an aesthetic education of preschoolers. For this purpose a variety of books are implemented:

- Greek/other countries folklore, fairytales and stories (e.g. Ch. Perault, Grimm, Andersen and the like);
- Fables (e.g. Aesop's Tales), legends, customs and traditions rendered in a literary form;
- Nursery Rhymes, lullabies and poems both anonymous and by well-known poets;
- Contemporary stories that deal with current reality by well-known children's writers;
- Poems and prose written for adults but which can easily be comprehended and enjoyed by children (Greek Ministry of Education, 1990).

Apart from the different types of reading activities mentioned above, whose objective is to familiarize kids with the great variety of written forms of expression, books comprise the basic material for activities aiming to develop pre-reading abilities in children (Greek Ministry of Education, 2003). Both Greek and foreign children's books can be used to meet the above objectives. When using foreign books, the educator must select books that have been well translated into the Greek language (Greek Ministry of Education, 1990).

In the Standard Regulation Manual for the Operation of Early Childhood and Preschool Centers (Greek Ministry of Inner Affairs, 2002) it has been specified that these institutions are the principal facilities that provide children of preschool age with education and safe accommodation. In the same manual, although there is a fair amount of flexibility in the program of each preschool center (e.g. opening and closing hours, meal time, activities schedule etc), there is no direct mention of an organized children's library. However, there is explicit reference to pedagogical activities related to reading books, narrating stories, and pre-reading exercises, which presupposes the existence of one. The types of pedagogic activities are defined so that they cover all aspects of the child's development, including the time that these should be carried out without, however, determining the aim, content, methodology, or the evaluation procedure of these activities. It must be noted that although it is a very general program, it leaves great leeway for the educator to take initiative in organizing her/his educational duties. Research has shown that the majority of educators apply educational programs based not only on what they had learnt during their studies at university, but also on information acquired during lifelong learning programs and other sources (e.g. Books, journals, Internet etc). While implementing their individual programs educators make use of illustrated children's books in order to reinforce certain knowledge imparted to the kids during the teaching of various subjects, especially in activities on linguistic and aesthetic development (Natsiopoulou, 1999).

AIM

The aim of the present research study was to ascertain the position of children's books generally, but more specifically translated children's books, at Greek preschool centers, as well as to examine educators' views in relation to the implementation of translated children's books on preschoolers.

METHODOLOGY

The research was conducted in the spring of 2007. The recording and quantitative analysis of the data comprises of two parts: a) making a record of the children's books at preschool centers in a large urban area; and b) examining educators' views on the implementation of translated children's books through a structured interview. The questions of these interviews were on how often they used these books, the reasons for using them, their selection criteria, and whether or not the educators question the fact that the majority of books for this age group are translations.

Depending on book content, they were divided into two categories: fiction or non-fiction (Cullinan & Galda, 1998). The first group consisted of books narrating stories, imaginary or real, whose main aim was to entertain the audience. The second category comprised of books whose main objective was to provide factual information. Such books include: a) concept books; b) informative storybooks; and c) question and answer books (Lukens, 1999; Glazer, 1991).

During the processing of the interviews, in the case where some subjects provided more than one answer, their first response was considered as being the most important.

DATA

1,584 books were recorded in 20 preschool centers. 76 preschool teachers participated in the structured interview.

RESULTS

The majority of children's books available in the preschools centers that took part in this study were fiction, whereas there were a limited number of non-fiction (71% and 29% respectively).

Most of the books in these centers were translations (Figure 1.).

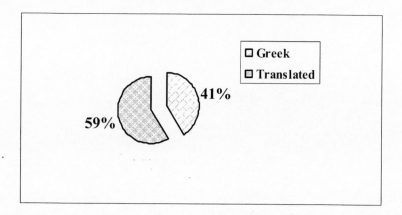

Figure 1. Greek and translated children's books in preschool centers

The percentage of translated non-fiction books was significantly higher than translated fiction books (Figure 2).

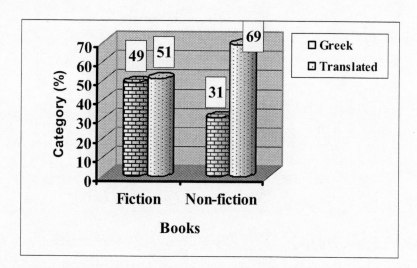

Figure 2. Greek and translated children's books in preschool centers

Only 5% of the research participants did not use any translated children's books, claiming that they found Greek books were able to meet their program needs. The majority of educators used translations (Figure 3), since they judged them as being of high quality (26%) with a wide subject range (27%), and thus served the needs of the preschool's program. 5% of educators used translations to familiarize children with other cultures, while 16% used translations by necessity, since they were the only books available at the center. A high percentage of subjects did not respond to the question why they use translated books (Figure 4).

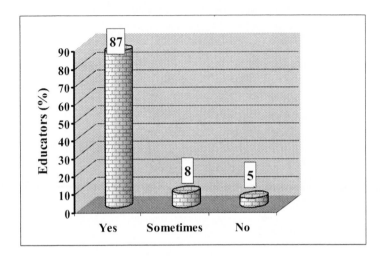

Figure 3. Use of translated children's books by educators

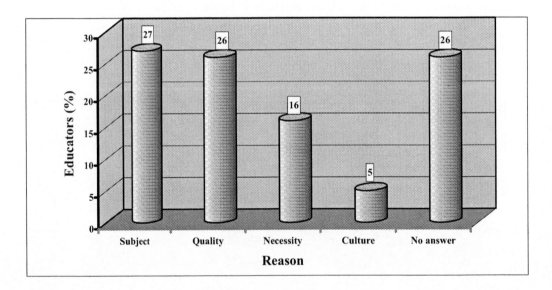

Figure 4. Reasons for using translated children's books

All educators stated that the book's subject and the children's age were the most important criteria in their choice of translated books. Only one educator responded that she was attentive to the quality of the translation. 33% of educators were concerned that the majority of children's books available on the Greek market were translations, while the remaining majority did not think to question this fact (Figure 5).

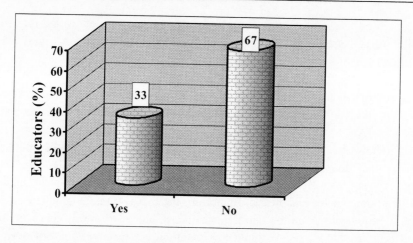

Figure 5. Reasons for using translated children's books

CONCLUSION

Literacy and the love for books are components of a child's cultural development that are not inherited but reinforced through the beneficial influence of their social environment (Vygotsky, 1974). The pedagogic viewpoint states that the earlier the child comes into contact with books through pleasant experiences, the more likelihood there is that it will develop a positive relationship with reading. That is why educators recommend that adults, who are the first to introduce the child to reading, should expose it to books from the age of 6 –9 months and read to preschoolers two to three times a day (Huck, 1997). This task initially is the responsibility of the family, which gradually is assisted by the wider social environment and in particular the state through the education system.

In Greece, besides the family, the next most structured social environment that brings the child into contact with books is preschool centers. As already mentioned, in the Standard Regulation Manual for the Operation of Early Childhood and Preschool Centers, although not directly stated, it is implied that an organized library is needed to achieve the prescribed educational goals of these institutions. Our research findings show that Greek preschool centers have a satisfactory number of children's books, most of which are translations. The majority of translated books in our study are in the literature genre, while the number of non-fiction books is limited. Similar results were found in research concerning Greek kindergartens (Makri & Tsilimeni, 2007). These data could be related to how the directives from the Ministry of Education are interpreted by educators. More specifically, the use of children's books as a means for language (Greek Ministry of Education, 1980) and aesthetic development (Greek Ministry of Education, 1989), has most probably contributed to the greater interest shown by Greek educators to literature books rather than non-fiction books. However, in other countries, school libraries tend to have a larger percentage of the latter (Cullinan & Galda, 1998), most probably due to the fact that they have a more student-centered approach to learning, which requires the child to actively seek out and acquire, on its own, information taught in the curriculum. We are confident that in the future more non-fiction books, both Greek and translated, will be available in the classrooms since the official guidelines state that Greek kindergartens are required to encourage children to "use" the class library to search for knowledge by choosing books that are appropriate to the set task or to their particular interest area (Greek Ministry of Education, 2003, p. 706), and preschool children are prompted to spend time in "reading and information learning corners" (Greek Ministry of Inner Affairs, 2002, p. 6669).

In the last decades of the 20th century, children's storybooks for preschoolers comprised the largest section of books on the Greek market, while there was only a small percentage of non- fiction books (Anagnostopoulos, 1999). Today, this trend is rapidly changing as more interest is being shown in factual children's books. The number of such books published in 2006 was more than double that of 2001 (National Book Center, 2007). This fact was apparent in our research, since the percentage of translated non-fiction books was higher than that of the fiction books. A reasonable explanation for the increase in the number of translated non-fiction children's books could be that publishers are interested in this genre as it is both profitable and popular. However, we hope that eventually Greek writers will develop the special skills and expert knowledge that is required in writing such books. Up to now research showed that Greek authors were probably discouraged from taking on such projects as they were time-consuming and demanding. The majority of translated non-fiction children's books deal with technology and science, while Greek authors prefer themes such as Greek history and archaeology (Ichneftis, 1995).

In our research, educators in preschool centers used mostly translated books because they found them to be of better or equal quality: "better illustrations"; or for practical reasons: "they better fulfill the needs of the educational program" and "deal with a wide variety of topics". The above views seem to agree with the policies of the Greek publishing houses, which translate good-quality, popular books; at the same time taking into consideration the needs of the Greek children's book market. Indicatively, Greek market researchers refer to the exceptional illustration of German children's books, especially storybooks (Ichneftis, 2000); to the high quality of English non-fiction books (Ichneftis, 1995); and the demand for factual children's books on Greek flora and fauna (Ichneftis, 1998).

An interesting finding was that the educators who took part in our study stated that they did not apply any particular selection criteria (e.g. country of origin, author or illustrator etc) for choosing translated books. It appears that educators select the translated books based on the children's age and the book topic; they were not overly concerned about the actual quality of the books' translation into Greek. This was surprising because even though they were aware that language is a fundamental element in the quality of a children's book they did not consciously take it into consideration. Needless to say that language quality is of the utmost importance in a work of translation. The effects of a bad translation can be seen when a remarkable, exciting and captivating foreign work is transformed into an insignificant, boring book (Aggelopoulou & Valasi, 1989). The same outcome applies to the tendency of some translators to interfere with the information given in the original text by changing words and phrases that they consider difficult for the children to comprehend and/or which are foreign to their culture (O'Sullivan, 2005).

Although translated books were implemented, quite a number of educators questioned the use of translation on very young children. This could be a result of misplaced national pride, e.g. "Greek children's books should take the lead in the books read" or an overestimation of the socialization role that children's books play, e.g. "books are mediums of culture and the large number of translated books endangers the Greek cultural element". The majority of educators, however, do not share these views, nor are they concerned by the large number of translated children's books available on the Greek market because for them translated books "have a high quality", "serve their work needs", "because all the world's children are the same" and "because it is not the author that is important but how enjoyable and appropriate the book is for children". The above expressions echo the prevailing view in Greece that translated books, when they are carefully chosen and well written, not only do no harm but in effect are useful (Aggelopoulou, 1991). In our opinion, this usefulness would be greater if in institutions of early education there were more non-fiction children's books and if the educators implemented books more as a tool to familiarize children with other cultures. The Ministry's Kindergartens Program anticipates the provision of opportunities to children, so that "they become aware of their uniqueness and that they identify the similarities and differences they have with others, while learning to respect them". "(Children) must be encouraged to accept people with language, cultural or religious differences, to cooperate and build friendship ties with them" (Greek Ministry of Education, 2003, p. 712). Unfortunately, our findings show that educators at preschool centers who use children's books for the above purposes are few and far between. However, multiculturalism is now the rule in contemporary Greek society. This is also the case in most schools, which renders it necessary to begin sensitizing children to the presence of foreigners at a very early age. The use of children's books at preschool centers where different behaviors and foreign cultures are described in an appropriate (i.e. politically correct) way would contribute to the prevention and the suppression of discrimination; it would also foster an appreciation of "foreigners", and lead to the acknowledgement of cultural equality.

Books were and are, a part of the communication and cultural processes with which people comprehend the world around them. In these processes translations play an important role, which serve to promulgate knowledge internationally, facilitate communication between peoples, and contribute to a country's intellectual level. In the last two centuries translations of foreign works have augmented Modern Greek literature, not only that geared to adults (Savvidis, 1989) but also that geared to children (Delopoulos, 1995). Today, in Greece intense endeavors are made to support and to promote children's books written in Greek by the state, the publishing houses, and the Greek intellectual community at large through the participation of Greek authors in children's book exhibitions both domestically and abroad, the translation of Greek children's books into other languages as well as into Braille, and the instigation of national children's book awards. All these activities in conjunction with the deluge of translated publications show that translations continue to "enrich" Greek children's literature, perhaps in a different way to what it did in the past. Nowadays, translated children's books are widely implemented in Greek preschool centers and contribute in much more constructive and creative ways to the personality development of young children. In conjunction with Information Technology, it appears that books are here to stay.

ACKNOWLEDGMENTS

Reviewed by: Andreas Karakitsios, Associate Professor, Aristotelian University of Thessaloniki, School of Preschool Education Sciences, 54124 Thessaloniki, Greece. Tel. 2310995026, 6942056306. Email: akarakit@nured.auth.gr.

REFERENCES

Agglelopoulou, V. (1991). Literature translations for children. In The Circle of the Greek Children's Book, D' Seminar Proceedings, *Modern trends and opinions on children's literature* (pp. 73-80). Athens: Psychoyios.

Aggelopoulou, V., & Valasi, Z. (1989). *Choosing books to form an essential library.* Athens: Gutenberg.

Anagnostopoulos, B. (1999). *Trends and developments of children's literature.* Athens: Friends' Publications.

Cullinan, B. & Galda, L. (1998). *Literature and the child.* San Diego: Harcourt Brace College Publishers.

Delopoulos, K. (1995). *Children and adolescent books of the nineteenth century. Bibliographical records of comments and pictures. First approach. Contribution to Neohellenic Literature.* Athens: Kastanioti.

Ghesquiere, R. (2007). We need our neighbours! Children's literature and translation: the case of a small culture. Retrieved December 20, 2007, from http://www.bookfair. bolognafiere.it/File?RitaGhesquiere.pdf

Glazer, J. I. (1991). *Literature for young children.* New Jersey: Upper Saddle River.

Greek Ministry of Inner Affairs, Governmental Paper No 497 (2002). *Standard Regulation Manual for the Operation of Early Childhood and Preschool Centers.*

Greek Ministry of Education, Governmental Paper No 1376 (2003). *Interdisciplinary Unified Framework Program of Education for Kindergarten.*

Greek Ministry of Education (1990). *Book on Preschool Activities. Preschool Teacher's Guide.*

Greek Ministry of Education, Governmental Paper No 208 (1989). *Program of Education for Kindergarten.*

Greek Ministry of Education, Governmental Paper No 132 (1980). *Program of Education for Kindergarten.*

Escarpit, D. (1993). *La littérature d'enfance et de jeunesse en Europe; panorama historique.* Presses Universitaires de France.

Huck, Ch., Hepler, S., Hickman, J., & Kiefer, B. (1997). *Children's Literature in the Elementary School.* Chicago: Brown & Benchmark publishers.

Ichneftis (2000). *Statistics on book production 1999.* vol. 27.

Ichneftis (1998). *Statistics on book production 1997.* vol. 23.

Ichneftis (1995). *Greek book production 1994.* vol. 12.

Karpozilou, M. (1994). *The Child in the land of books.* Athens: Kastanioti.

Lukens, R. J. (1999). *A critical handbook of children's literature.* Glenview, IL: Scott, Foresman.

Makri, B., & Tsilimeni, T. (2007). Non-fiction children's books in preschool education. Paper presented at the 1st Pan-Hellenic Congress of Preschool Education, Thessaloniki, September 29-30, 2007.

National Book Centre of Greece (2007). *The Book Market in Greece 2006.*

Natsiopoulou, T. (2007). Children's Literature in Greece at the End of the Twentieth Century. *The Journal of Children's Literature Studies,* 4(1), 55-69.

Natsiopoulou, T., Souliotis, M., & Kyridis, A. (2006). Narrating and reading folktales and picture books: Storytelling techniques and approaches with preschool children. *Early Childhood Research & Practice,* 8(1), Retrieved June 6, 2006, from http://ecrp.uiuc.edu/v8n1/natsiopoulou.html

Natsiopoulou, T., Souliotis, D., Kyridis, A. and Hatzisavvides S. (2006). Reading children's books to the preschool children in Greek families. *International Journal of Early Childhood,* 38(2), 69-79.

Natsiopoulou, T. (1999). Language arts at Greek Preschool Centers. *Sygchroni Ekpaidevsi,* 105, 32-42.

O'Sullivan, E. (2005). *Comparative Children's Literature.* London: Routledge.

Patakis, St. (1994). The recipients of children's books promotion. In Katsiki-Gkibalou, A. (ed.) *Children's Literature: Theory and Action* (pp. 255-262). Athens: Kastanioti.

Savvidis, G. P. (1989). French-Greek poems. Newspaper, *To Vema,* 19 Feb, p. 65.

Sakellariou, H. (1991). *History of Greek and foreign children's literature. From ancient times till today.* Athens: Stratis G. Filippotis.

Vygotsky, L. (1978). *Mind in society: The development of higher psychological processes.* Cambridge, M.A.: Harvard University Press.

In: Early Education
Editors: J.B. Mottely and A.R. Randall

ISBN 978-1-60456-908-7
© 2009 Nova Science Publishers, Inc.

Chapter 8

EARLY LEARNING-RELATED SKILLS IN RELATION TO PREPARATORY MATHEMATICS

Evelyn H. Kroesbergen, Meijke E. Kolkman and Willemijn G. Bolier
Utrecht University, The Netherlands

ABSTRACT

Learning-related skills refer to a set of skills that are necessary for the adequate acquisition of new knowledge in school and include cognitive and behavioral self-regulation. It is assumed that the behavioral regulating skills stem from the domain-general executive functions. Learning-related skills can be seen as the behavioral and social manifestation of these executive functions, such as listening and following directions, but also planning and self-control. The chapter elaborates on the possible relations between executive functions, self-regulation and academic skills.

The topic is illustrated with an empirical study, which was meant to investigate if the learning-related skills can explain part of the individual variance in preparatory mathematics skills of children attending Kindergarten. As individual differences in mathematical development in elementary school often have their origin already before formal schooling starts, this study aims at revealing the skills that are related to later mathematical learning difficulties. A total of 30 5- and 6-year old children participated in the study. Cognitive and behavioral regulation was measured, as well as the counting skills of the children.

The results of this study support our hypothesis that learning-related skills are related to academic outcomes already in Kindergarten. The different learning-related skills were indeed related to children's counting skills. The highest correlations were found between executive functions and counting, whereas behavior regulation was only marginally related to counting. Furthermore, we found that executive functions explained about half of the variance in counting. Behavioral regulation added no further prediction. The results have implications for practice as they give new directions for early screening and possible interventions for young children at-risk for learning disabilities.

INTRODUCTION

Although cognitive differences between children are already present very early in life, the effects of these differences are not quite evident until the children enter Kindergarten and differences in learning skills become apparent. Interindividual variations come forward in the ease of learning new skills and in switching between these new skills, in task persistence and attention, in meta-cognition and self-control, but also in preparatory reading and math skills (Kroesbergen, Van de Rijt, & Van Luit, 2007; McClelland, Morrison, & Holmes, 2000). Next to these differences in cognitive skills, differences in social skills are also manifest in young children. For example, some children are more than others capable of expressing their emotions, displaying appropriate behavior and following directions. Lin, Lawrence and Gorrell (2003) found that kindergarten teachers tend to view that preparing children to satisfy social demands of schooling is more important than academic skills development.

Much of the literature on school readiness point to the importance of both cognitive and behavioral regulatory skills for successful school adjustment. Moreover, cognition and emotion seem to be inextricably linked in the development of self-regulation in young children (Blair, 2002; Wolfe & Bell, 2007). Self-regulation consists of both the regulation of attention and selective strategy use in the execution of cognitive tasks, and the regulation of emotion in appropriate social behavior (Blair, 2002). Furthermore, self-regulatory skills are good predictors of school achievement, both in kindergarten years (McClelland et al., 2007; Wolfe & Bell, 2007) and in later years of elementary education (McClelland, Acock, & Morrison, 2006).

According to McClelland and colleagues (2006) differences between children can largely be attributed to 'learning-related skills'. These skills facilitate learning processes because they are required for the acquisition of knowledge (McClelland, Cameron, Wanless & Murray, 2006) and these skills are closely related to the concept of self-regulation (McClelland et al., 2007). Cognitive aspects of learning-related skills refer to the basic executive functions that are important in goal-directed behavior such as inhibition, switching and updating abilities (Miyake et al., 2000). Social and emotional aspects of learning-related skills can be seen as the behavioral manifestations of the executive functions and include regulation skills and social competence (McClelland & Morrison, 2003). In this chapter we will discuss learning-related skills in relation to self-regulation. An empirical study is presented to illustrate the relation between these skills and preparatory mathematics. First, we will discuss both the cognitive executive functions and the social aspects of behavioral regulation in relation to learning-related skills before elaborating on the empirical study.

Executive Functioning

Self-regulation is not a single construct, but consists of several aspects of controlling, directing, and planning, including emotion regulation and behavioral regulation. It is related to and involves elements of cognitive processing, in specific executive functioning. Executive functions are necessary for the adequate acquisition of complex goal-directed behavior (Welsh, 2002), and they are considered as control mechanisms in working memory (Miyake et al., 2000). No consensus exists about the exact nature of the different executive functions.

Miyake and colleagues (2000) proposed, based on a confirmative factor analysis, that three executive functions can be distinguished in adults: 'Shifting' concerns the ability to shift between different tasks and different strategies. 'Updating' is about the monitoring and coding of information relevant to the task and replacing non-relevant information with new input. Thirdly, 'inhibition' is related to the control of natural, unnecessary, automatic responses and concerns replacing these with appropriate responses. Executive functions develop rapidly during childhood, with substantial changes occurring between 3 and 5 years (Müller, Dick, Gela, Overton, & Zelazo, 2006). These three distinguished executive functions can be found in children early in life (Espy et al., 2004; Lehto, Juujärvi, Kooistra, & Pulkkinen, 2003). However, the role that the different functions play in regulating overt behavior is discussed (McClelland et al., 2007; Müller, Zelazo, Hood, Leone, & Rohrer, 2004).

Several studies have found a correlation between executive functions and school performance in children (Kroesbergen et al., 2007; McClelland et al., 2006; Van der Ven & Kroesbergen, 2008). Inhibition enables children to focus their attention and ignore irrelevant information. Problems in academic tasks arise when children experience problems with focusing their attention (McClelland et al., 2006). Inhibition has been found to be significantly related to academic skills (e.g. Bull & Scerif, 2001; Kroesbergen, et al., 2007). Shifting, or the ability to switch between tasks or strategies, is involved when children have to solve more complex tasks and when they have to alternate between strategies. The relation between shifting and academic competence is confirmed in studies including children with mathematical and/or reading problems (e.g., Bull & Scerif, 2001; Van der Sluis, De Jong & Van der Leij, 2004). Children with learning problems also experience difficulties with updating tasks (Van der Ven & Kroesbergen, 2008). Moreover, children who have problems with mathematical tasks are less competent in recalling information in their working memory compared to peers with better developed math skills (Passolunghi & Siegel, 2001). Updating seems to be an important factor in understanding, processing and manipulating information. To update information in working memory, children need to focus on relevant information. Therefore, inhibition is suggested to play a mediating role in the correlation between updating and learning skills (Passolunghi & Siegel, 2001). However, inhibition also has a direct effect on school achievement. Van der Sluis and colleagues (2004) found that ten year old children with mathematical problems and/or reading problems have difficulties with both inhibition and shifting. The correlation between low mathematical performance and low inhibition skills is found by Bull and Scerif (2001) as well, in their study on the influence of inhibition on mathematical skills in seven year olds.

It is assumed that executive functions do have a direct effect on children's learning abilities since cognitive regulation takes place while children are working on academic tasks. However, it is also possible that executive functions are related to academic achievement as they influence a child's regulation of behavior, which makes learning possible and more effective. In the next part of this chapter we discuss the concept of behavioral regulation.

Behavioral Regulation

Not only cognitive skills (executive functions) but also social and emotional skills contribute to the construct of learning-related skills as described in the former paragraph.

These social and emotional skills can be divided in behavioral regulation and social competence. Behavioral regulation originates from the executive functions discussed earlier (McClelland et al., 2006). For example, inhibition predicts to what extent children are able to adjust their behavior to specific situations (e.g., taking turns, listening and following directions). Self-regulation can thus be seen as the behavioral output of the executive functions and is an active, cognitive, meta-cognitive and motivational process. In this process attention and emotion are planned and managed to assimilate strategies and achieve goals (Lin, et al., 2003; Shonkhoff & Philips, 2003). These skills influence the school performance of children in several ways. Young children with more developed self-regulating skills are better able to apply these skills to regulate behavior, such as planning and organization (Howse, Lange & Farran 2003; Lin et al., 2003). Furthermore, children with less developed regulative skills are easily distracted and experience more problems in focusing their attention or listening to the teacher, which will eventually result in lower school performance (Howse et al., 2003). Problems in behavioral regulation can thus contribute to learning problems (Howse et al., 2003; Shonkhoff & Philips, 2003). Therefore, behavioral regulation is considered as an important factor in the construct of learning-related skills.

Self-regulation also includes the regulation of emotions which is a crucial aspect in social appropriate behavior (Kemple & Han, 2006). Social competence can be defined as appropriate social behavior and the cognitive and affective antecedents included (Schneider, Ackerman & Kanfer, 1996). Cooperation, independency and responsibility are the aspects of social competence in the construct of learning-related skills (McClelland & Morrison, 2003). Cooperation concerns playing with other children, following instructions and sharing toys and tools. The term independency refers to finishing tasks independently and managing actions in an appropriate way. Children are independent when they can solve problems without any help from others and when they are able to start a task spontaneously after instructions. The level of independence predicts school performance and is related to responsibility. Responsibility indicates that the child is able to select an appropriate working place, choose and organize tools and finish tasks adequately in cooperation with others. These components influence the school performance of children. Children with lower levels of independency and responsibility show more behavioral problems and achieve poorer school results (McClelland & Morrison, 2003; McClelland, Cameron, et al., 2006). Independency and responsibility are also related to successful interactions and cooperation with other children (Folks & Morrow, 1989; Rimm-Kaufman, Pianta & Cox, 2000; McClelland et al., 2006).

According to McClelland and colleagues (2000) children with strong social competencies have higher scores on math and reading tests compared to peers with less developed social skills. Dobbs, Doctoroff, Fisher, and Arnold (2006) examined the relation between mathematical skills and social emotional behavior in five year old children. The results showed that positive social emotional behavior is related to better developed mathematical skills. Higher levels of initiative, self-control and attachment predicted better math skills in young children. Social competence thus has an effect on the learning outcomes of children and is therefore another important factor in the construct of learning-related skills.

Learning-Related Skills and Academic Functioning in Early Childhood

The different components of learning-related skills, executive functions, behavioral regulation and social competence, are related to the academic achievement of young children. Although these three concepts all seem to have an individual influence on learning outcomes, they also seem to be related to each other (McClelland et al., 2006). They suggest that the executive functions of children lead to self-regulated skills that facilitate the development of social competence. Eventually this will enable children to develop (new) academic knowledge. These learning-related skills thus provide a basis for academic performance (McClelland, et al., 2000).

In this chapter, we focus on one of the most important basic academic skills that a child is supposed to learn during the first years of his school career: preparatory mathematics. Adequate mastery of preparatory math skills enhances development of mathematical knowledge in later grades, when children receive their first formal math instruction (Kavkler, Tancig, & Magajna, 2003; Van de Rijt & Van Luit, 1998). However, the development of math skills receives little attention in early childhood. Normally, children develop early math abilities by experimenting and manipulating with quantities, and by gaining insight in the logical and linguistic aspects of math. Preparatory skills are necessary for the development of more complex math skills later in life. An important preparatory math skill concerns number conservation. This relates to the ability of children to count and to estimate numerical magnitudes. Van de Rijt and Van Luit (1998) distinguish four components of early mathematical counting skills: 'using counting words', 'structured counting', 'resultative counting' and 'general knowledge of numbers'. Individual differences between children in these counting skills often have their origin before formal education starts. It is important to distinguish the factors that contribute to these differences to prevent later mathematical learning difficulties. In this study, it is proposed that learning-related skills can explain a large part of the variance in preparatory math skills.

Clear relations between executive functions and math outcomes have been demonstrated in children in elementary education. Bull and Scerif (2001) found that within a group of children aged 7 to 9, tests that measured inhibition, updating and shifting all correlated with performance on a test of mathematical performance and explained more variance in mathematical performance than IQ did. Barouillet and Lépine (2005) found that children in third and fourth grade who scored high on updating measures were also faster at solving single-digit addition problems than low-scoring children. A study by Rasmussen and Bisanz (2005) showed that scores on an updating task and a phonological loop task predicted performance on a verbally presented mathematical test in first grade children, and Van der Sluis, De Jong, and Van der Leij (2005) found that updating was related to arithmetical performance in children in fourth and fifth grade. This was found by Adams and Hitch (1997) as well with 7 to 11 old children. Little research, however, has focused on the relationship between learning-related skills and early school achievement. McClelland et al. (2007) have demonstrated that self-regulation is significantly related to emergent math skills in preschoolers. They used one single task to measure self-regulation, the Head-to-Toes task. This task was assumed to directly measure children's behavioral regulation by requiring them to integrate three executive functions: attention, working memory and inhibition. Kroesbergen et al. (2007) showed that three different executive functions, planning, inhibition, and shifting, all were related to preparatory math skills. McClelland and colleagues

(2006) also showed that early learning-related social skills in kindergarten are important predictors for math development.

When children show deficits in learning-related skills they are at risk for learning problems (McClelland, et al., 2006), and, therefore, it is important to monitor the development of learning-related skills from an early age on. To understand the effects of learning-related skills on learning, we will examine the variance in preparatory math skills as explained by learning-related skills. The hypothesis is tested that the relationship between executive functions and preparatory mathematics is mediated by behavioral regulation. The findings will be discussed in the next section of this chapter.

METHOD

Participants and Procedure

The children that participated in this study, were all Dutch natives in their second year of kindergarten (mean age = 5.9 years; SD = 0.4). The sample consisted of 30 children (11 girls, 19 boys). The children were randomly selected from four schools. Each child completed four tests on cognitive learning-related skills, and a test that measured preparatory math skills. Moreover, the teacher of each class was asked to complete a questionnaire about the child's social learning-related skills.

Measures

Preparatory Math Skills

The Early Numeracy Test (ENT, Van Luit, Van de Rijt & Pennings, 1994) was used to measure the preparatory math skills of the children. This test is developed for children from 4 to 7 years old and measures the level of early mathematical competence. The ENT consists of eight parts; the tasks are spread over these parts in groups of five. In this study four parts are used, measuring the counting skills. (1) *Using counting words*. The child's skills counting forwards and backwards as well as using the cardinal and ordinal numbers are evaluated. (2) *Structured counting*. These items help determine if the child can correspond numbers with numbers of objects. Children are asked to point to the objects with their fingers while counting. (3) *Resultative counting*. Counting structured and unstructured quantities as well as counting hidden quantities are assessed. (4) *General knowledge of numbers*. Being able to use knowledge of the number system in a simple problem situation is also evaluated. Items determine if children are able to use numbers under twenty in simple daily problem situations. The raw total score of the test consists of the total number of tasks that are answered correctly by the child (maximum score is 20).

Learning-Related Skills: Executive Functions

Digit Span Backwards

The Dutch version of Digit Span Backwards from the AWMA test battery (Alloway, Gathercole, & Pickering, 2004), was administered to measure updating. The child heard a sequence of digits and had to repeat the sequence in reversed order.

Animal Shifting

This task has been adapted from the Symbol Shifting task developed by Van der Sluis and colleagues (2005), which had been shown to load high on a shifting factor. The child was shown a sheet with boxes. Within each box a pair consisting of an animal and a vehicle was printed. The boxes and figures within them were printed in yellow and blue in a random fashion, but each box with its letter and digit had the same color. The child was instructed to name the animal when the color was blue and the vehicle when the color was yellow. There were eight practice items, followed by forty test items. The time taken to complete the test sheet and the number of mistakes were recorded.

Animal Stroop

A task similar to the Expressive Attention task from the Cognitive Assessment System (Naglieri & Das, 1997) was used to measure inhibition. The task measures inhibition in young children and requires the child to name the real life size (big or small) of an animal, while ignoring the size of the drawing. First, the child was familiarized with the ten animal pictures in the task and the sizes of these animals in real life (big or small). Then, in the control task, the child was shown a page with these same animal pictures, all drawn equally large, and it had to name the real life sizes of all the animals on the page as rapidly as possible. In the interference task most animals that are big in real life were depicted small, and the small animals were drawn big. The child's task was to ignore the size of the drawings and mention the animals' sizes in real life as rapidly as possible.

Tower of London

The Tower of London (Shallice, 1982) was used to measure inhibition and planning. The Tower of London involves three differently colored balls that are placed on three pegs of unequal sizes: the first peg can hold only one ball, the second two balls and the third peg can hold all three balls. The child was shown a goal configuration of the balls and was asked to copy this configuration by moving the balls one by one to other pegs. This had to be done in a minimum number of moves, which the child was given in advance. There was one practice trial and twenty test trials. The difficulty of the trials gradually increased by increases in the number of required moves.

Learning-Related Skills: Behavioral Regulation

The Social Skills Rating System (SSRS; Gresham & Elliott, 1990) was used to measure social behavior. The SSRS is an assessment tool for evaluating students considered to be at risk for serious interpersonal difficulties resulting from their poor social behaviors. Ratings are based on a 3-point scale (never, sometimes, and very often). Three subscales from the social skills scale were assessed: (1) Assertion: Initiating behaviors, such as asking others for information, Introducing oneself, and responding to the actions of others; (2) Self-control: Behaviors that emerge in conflict situations, such as responding appropriately to teasing, and in nonconflict situations that require taking turns and compromising; and (3) Cooperation: Helping others, sharing materials and complying with rules and directions.

In addition, the Master Scale of the Child Behavior Rating Scale was used (CBRS; Bronson, Tivnan, & Seppanen, 1995). The CBRS is designed to evaluate a child's task behavior and social behavior with peers and adults. The 32 behaviors are rated on a 5-point scale ranging from 1 (never) to 5 (usually/always) to indicate how frequently they occur.

Data Analysis

All scores were transformed to z-scores. If necessary, the variables were recoded to obtain variables in which higher scores mean higher functioning on the specific task. To reduce the effect of outliers, the range of the scores on all the variables had a maximum of two standard deviations from the mean score. All tasks measuring learning-related skills were combined in one scale score ($\alpha = .84$). Furthermore, a factor analysis was conducted to find whether the scale could be divided in different subscales. This would allow a more detailed description of the relation between learning-related skills and mathematics. A Principal Component Analysis with oblimin rotation resulted in two factors with Eigenvalue > 1. These factors explained respectively 54.9 and 18.4 per cent of the variance. All behavior related variables loaded on the first factor and the cognitive skills loaded on the second factor (factor loadings > .40). Two different subscales were defined: Behavior regulation ($\alpha = .97$) and executive functioning ($\alpha = .49$). For all statistical tests, a significance level of $\alpha = .05$ was used.

RESULTS

The goal of this study was to investigate if the relationship between executive functions and preparatory math skills is mediated by behavioral regulation. In Table 1, the descriptives of the learning-related skills and preparatory mathematics are given.

The mean scores on *using counting words* and *general knowledge of numbers* are higher than the mean scores on the other two ENT-scales. This indicates that children are more able to use counting words and apply general knowledge of numbers in their second year of kindergarten. Apparently, using counting words is a skill that most children of this age already have obtained. Furthermore, the small standard deviation indicates little variance in this variable which could be contributed to a ceiling effect. The variable *general knowledge of numbers* concerns the application of general knowledge of numbers in simple problem situation, not necessarily inside the classroom. *Structured counting* and *resultative counting* may be the more important preparatory math skills that are developing in the second year of kindergarten.

To examine the relationships between both independent variables (executive functions and behavioral regulation) and between the independent variables and the dependent variable math (all subscales of the ENT), a correlation analysis was performed (see Tables 2 and 3).

Table 1. Descriptives of learning-related skills and preparatory math (N=30)

	M	S.D.
Learning-related skills	44.94	5.16
Executive functions	28.94	3.34
Digit span backwards	4.60	1.3
Tower of London	12.13	2.64
Animal shifting	7.91	0.55
Animal stroop	91.10	12.89
Behavioral regulation	60.95	9.09
SSRS	116.47	17.63
Cooperation	39.43	6.55
Assertion	38.43	6.43
Self-control	38.60	5.94
CBRS	127.33	19.14
Preparatory math skills		
Early Numeracy Test - Total score	11.97	3.93
Using counting words	3.40	1.1
Structured counting	3.00	1.31
Resultative counting	2.30	1.34
General knowledge of numbers	3.27	1.31

Table 2. Correlations between executive functions and behavioral regulation (N=30)

	Behavioral regulation	Cooperation	Assertion	Self-control	CBRS
	r	r	r	r	r
Executive functions	.27	.30	.24	.15	.32*
Digit span backwards	.39*	.44**	.43**	.17	.44**
Tower of London	.09	0.09	.06	.04	.13
Animal shifting	-.07	-.08	-.15	-.01	-.03
Animal stroop	.32*	.31*	.34*	.23	.32*

*Correlation is significant at the 0.05 level (1-tailed)
**Correlation is significant at the 0.01 level (1-tailed).

In Table 2 the correlations between the independent variables are displayed. Although there is no significant relationship between the general scales of executive functioning and behavioral regulation, several correlations are found between the subscales of both variables. A correlation was found between *digit span backwards* and *cooperation, assertion* and the *CBRS* and between *animal stroop* and *cooperation, assertion* and the *CBRS*.

Table 3. Correlations between learning-related skills and preparatory mathematics (N=30)

	ENT-total	Using counting words	Structured counting	Resultative counting	General knowledge of numbers
	r.	r.	r.	r.	r.
Learning-related skills	.62**	.32*	.63**	.52**	.44**
Executive functions	.71**	.44*	.68**	.53**	.54**
Digit span backwards	.69**	.48**	.63**	.54**	.49**
Tower of London	.31*	.03	.36*	.34*	.19
Animal shifting	.43**	.42**	.29	.21	.43**
Animal stroop	.36*	.16	.43**	.25	.26
Behavioral regulation	.23	.03	.29	.27	.10
SSRS	.17	-.02	.22	.23	.07
cooperation	.29	.08	.33*	.32*	.14
assertion	.15	-.07	.25	.14	.12
self-control	.02	-.09	.03	.17	-.07
CBRS	.28	.07	.35*	.30*	.13

*Correlation is significant at the 0.05 level (1-tailed)
**Correlation is significant at the 0.01 level (1-tailed).

As shown in Table 3, learning-realted skills are related to all four subscales of the ENT. However, major differences in correlations can be observed when the executive functioning variables and the behavioral regulation skills are examined separately. The subscale executive functions correlates with all subscales of the ENT and also correlations are found between the different measurements of executive functions and ENT. However, no relationships are found between the behavioral regulation scale and ENT although some of the regulation skills do correlate with *structured counting* and *resultative counting*.

Apparently, behavioral regulation skills correlate with the subscales of the ENT that concern the important aspects of math development in second year in kindergarten. Taken into account the mean scores and the correlations on the subscales of the ENT, *using counting words* and *general knowledge of numbers* are excluded from the further analyses. Then, a new math variable was computed out of the scores on *structured counting* and *resultative counting*. Regression analysis revealed that the variance in this new math variable can be explained by the four executive functions ($R^2 = .56$, $p < .01$) and by the four behavioral regulation skills ($R^2 = .32, p < .01$).

Secondly, in spite of the small group, but justified by the significant correlations as decribed above, a standard multiple regression analysis was performed to examine the effect of both executive functioning and behavioral regulation on preparatory math skills. Table 4 shows the findings of multiple regression analyses.

Table 4. Standard multiple regression of executive functions and behavioral regulation on preparatory math skills (N=30)

	R	R^2	$R^2_{adjusted}$	R^2_{change}
model 1: executive functions	.70**	.49	.47	-
model 2: executive functions & behavioral regulation	.71**	.50	.46	.01

*Correlation is significant at the 0.05 level (1-tailed)
**Correlation is significant at the 0.01 level (1-tailed).

In model 1, with only executive functions in the equation, $R^2 = .49$ ($p < .01$). The adjusted R^2 value of .47 indicates that almost half of the variance in preparatory math skills is predicted by executive functions. In model 2, with behavioral regulation added to prediction of preparatory math skills, $R^2 = .50$ ($p < .01$). The adjusted R^2 value of .46 indicates that behavioral regulation does not add to the prediction. Furthermore, addition of social skills to the equation with behavioral regulation does not result in a significant change in R^2 ($R^2_{change} = .01$) either. The results, therefore, suggest that half of the variance in preparatory math skills can be explained by executive functions. Behavioral regulation adds no further explanation.

CONCLUSION

Two distinct aspects could be distinguished in the concept of self-regulation: cognitive and behavioral regulation. Cognitive regulation takes place at a basic neuropsychological level and is defined as executive functioning. Executive functions are necessary for the control of behavior and are, therefore, assumed to facilitate behavioral regulation. In this chapter, the relations between different components of self-regulation were investigated and it was studied how the distinct components could influence learning in early education. For the study of self-regulation skills, we used the concept of learning-related skills as described by McClelland and colleagues (2000, 2003, 2006, 2007). According to McClelland and colleagues (2007), executive functions, such as inhibition and updating, are involved in regulating overt behavior. Furthermore, they found that behavioral regulation skills are an important predictor of (early) academic skills. However, executive functions are also found to have a direct relation with (early) academic skills (Espy et al., 2004; Kroesbergen et al., 2007). In this chapter it was studied if the relation between executive functions and academic skills is mediated by behavioral regulation. Our hypothesis was that executive functions enhance behavioral regulation, which will have a positive effect on children's learning skills and thus on academic outcomes. This hypothesis was tested in a sample of 30 children attending kindergarten. The results of this study should be interpreted with caution, due to the small sample size.

The first hypothesis was that high correlations would exist between executive functions and behavioral regulation. In this study, however, only a small, non-significant correlation was found between the executive functions scale and the behavioral regulation scale. However, significant relations were found between social and task behavior and the executive functions scale. Furthermore, both inhibition and updating were significantly related to the behavioral regulation scale. The conclusion is therefore that although the cognitive and behavioral regulation scales were not significantly correlated, significant relations were found between subcomponents of cognitive and behavioral regulation. A possible explanation for the fact that the correlations were lower than expected may be found in the instruments that were used to measure self-regulation. Cognitive regulation was assessed with experimental tasks, directly with the children, while behavioral regulation was assessed by a behavior questionnaire filled in by the teacher, since the children of the sample could not read. So both the form and the informant were different. Although McClelland and colleagues (2007) reported that the used questionnaires (SSRS and CBRS) are related to child measures, the differences between both measures are large. We, therefore, recommend for future research to cross-validate the teacher questionnaire with child measures and behavior observations. Because some aspects of cognitive and behavioral regulation are related, it seems relevant to further investigate this relationship.

This study confirmed former research (e.g., Passolunghi, Vercelloni, & Schadee, 2007) that executive functions are related to preparatory mathematics. All executive functions were related to the children's scores on the Early Numeracy Test. The four executive function measures together explained 56% of the variance in mathematics. Apparently, cognitive self-regulation skills are very important in academic performance. The results confirm the hypothesis that planning, inhibition, shifting and updating are necessary for adequate learning and performing on academic tasks.

Contrary to our expectations and to former research (e.g., McClelland et al., 2006) the relation between behavior regulation and preparatory mathematics was small and non-significant. However, some subscales of behavior regulation correlated with two subscales of the ENT. These two subscales measure children's abilities to use counting principles and represent the academic skills that children learn in their second year of Kindergarten. The other two subscales of the ENT measure children's counting skills (saying the counting row) and more applied math skills. The first scale is relatively easy for 5- and 6-year old children, and a ceiling effect was found for this scale. The latter scale may measure skills that are not closely related to the tasks children learn in schools. Therefore, a new scale was made of only two of the four ENT scales. It was found that the behavioral regulation measures together explained 32% of the variance in this scale of school related early mathematics skills. In spite of the small correlation, we found some evidence that behavioral regulation is related to early mathematics. To enlarge the power, however, this study should be replicated with more children. Furthermore, the different nature of the test measures could be a complicating factor once more, because early numeracy was tested with the children as informants, in contrast with the teacher questionnaires for behavioral regulation.

Finally, relative contributions of social and behavioral regulation in mathematical performance were investigated. Regression analysis confirmed that executive functions were more related to preparatory math skills than behavioral regulation. Furthermore, it was found that behavioral regulation could not add further explanation to the model in which mathematics performance was explained by only executive functioning. The hypothesis that the relation between executive functioning and learning is mediated by behavioral regulation could thus not be confirmed with these data. However, it should be noted that the small sample may not be representative for the population.

The implications of this study for early education are twofold. First, the relevance of behavioral regulation needs further investigation. Kindergarten teachers should be aware of the relevance of self-regulating behavior, and of the possibilities to improve self-regulating skills of children. Second, since executive functions are much more important for academic learning, the possibilities to improve executive functions should be investigated. If executive functions are necessary prerequisites of math ability, it is assumed that improving the executive functions would lead to better math performance of children. No research is available yet on the possibilities of improving executive functions in kindergarten children. However, since executive functioning training in older children, including children with mild intellectual disabilities, shows significant effects, even at a delayed posttest (e.g., Van der Molen, Van Luit, Van der Molen, Klugkist, & Jongmans, 2008), it is assumed that executive functions are also trainable in younger children. Furthermore, the relations that are found between executive functioning and preparatory mathematics give direction to alternative screening procedures at young ages to select children at risk for later learning difficulties.

REFERENCES

Adams, J. W., & Hitch, G. J. (1997). Working memory and children's mental addition. *Journal of Experimental Child Psychology, 67*, 21-38.

Alloway, T. P., Gathercole, S. E., & Pickering, S. J. (2004). *The automated working memory assessment*. Computer version.

Barouillet, P., & Lépine, R. (2005). Working memory and children's use of retrieval to solve addition problems. *Journal of Experimental Child Psychology, 91*, 183-204.

Blair, C. (2002). School readiness: Integrating cognition and emotion in a neurobiological conceptualization of children's functioning at school entry. *American Psychologist, 57*, 111-127.

Bronson, M. B., Tivnan, T., & Seppanen, P. S. (1995). Relations between teacher and classroom activity variables and the classroom behaviors of pre-kindergarten children in Chapter 1 funded programs. *Journal of Applied developmental Psychology, 16*, 253-282.

Bull, R, & en Scerif, G. (2001). Executive functioning as a predictor of children's mathematics ability: Inhibition, switching and working memory. *Developmental Neuropsychology, 19*, 273-293.

Dobbs, J., Doctoroff, G. L., Fisher, P. H., & Arnold, D. H. (2006). The association between preschool children's socio-emotional functioning and their mathematical skills. *Applied Developmental Psychology, 27*, 97-108.

Espy, K. A., McDiarmid, M. M., Cwik, M. F., Stalets, M. M., Hamby, A., & Senn, T. (2004). The contribution of executive functions to emergent mathematic skills in preschool children. *Developmental Neuropsychology, 26*, 465-486.

Folks, B., & Morrow R. D. (1989). Academic survival skills for the young child at risk for school failure. *Journal of Educational Research, 82*, 158-165.

Gresham, F. M., & Elliott, S. N. (1990). Social skills rating system. Circle Pines, MN: American Guidance Services.

Howse, R. B., Lange, G., & Farran, D. C. (2003). Motivation and self-regulation as predictors of achievement in economically disadvantaged young children. *Journal of Experimental Education, 71,* 151-174.

Kavkler, M., Simona, T., & Lidija, M. (2003). *Follow-up study of children with very low and very high mathematical competence in preschool years.* Paper presented at EARLI-2003, Padova, Italy.

Kemple, K. M., & Han, H. S. (2006). Components of social competence and strategies of support: Considering what to teach and how. *Early Childhood Education Journal, 34,* 241-246.

Kroesbergen, E. H., Van de Rijt, B. A. M., & Van Luit, J. E. H. (2007). Working memory and early mathematics: Possibilities for early identification of mathematics learning disabilities. In T. E. Scruggs, & M. A. Mastropieri (Eds.), *Advances in learning and behavioral disabilities. Vol. 20: International perspectives* (pp 1-19). Oxford, UK: Elsevier.

Lehto, J. E., Juujärvi, P., Kooistra, L., & Pulkkinen, L. (2003). Dimensions of executive functioning: Evidence from children. *British Journal of Developmental Psychology, 21,* 59-80.

Lin, H. L., Lawrence, F. R., & Gorell, J. (2003). Kindergarten teachers' view of children's readiness for school. *Early Childhood Research Quarterly, 18,* 225-237.

McClelland, M. M., Acock, A. C., & Morrison, F. J. (2006). The impact of kinderkarten learning-related skills on academic trajectories at the end of elementary school. *Early Childhood Research, 21,* 471-490.

McClelland, M. M., Cameron, C. E., McDonald Connor, C., Farris, C. L., Jewkes, A. M., & Morrison, F. J. (2007). Links between behavioral regulation and preschoolers' literacy, vocabulary, and math skills. *Developmental Psychology, 43,* 947-959.

McClelland M.M., Cameron, C.E., Wanless, S.B., & Murray, A. (2006). Executive function, behavioural selfregulation and social-emotional competence. *Contemporary Perspectives in Early Childhood Education, 7,* 1-39.

McClelland, M.M., & Morrison, F.J. (2003). The emergence of learning-related social skills in preschool children. *Early Childhood Research Quarterly, 18,* 206-224.

McClelland, M.M., Morrison, F.J., & Holmes, D.H. (2000). Children at-risk for early academic problems: The role of learning related social skills. *Early Childhood Research Quarterly, 15,* 301-329.

Miyake, A., Friedman, N., P., Emerson, M., J., Witzki, A., H., Howerter, A., & Wager, T. D. (2000). The unity and diversity of executive functions and their contributions to complex 'frontal lobe' tasks: A latent variable analysis. *Cognitive Psychology, 41,* 49-100.

Müller, U., Dick, A. S., Gela, K., Overton, W. F., & Zelazo, P. D. (2006). The role of negative priming in preschoolers' flexible rule use on the dimensional change card sort task. *Child Development, 77,* 395–412.

Müller, U., Zelazo, P. D., Hood, S., Leone, T., & Rohrer, L. (2004). Inference control in a new rule use task: Age-related changes, labeling, and attention. *Child Development, 75,* 1594–1609.

Naglieri, J. A., & Das, J. P. (1997). *Cognitive assessment system.* IL: Riverside: Itasca.

Passolunghi. M. C., & Siegel, L. S. (2001). Short-term memory, working memory, and inhibitory control in children with difficulties in arithmetic problem solving. *Journal of Experimental Child Psychology, 80,* 44-57.

Passolunghi, M. C., Vercelloni, B., & Schadee, H. (2007). The precursors of mathematics learning: Working memory, phonological ability and numerical competence. *Cognitive Development, 22,* 165-184.

Rimm-Kaufman, S. E., Pianta, R. C., & Cox, M. J. (2000). Teachers's judgments of problems in the transition to kindergarten. *Early Childhood Research Quarterly, 15,* 147-166.

Rasmussen, C., & Bisanz, J. (2005). Representation and working memory in early arithmetic. *Journal of Experimental Child Psychology, 91,* 137-157.

Ruijssenaars, A.J.J.M., Van Luit, J.E.H., & Van Lieshout, A.C.D.M. (2004). *Rekenproblemen en dyscalculie: Theorie, onderzoek, diagnostiek en behandeling* [Mathematics learning problems and dyscalculia: Theory, research, assessment and treatment].. Rotterdam: Lemniscaat B.V.

Schneider, R. J., Ackerman, P. L., & Kanfer, R. (1996). To "act wisely in human relations:" exploring the dimensions of social competence. *Personality and Individual Differences, 4,* 469-481.

Shallice, T. (1982). Specific impairments of planning. *Philosophical Transactions of the Royal Society of London (Biology), 298,* 199-209.

Shonkhoff, J. P., & Phillips, D. A. P. (2003). *From neurons to neighbourhoods: The science of early childhood development.* Washington, D.C.: National Academy Press.

Van de Rijt, B. A. M., & Van Luit, J. E. H. (1998). Effectiviness of the additional early mathematics program for teaching children early mathematics. *Instructional Science, 26,* 337-358.

Van der Molen, M., Van Luit, J. E. H., Van der Molen, M., Klugkist, I., & Jongmans, M. (2008). The effectiveness of a computerized working memory training in adolescents with mild intellectual disabilities. *Manuscript submitted for publication.*

Van der Sluis, S., De Jong, P. F., & Van der Leij, A. (2004). Inhibition and shifting in children with learning deficits in arithmetic and reading. *Journal of Experimental Child Psychology, 87,* 239-266.

Van der Sluis, S., De Jong, P. F., & Van der Leij, A. (2005). Executive functioning in children, and its relations with reasoning, reading, and arithmetic. In S. van der Sluis (Ed.), *Working memory capacity and children's achievement.* Amsterdam, The Netherlands: University of Amsterdam (PhD thesis).

Van der Ven, S. H. G., & Kroesbergen, E. H. (2008). Executive functions and learning mathematics. *Manuscript submitted for publication.*

Van Luit, J. E. H., Van de Rijt, B. A. M., and Pennings, A. H. (1994) '*Utrechtse Getalbegrip Toets'* [Utrecht Early Numeracy Test]. Doetinchem, The Netherlands: Graviant.

Welsh, M. C. (2002). Development and clinical variations in executive functions. In D.L. Molfese & V.J. Molfese (Eds.), *Developmental variations in learning. Applications to social, executive function, language, and reading skills.* Mahwah, NJ: Lawrence Erlbaum.

Wolfe C. D., & Bell, M. A. (2007). The integration of cognition and emotion during infancy and early childhood: Regulatory processes associated with the development of working memory. *Brain and Cognition 65,* 3-13.

In: Early Education
Editors: J.B. Mottely and A.R. Randall

ISBN 978-1-60456-908-7
© 2009 Nova Science Publishers, Inc.

Chapter 9

LEARNING MATHEMATICS BY INTERACTION IN YOUNG STUDENTS WITH SPECIAL EDUCATIONAL NEEDS

Johannes E. H. Van Luit[1], Jo M. C. Nelissen[2] and Marjolijn C. Peltenburg[2]

[1]Utrecht University, The Netherlands; Department of Special Needs Education
[2]Utrecht University, The Netherlands; Freudenthal Institute

ABSTRACT

The common instruction format for students with special educational needs in mathematics education is individually based instruction. We challenge this approach by guided, interactive instruction. The starting point is the student's own informal way of thinking, or in other words, their 'common sense'. This is the basis for construction, and student interaction in the classroom. The confrontation with each other's ways of thinking can stimulate students' reflection, leading to a higher level of semantization and formalization. We translate this theory into school practice by presenting an instruction format in which students are confronted with rich math problems that are embedded in a context. Working in pairs the students discuss, inquire and construct solutions. Through writing down solutions and conjectures, they have a means to communicate their ideas to their classmates and their teacher. The arising interaction, we think, is an essential element for the emergence of reflective thinking in learning mathematics.

Keywords: Realistic mathematics education, special needs education, guided instruction, learning by interaction

INTRODUCTION

The focus of this study is on the kind of instruction (guided instruction) and mode of interaction (simultaneous interaction) that can be used in mathematics education. Guided instruction has been proved to be effective in a study of students with special mathematical needs (Kroesbergen & Van Luit, 2002), where other research is more pessimistic about the possibilities of this form of instruction for these students (Geary, 2004). In this study we will provide arguments for optimizing mathematics education (curriculum and instruction) for students with special educational needs, in particular learning disabled (LD) and mild mentally retarded (MMR) students.

A general question in education research is that of how an appropriate changeover from traditional to realistic mathematics education (RME) for students with special educational needs can be achieved. The implementation of this type of education is a complicated endeavor and no mean feat at all. The effort should be focused especially on the following issues of discussion and controversy which are connected with the RME theory (Gravemeijer, 1994; Nelissen, 1999; Treffers, 1987).

Students with special educational needs suffer, as is known, from low confidence in their own abilities. For that reason 'drill and practice' is thought to be the best instruction method for these students. This point of view, however, is challenged by Woodward and Montague (2002) who argue in favor of a school practice in which students do have the opportunity to find their own constructions. The next subject of debate is that of whether the use of contexts is distracting for these students, or do contexts contribute to insightful learning? What should be the nature of these contexts? In most cases until now teachers have been inclined to use contexts only rarely. Are students with special educational needs able to learn mathematics in that they are confronted with context problems? It is thought that they are not able to solve problems and many teachers therefore confront these students only with traditional tasks (addition, subtraction, multiplication, division tasks and so on) in line with the 'step by step' instruction philosophy.

The next question is whether students with special educational needs are able to achieve insights through student discussion in the classroom. Until now it has been thought that they should just individually accomplish their tasks, and that therefore the teacher should focus on drill and practice. In this study we argue that these children are able to interact, learn meaningfully and reflect on their own strategies and those of others. This argumentation is supported by data collected during classroom experiments. In these lessons students are confronted with meaningful context problems. In pairs the students (learn to) discuss and try to find a solution. They use large size scrap paper, also called a poster, to write down and remember their strategy. During classroom discussion the posters are a means to discuss the approaches of the students. This discussion will be the basis for the students to come to reflection (Nelissen & Tomic, 1996). In one of the next sections we will elaborate on this.

'Interaction' is seen as an important concept in this study (Nelissen, 2002). So far the most suitable approach for students with special educational needs was considered to be individually based instruction. The idea is that all students have to cope with their own unique problems and learning trajectory. The consequence of this idea is that there is hardly any meaningful communication between students, and only limited communication between teacher and student, in fact only when the teacher is explaining or correcting work of the students. It was thought, because of language deficiencies, that too much communication would only harm the student's learning. So, in the math lessons, the students miss the encouragement they most need: the encouragement to practice the language that is typical for problem solving, for reflection, for explaining one's own strategies, for comparing different thinking procedures and so on. Moreover they miss the stimulation of the 'thinking processes' that all this is built on.

This individual instructional approach in school practice is often strongly connected with so-called *direct* instruction and with what Woodward, and Montague (2002) typify as 'step by step' instruction. This type of instruction does not fit well with the RME ideas and, moreover, research findings suggest that insights quickly atrophy and fade again (Baxter, Woodward, & Olson, 2001). In contradiction with daily school practice of 'step by step' instruction, and in line with a lot of research, though mostly aimed at 'normal' students (Fosnot & Dolk, 2005; Mercer, 1995; Stone, 1998), we suggest that a suitable instruction form for students with special educational needs can be 'interactive teaching'.

In the next section we elaborate in more detail on the theoretical background. We discuss the alignment of three core concepts of RME: construction, interaction and reflection. Subsequently we discuss several modes of interaction and we clarify how students with special educational needs can take advantage of what is meant in the RME paradigm by meaningful learning, increasing formalization and increasing semantization.

THEORETICAL FOUNDATION

Before we discuss a distinction in several modes of interactive teaching, we present a model which contains an alignment of three core principles of RME. In this model, 'interaction' is placed in a clarifying theoretical context.

Learning Mathematics: A Cyclic and Continuous Learning Process

The first principle is the principle of 'construction'. This principle implies that the learning process should start with the student's own informal way of thinking, or in the words of Freudenthal (1991), with 'common sense'. This way of thinking is elicited in confrontation with meaningful *contexts,* i.e. contexts that derive from the every day life of the students. Construction often leads to interaction, because it makes sense (to stimulate) that the students exchange and discuss the findings that emerged (Kroesbergen & Van Luit, 2002). And so we arrive at a second principle, 'interaction'. In interaction students discuss their ways of thinking, their solutions, the similarities and differences in their approaches. The dialogue with others transforms into dialogue with oneself, and so we arrive at the third principle: 'reflection'. Reflection is interpreted as internalized dialogue and in this statement we recognize the theory of the notable Russian scholar Vygotsky (1978), that all higher functions (speech, thinking, reflection and so on) are originally social functions. In the dialogue the student will anticipate on the expected comments of the discussion partners. This evokes intern dialogue, meaning critical analysis of one's own thinking processes, and that is what we call *reflection* (Nelissen & Tomic, 1996; Slobodcikov & Cukerman, 1990). Moreover, reflection as internalized dialogue emerges, as the Russian psychologists Stepanov, and Semenov (1982) suggest, as a *personal* act as well as an *intellectual* act. Personal means that students attribute sense to their own actions. This is a condition for intellectual reflection, which is aimed at constructing new strategies and modes of thinking.

Reflection is an essential feature of mathematical thinking (Freudenthal, 1991; Nelissen, 1999) and can be considered as a foundation for the development of processes of transfer and generalization as research suggests (Zak, 1976). Figure 1 represents the three principles in connection. In the scheme, learning mathematics is represented as a cyclic and continuous process: construction leads to interaction; interaction or discourse is the basis for reflection and reflection leads to construction on a higher level (Construction 2). And so the process of mathematizing proceeds, because construction again leads to interaction on a higher level (Interaction 2) and so on.

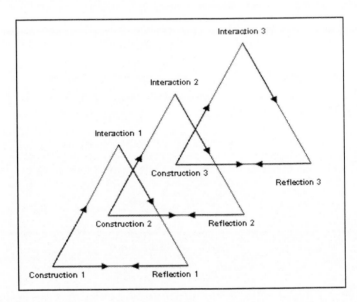

Figure 1. Interaction – construction – reflection (Nelissen, 2002)

Modes of Interaction

An important question is: do students with special educational needs profit from interactive teaching and learning? Both Stone (1998) and Palinscar (1986) advocate that 'scaffolding' (a term that stems from Bruner, 1967) is feasible for students with learning disabilities. Scaffolding is considered a form of what is called 'interactive teaching'. Whether this succeeds depends on how the dialogue in the classroom is designed and organized. We propose a distinction in three modes of interaction designs: horizontal, vertical and simultaneous. In figure 2 three modes of interaction are represented.

'Horizontal interaction' refers to communication and discussion among students. Advantages of horizontal interaction are that students feel free to discuss (Mercer, 1995), that they exchange ideas, that they learn how to put arguments and to improve their speech if needed. A disadvantage however is that students may go under in the group and that the bolder students may dominate the discourse.

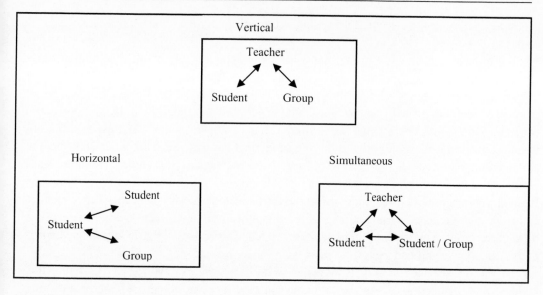

Figure 2. Three modes of interaction (Nelissen, 2002)

We call the interaction between the teacher and a single student, small groups or the whole class '*vertical* interaction'. Some special forms of vertical interaction are scaffolding, revoicing and reciprocal teaching (Palinscar, 1986). Scaffolding offers students an opportunity to play a role in their own learning, as Reid (1998, p. 388) stipulates: scaffolding 'redirects our focus to the bi-directional interactive influences'. The student's contribution during the lessons is taken seriously, but that does not imply that the teacher's role is submerged. However, there is sometimes a danger that the teacher will just play a formal role. In such cases interaction shrivels into a mere ritual, a ritual without real *negotiation*. An advantage of vertical interaction is however that the teacher can manage the complicated processes that may emerge during the interaction in the group.

'Simultaneous interaction' reconciles the advantages of horizontal and vertical interaction. For this reason we advocate to use a mix of these two modes of interaction. In the poster lessons all three modes of interaction are incorporated.

Meaningful Learning: Physical Concrete or Common Sense Concrete?

Once (Nelissen, 1999) we asked students - all 10 years old weak students - if they had an idea *why* they were learning math (particularly fractions). Some answers: "Fractions are in our textbooks", "I don't know", "Fractions are very difficult", "For later perhaps?", and so on. How can students like and do math when they don't have any idea why they are learning all these subjects? Several authors (Bottge, 2001; Goldman & Hasselbring, 1997) stress the importance of meaningful learning. Bottge pleads for 'anchored instruction': meaningful problems and contexts. In his research students are asked to manage the problems in cooperation. They should call upon their intuitions or - as we say in RME - informal knowledge. But now the question arises whether it would not be more useful for students with special educational needs to teach them on the basis of concrete and straightforward manipulatives, for after all students would understand what is concrete and tangible such as the well-known Dienes material (MAB-blocks) or the Cuisenaire material, the abacus, cubes and so on. The dilemma seems to be 'concrete or meaningful?'. But what is conceived as concrete?

We propose a distinction in (a) 'material or physical concrete' and (b) 'common sense concrete'. Physical concrete, we believe, mainly ensues from the adult world and is as such not always very meaningful for students. The concept of concrete, however, can also be considered in cohesion with the students' own experience and this we entitle common sense concrete. That is the concrete that stems from a student's own intuitions and experiences, for instance, playing games with dice or sharing candy in a fair way. Such activities contribute to the emergence of number sense, as Woodward, and Montague (2002) assert. Number sense establishes a basis for the use of strategies for addition and subtraction and this illustrates how students achieve progressively more insight in the denotation of math concepts and strategies, and in how these concepts and strategies are semantically related, such as for instance how procedures of addition and multiplication are related. This process of growing understanding of mathematical significance we call 'increasing semantization'.

Increasing semantization goes together with increasing formalization. Formalization alludes to a distinction in levels of mathematizing, as Gravemeijer (1994) points out. Gravemeijer discerns four levels: a situational, a referential, a general and a formal level. The referential level contains the models, descriptions, concepts, procedures and strategies that refer to concrete or paradigmatic situations. By generalization and further exploration, reflection about different strategies becomes more prominent. Then, a formalization of the general level takes place. This means that the general level is the referential level for the formal level.

We find the idea of increasing semantization and increasing formalizations pictured in the metaphor of the iceberg (see figure 3) by Boswinkel, and Moerlands (2003). They use this metaphor in their project 'Speciaal Rekenen' (2001) to make clear the need to invest in activities and insights that are needed to reach a formal level of mathematics, which they call the top of the iceberg. The basic level in the iceberg metaphor can be seen as the situational level of Gravemeijer. Meaning is here the basis for the process of formalization.

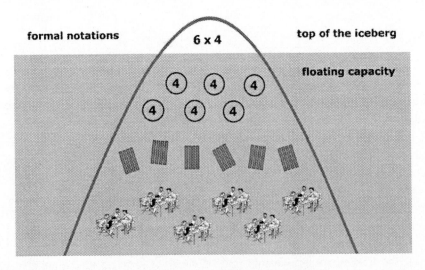

Figure 3. Iceberg metaphor borrowed from Boswinkel & Moerlands (2003)

The highest level represented in the iceberg metaphor is the formal level. The problem is that the attention of most teachers is focused on this formal level, and so on what is regarded as the final results of the teaching process. These are calculations expressed in formal notations, for example 5+2=7 and 7x3=21. The activities leading to this result are more or less neglected and not seen as valuable. These activities are typified as 'floating capacity', for example activities during which students discover the multiplicative structures in packaging. Different models and strategies are discussed in these activities. The problem however is that the 'floating' capacity is not solid enough. Hence learning problems of students with special educational needs do have deeper roots and arise earlier in the learning process and not only at the most formal level. The problems are hidden and not always recognized as such. Moreover, in daily practice it appears that not all students achieve a formal level of addition, multiplication, fractions and so on. If a teacher is confronted with this problem, she should not proceed with 'drill and practice', but be tolerant and leave off the instruction. We should realize that the highest formal level is not attainable for all students with special educational needs (Kroesbergen & Van Luit, 2003).

Just as Boswinkel and Moerlands (2003) Whitson's (1997) represents, as we believe, the way in which semantization and formalization are *interwoven* with each other. The learning process starts with concrete people with whom the student can feel emotionally connected (see Figure 4). Just as in the iceberg metaphor, this is a meaningful start of the learning process. These persons have names. On a higher level one can represent them by fingers and subsequently with numbers et cetera. Students achieve a higher level over and over again but the meaningful basis never disappears. In other words, as Whitson (1997) put it, the signifier or representation always arises from signifiers at a lower level, and are meaningful experiences.

Figure 4. Levels of formalization (See Whitson, 1997)

At a higher level students come to understand that (for instance) counting and addition are related math activities. This process, which we characterize as increasing semantization, is of great significance when students with special educational needs learn mathematics. After all, for many of these students mathematics does currently not have much meaning, if any at all.

But not only these students, every individual, as research suggests (Girotti, 2004, p.122) is inclined to reason on the basis of meaningful information, *more* than on the basis of formal and fixed rules of reasoning. Girotti (2004, p.111): "inferences may be based on mental models, rather than on rules". Stenning, and Monoghan (2004, p.146) as well as Girotti characterize human reasoning as logic "that is not about mechanisms", but about meaningful interpretation.

Learning Mathematics by Interaction

The core question of this study is: Can the access to mathematics of students with special educational needs be increased by guided, interactive instruction, meaningful learning and learning to solve problems reflectively? These core concepts are reconciled in the idea of interactive problem solving lessons.

What Is Meant by Interactive Problem Solving Lessons and How Are These Lessons Designed

In the poster lessons the students will be confronted with context problems. In small groups (two or three students) they try to find their own approach and they discuss possible solutions for the problem. This first phase of the students' activities is called the 'construction phase' or better the 'co-construction phase', because in the small groups the students are involved in close cooperation. This is similar to what Fosnot, and Dolk (2001) call a 'math workshop'- when learners are inquiring, investigating and constructing. As a result of the small group activities, the students exchange their thoughts and findings with the members of the other groups. This is the 'interaction phase'. Interaction can result in new insights in the way of thinking of other students as well as in a growing awareness of one's own problem solving activities, which leads to reflection. Fosnot, and Dolk (2001) call this a 'math congress' as a follow up of the math workshop. After investigating and writing down solutions and conjectures, the students communicate their ideas, solutions and thinking to each another. Posters can be helpful in this.

The whole process of interaction, reflection and construction is represented in Figure 1. As one can see, we try to integrate meaningful problem solving and interactive teaching and learning. The lessons are organized in such a way that there is plenty opportunity for both horizontal and vertical interaction, hence for simultaneous interaction. Students are confronted with meaningful problems, and of course it is an important research activity to find out what kind of contexts are inviting and appreciated the most by the students. The lessons supply enough opportunity for interaction to create a basis for the emergence of reflective thinking, which is of great significance for the learning of mathematics.

How the Lessons Actually Take Place

The role of the teacher during the poster lessons is crucial. She should not play a dominant role and the students should feel free to collaborate in their own way. At the same time the teacher has to carefully look at the complicated social processes that emerge during the lesson.

1. The teacher introduces the problem to be solved and she explains the working procedure:
   - look at the problem;
   - discuss the approaches you both favor;
   - try to find a shared approach;
   - write down your ideas and discuss these with your partner (in each pair);
   - a scratch paper or poster can be helpful for yourself and a resource for reflection,
   - the teacher explains what will be her function and role while the students are collaborating; she will not intervene, but she is always available to give information or to support when a pair has a problem.
2. The students work in pairs and try to solve the problem.
3. The students are encouraged to present their work and thinking activities to the whole group. However, special attention has to be paid to shy students. In the try-outs it was observed that for them intervening questions by the teacher was a stimulus for informing the other students about their own work.
4. In a whole class discussion, guided by the teacher, the couples inform each other about their findings and solutions.
5. The teacher looks back, in retrospection, together with all the students, on the merits of the different proposals. The proposals are discussed and the students are requested to review critically their own strategies and solutions.

PRACTICAL IMPORTANCE

Mathematics education for students with special needs was in the past mostly characterized by a practice of step-by-step instruction, and drill and practice. Teachers believe that they should always give these students a helping hand, because of their learning weaknesses. The consequence of this pedagogic is that the students do not get the opportunity to learn to think and reflect on their own. This results in a growing dependency of the students and thus a self-fulfilling prophecy, because the students' low confidence will lead to continuous requests for support which the teachers mostly are inclined to supply.

In two pilot studies (Abels, Peltenburg & Verbruggen, 2007; Verbruggen, 2005) we have seen that students with special educational needs are in fact more capable than is often thought in current school practice and that this competence can be stimulated by realistic mathematics education, especially by interactive teaching. Interactive problem solving lessons, we believe, can be a suitable resource to enhance skill in solving problems and the interactive and reflective skills of students with special educational needs.

RESEARCH IN YOUNG STUDENTS WITH SPECIAL NEEDS

Mathematics learning has been conceptualized as a constructivist process through which students construct mathematical knowledge by linking newly learned knowledge to previously acquired concepts (Van Luit & Naglieri, 1999). The premise of this perspective is that individuals set goals that lead to the construction of new knowledge, which in turn leads to new goals and new knowledge, thus producing a spiral effect in learning. In this view, social and affective development, and the context of learning, are regarded as influential factors in mathematical learning, next to cognitive development (Montague, 1997). Appropriate problem solving behavior in mathematics requires different skills: adequate orientation, planning, and systematic working, controlling and evaluating the solution process and elaborating the most important results (Veenman, Kerseboom & Imthorn, 2000).

In education for students with special educational needs, especially for the learning disabled (LD) and the mild mentally retarded (MMR) students, the number of students with mathematics disabilities seems to increase (Ruijssenaars, Van Luit & Van Lieshout, 2004). These difficulties begin at an early stage in the student's school life. Many students in special education schools are unable to learn the four basic math operations of addition, subtraction, multiplication and division before leaving primary education at the age of about twelve years. Since the seventies, many studies have investigated whether students, either mentally retarded students or learning disabled are better able to learn and/or memorize by teaching them skills like executive processes, performance and learning processes (Van Luit & Naglieri, 1999). It has been shown that education based on the use of open verbalizations by students about the choices they make in the solution procedure has a number of advantages. For example: two students have to solve problems like 'You can put 8 eggs in a box. How many eggs can you put in 7 egg boxes?' The students have to solve 7x8 or 8x7. If they do not know the answer automatically, they can use a backup strategy to solve this problem (Siegler, 1998). One possibility would be 5x8 + 2x8 = 40+16 = 56, while a less efficient strategy could be 1x8 = 8, 2x8 = 16, ..., 7x8 = 56.

In interactive problem solving lessons the students' problem solving and mathematical thinking within and between domains (especially addition, subtraction and multiplication) has to be taken into account. For example, students with mathematics disabilities usually do not combine new information with already known information. Within the domain of multiplication they do not make the connection between an already known task (5x9 = 45), and a new task (6x9 =?). In the lessons the following goals are designed to increase the student's:

- orientation on the problem and making a first plan for a possible solution.
- application of addition, subtraction and multiplication in real and imagined situations (for example by making a picture of the situation).
- understanding of number system and the premises of some problem solving strategies like reversibility (5x9 = 9x5), associations (9x7 = 10x7 - 1x7), and doubling (8x6 = 4x6 + 4x6) in discussion with another student.
- understanding and using control activities to check the chosen solution strategy and the answer together with another student.

A new math domain or a new level within a domain always starts with an orientation phase, and then the task can be solved with the help of materials or drawings, or later on through imagining. After that the connection will be made with the solution for adequate (mental) problem solving. The students then have to learn to check these solutions together. Finally, this cycle ends with the control phase - shortening - elaborating- reflection - generalization. The most common and adequate strategy can be elaborated on a poster (see Figure 5).

Figure 5. Students working in pairs on a problem

At the end of each lesson some pairs will present their poster to their fellow students. This will result in discussions in which the presenting duo will defend their solution or will choose an idea of one of the other students in the class (see Figure 6).

Figure 6. Students presenting their strategy and solution to their classmates

The poster lessons involve an opportunity for problem solving strategy generation and use. Students are given the opportunity to apply their own solution or strategy to problems.

The teacher's task is to lead the discussion in the direction of the use of adequate strategies and to facilitate the (group) reflection of the strategies put forward by the students. Student can use any problem solving strategy they wish, but the teacher assists the students in discussion and reflection about the choices made. For example an initial strategy for 8x7 could be: $7 + 7 + 7 + 7 + 7 + 7 + 7 + 7$. Some students may find this strategy too long and use: 4x7 + 4x7, or 5x7 + 3x7, for example. The teacher ensures that each student understands the different strategies and encourages them to use and to reflect on the most efficient strategy. The main goal is to help students to think mathematically about an adequate strategy with the use of simple facts in solving more complex problems.

DISCUSSION

With this study we suggest that interactive problem solving lessons can be employed in teaching mathematics to students with special educational needs who have mathematics difficulties. This idea is based on other research results (Van Luit & Kroesbergen, 2005; 2006). The lessons facilitate, as we have seen in two pilot studies (Abels, Peltenburg & Verbruggen, 2007; Verbruggen, 2005), students learning to think about different ways of problem solving, and learning from presenting their own solutions and discussions about alternatives. We expect that students who have worked with the lessons will become capable of thinking about the best possible problem solving strategy for regular mathematics tasks and their capacity for reasoning and using arguments will be better than before.

·We suggest that students with special educational needs may improve in mathematics if they are provided with the underlying principles and given the opportunity to reflect and to generate their own procedures for solving mathematical problems, and that this may result in generalization of knowledge. In an earlier experiment (Van Luit & Kroesbergen, 2006), generalization was possible for most of the LD-students, but not for the MMR-students. Geary (2004), noting the complexity of the difficulties faced by the latter students, remarks that the most likely consequence of these difficulties is the lack of transfer. One important reason for the lack of transfer is that students who show transfer are also proficient in strategy use (Van Luit & Naglieri, 1999).

We will conclude with the expectation that interactive problem solving lessons will have a positive influence on the achievement of students with special educational needs, especially on their adequate problem solving strategies and transfer. Furthermore the arguments mentioned before facilitate regular and remedial teachers with ideas to help students with disabilities improve their math thinking performance.

REFERENCES

Abels, M., Peltenburg, M. C., & Verbruggen, I. (2007). *Probleemoplossen in interactie* [Problem solving in interaction]. Utrecht: Freudenthal Instituut.

Baxter, J., Woodward, J., & Olson, D. (2001). Effects of reform-based mathematics instruction in five third grade classrooms. *Elementary School Journal, 101*, 529-548.

Boswinkel, N., & Moerlands, F. J. (2001). Speciaal Rekenen [RME for students with special needs]. *Tijdschrift voor Nascholing en Onderzoek van het Reken-WiskundeOnderwijs, 19*(3), 3-14.

Boswinkel, N., & Moerlands, F. J. (2003). Het topje van de ijsberg [The top of the iceberg]. In: K. Groenewegen (Ed.), Nationale Rekendagen 2002; Een praktische terugblik (pp. 103-114). Utrecht: Freudenthal Instituut.

Bottge, B. A. (2001). Reconceptualizing mathematics problem solving for low-achieving students. *Remedial and Special Education, 22*, 102-112.

Bruner, J. S. (1967). *Towards a theory of instruction.* Cambridge, UK: Harvard University Press.

Fosnot, C. T., & Dolk, M. (2001). *Young mathematicians at work: Constructing number sense, addition, and subtraction.* Portsmouth, NH: Heinemann.

Fosnot, C. T., Dolk, M., Cameron, A., & Hersch, S. B. (2005). *Turkey investigations.* Portsmouth, NH: Heinemann.

Freudenthal, H. (1991). *Revisiting mathematics education; China lectures.* Dordrecht, The Netherlands: Kluwer.

Geary, D. C. (2004). Mathematics and learning disabilities. *Journal of Learning Disabilities, 37*, 4-15.

Goldman, S. R., & Hasselbring, T. S. (1997). Achieving meaningful mathematics literacy for students with learning disabilities. *Journal of Learning Disabilities, 30*, 198-208

Gravemeijer, K.P.E. (1994). *Developing realistic mathematics education.* Utrecht, The Netherlands: CD-B Press.

Kroesbergen, E. H., & Van Luit, J. E. H. (2002). Teaching multiplication to low math performers: Guided versus structured instruction. *Instructional Science, 30*, 361-378.

Kroesbergen, E. H., & Van Luit, J. E. H. (2003). Mathematics interventions for children with special educational needs: A meta-analysis. *Remedial & Special Education, 24*, 97-114.

Kroesbergen, E. H., & Van Luit, J. E. H. (2005). Constructivist mathematics education for students with mild mental retardation. *European Journal of Special Needs Education, 20, 1,* 107-116.

Mercer, N. (1995). *The guided construction of knowledge: Talk amongst teachers and learners.* Clevedon, UK: Multilingual Matters.

Montague, M. (1997). Cognitive strategy instruction in mathematics for students with learning disabilities. *Journal of Learning Disabilities, 30,* 164-177.

Nelissen, J. M. C. (1999). Thinking skills in realistic mathematics. In J. H. M. Hamers, J. E. H. Van Luit, & B. Csapo (Eds.), *Teaching and learning thinking skills* (pp. 189-213). Lisse, The Netherlands: Swets & Zeitlinger.

Nelissen, J. M. C. (2002) Interactie: Een vakpsychologische analyse [Interaction: A psychological analysis]. In: R. Keijzer & W. Uittenbogaard (Eds.), Interactie in het reken-wiskundeonderwijs (pp. 11-41). Utrecht, The Netherlands: Freudenthal Institute.

Nelissen, J. M. C., & Tomic, W. (1996). Reflection in Russian educational psychology. *Educational Foundations, 10*(1), 35-57.

Palinscar, A. S. (1986). The role of dialogue in providing scaffolding instruction. *Educational Psychologist, 21*, 73-98.

Reid, D. K. (1998). Scaffolding: A broader view. *Journal of Learning Disabilities, 31*, 386-396.

Ruijssenaars, A. J. J. M., Van Luit, J. E. H., & Van Lieshout, E. C. D. M. (2004). Rekenproblemen en dyscalculie. Theorie, onderzoek, diagnostiek en behandeling [Mathematics disabilities and dyscalculia. Theory, research, assessment and intervention]. Rotterdam, The Netherlands: Lemniscaat.

Siegler, R. S. (1998). *Childrens' thinking*. Upper Saddle River, NY: Prentice Hall.

Slobodcikov, V. J., & Cukerman, G. A. (1990). Genezis refleksivnogo soznaniya v mladshem shkol'nom vozraste [Development of reflective thinking in young school children]. *Voprosy Psichologii, 9*, 25-36.

Stepanov, S. J., & Semenov, I. N. (1982). Problema formirovaniye tipo refleksii v reshenii tvorcheskih zadach [Problems in the development of types of reflection in solving (creative) tasks]. *Voprosy Psicholgii, 1*, 99-104.

Stone, C. A. (1998). The metaphor of scaffolding: Its utility for the field of learning disabilities. *Journal of Learning Disabilities, 31*, 344-364.

Treffers, A. (1987). *Three dimensions. A model of goal and theory description in primary mathematics education. Wiskobas*. Dordrecht, The Netherlands: Reidel.

Van Luit, J. E. H., & Kroesbergen, E. H. (2006). Teaching metacognitive skills to students with mathematical disabilities. In A. Desoete & M. V. J. Veenman (Eds.), *Metacognition in mathematics education* (pp. 177-190). Hauppauge, NY: Nova Science.

Van Luit, J. E. H., & Naglieri, J. A. (1999). Effectiveness of the MASTER program for teaching special children multiplication and division. *Journal of Learning Disabilities, 32*, 98-107.

Veenman, M. V. J., Kerseboom, L., & Imthorn, C. (2000). Text anxiety and metacognitive skillfulness: Availability versus production deficiencies. *Anxiety, Stress, and Coping, 13*, 391-412.

Verbruggen, I. (2005). Interactie in het reken-wiskundeonderwijs [Interaction in mathematics education]. Utrecht: Freudenthal Institute. (Internal report).

Vygotsky, L. S. (1978). *Mind in society*. London: Harvard University Press.

Whitson, J. A. (1997). Cognition as semiotic process: From situated mediation to critical reflective transcendence. In D. Kirshner & J. A. Whitson (Eds.), *Situated cognition* (pp. 97-151). London: Lawrence Erlbaum.

Woodward, J., & Montague, M. (2002). Meeting the challenge of mathematics reform for students with LD. *The Journal of Special Education, 36*, 89-101.

Zak, A. Z. (1976). Psichologichkiye osobennosti teoreticheskogo peshenii zadat [Psychological particularities in theoretical task solving]. *Novye Issledovanye v Psichologii, 2*, 17-20.

In: Early Education
Editors: J.B. Mottely and A.R. Randall
ISBN 978-1-60456-908-7

Chapter 10

DISTRACTOR INTERFERENCE EFFECTS AND IDENTIFICATION OF SAFE AND DANGEROUS ROAD-CROSSING SITES BY CHILDREN WITH AND WITHOUT MENTAL RETARDATION

A. Alevriadou[*1] and G. Grouios[2]

[1]Department of Early Childhood Education, Faculty of Education in Florina,
University of Western Macedonia, Greece
[2]Department of Physical Education and Sport Sciences,
Aristotle University of Thessaloniki, Greece

ABSTRACT

This study provides some reasoning to support the notion that individuals with mental retardation are less likely to actively inhibit response tendencies to irrelevant information in their visual field. Inherent in this idea is the notion that selective attention processes operate differently for subjects with and without mental retardation. Selection by individuals with mental retardation only involve facilitatory processes directed at the target stimulus, whereas selection by individuals without mental retardation involve both facilitatory processes directed toward the target and inhibitory processes directed against irrelevant information. The aim of the present study was to test the suppression of irrelevant information in a non-laboratory context (testing road crossing abilities of children with and without mental retardation). The sample of the study consisted of 104 young individuals. The participants were further subdivided into four groups (n=26 per group) matched on mean mental age, using the Raven's Colored Progressive Matrices: two groups with children with mental retardation (Group A and Group B) and two groups with children without mental retardation (Group C and Group D). Group A and Group C were matched on mental age at 5.6 yr.; Group B and Group D were matched on mental age at 8.0 yr. Ability to identify safe and dangerous road–crossing sites was assessed using computer presentations. The task featured the image of a child standing at the edge of a road facing towards the road. Two tasks were designed using a number of road-crossing sites in each one: recognition task without irrelevant information (i.e., distracting

---

* Address correspondence to Dr. Anastasia Alevriadou, University of Western Macedonia, Pedagogical School of Florina, Department of Early Childhood Education, Florina, GR 53 100, Greece, or mail alevriadou@uowm.gr

visual stimuli were removed from the scene, allowing the participant to focus on the road site) and recognition task with irrelevant information (i.e., distracting visual stimuli were included in the scene, obscuring the participant to focus on the road site). Every participant was asked to select the "safe" and "unsafe" (dangerous) road-crossing sites. Results demonstrated statistically significant differences between Groups A and C and Groups B and D in task conditions, especially in those in which irrelevant information was involved. Conclusions were drawn concerning the empirical and theoretical benefits for psychology and education, which arise from the study of safety road education in children with mental retardation.

INTRODUCTION

Attention is a multifaceted construct that is manifested in a variety of ways. Studies of visual selective attention (Broadbent, 1982; Parasuraman and Davies, 1984) have provided considerable information concerning the manner in which stimuli are selected for processing. The assumption that underlies much of the research in this area is that the environment provides individuals with a complex array of stimuli from which a subset of stimuli may be selected for processing. Selective attention implies that attention is directed toward some stimuli and away from other stimuli. The ability to narrow attention to those stimuli that are relevant to the performance of a given task and direct attention away from nonrelevant stimuli is considered to be a characteristic of optimal selective attention processing.

Since individuals with subnormal intellectual development consistently demonstrate attentional deficiencies (Bergen and Mosley, 1994; Merrill, 1990; Nugent and Mosley, 1987), selective attention processes represent a coherent focus on the search for important deficiencies in cognition associated with mental retardation. In particular, a significant number of theorists and researchers comparing the selective attention abilities of individuals with and without mental retardation have consistently shown that those with mental retardation are more distracted by the presence of irrelevant information in a stimulus array than are individuals without mental retardation (Crosby, 1972; Hagen and Huntsman, 1971). Neil and his colleagues (Neil, 1977; Neil and Westberry, 1987) and Tipper (1985) have proposed that selective attention may involve not only facilitory processes directed toward the selected target but also inhibitory processes operating on the unselected distractor stimuli.

Experimental evidence for inhibitory deficits in individuals with mental retardation has been found across many experimental tasks. In an early study, Terdal (1967) reported evidence that individuals with moderate to mild mental retardation were less able to inhibit attention to background stimuli during a simple looking task involving checkerboard stimuli. Additionally, in the presence of distractors, children with mental retardation had more difficulty in remembering information (Holowinsky and Farelly, 1988) and in inhibiting responses caused by distracting dimensions of task stimuli (Ellis, Woodley-Zanthos, Dulaney, and Palmer, 1989). A few years later, Merrill and O'Dekirk (1994), using a flanker task, found that individuals with mental retardation were affected negatively by flanking stimuli at much greater eccentricities than were individuals without mental retardation. These authors asserted that the differences observed may have resulted from the differential use of top-down processing resources across groups. Similar findings of susceptibility to distraction or interference have been reported on Stroop tasks (Ellis and Dulaney, 1991) and identity-based negative-priming tasks (e.g., Cha and Merrill, 1994). In one study, Cha (1992) measured the ability of retarded and nonretarded persons to focus attention during a visual selective attention task in which a central target stimulus letter was presented between two flanker stimuli. The results revealed that the performance of mentally retarded individuals was more influenced by the distracting effects flankers than was the performance of nonretarded individuals. In another study, Cha (1992) evaluated the degree to which retarded individuals are able to overcome the effects of the onset of distractors. The magnitude of the distractor effect differed between IQ groups. The researcher concluded that irrelevant stimuli are more powerful attractors of attention for retarded individuals than they are for nonretarded individuals. Recently, Merrill (2006) found that the failure to engage in inhibitory processes by the participants with mental retardation in tasks of selective attention was related to increased distractor interference. Taken collectively, these studies suggest that individuals with mental retardation have more difficulty than their peers without mental retardation in controlling the focus of their attention and that, at least part, this difficulty can be traced to deficits in selectively attending to relevant cues.

On the contrary, Merrill, Cha, and Moore (1994) demonstrated that individuals with and without mental retardation show similar negative-priming effects on a location-based task. Thus, individuals with mental retardation may be able to utilize top-down processing to inhibit attention to irrelevant information but did not do so in all experimental contexts (see also Crosby, 1972). Furthermore, the susceptibility of persons with mental retardation to distraction has been shown to be related to the level of task difficulty. For example, Sen and Clarke (1968) found that although adults with mental retardation were distracted by extraneous stimulation during a difficult task, they were unaffected by the same distractors when the task was easy. Similarly, Belmont and Ellis (1968) found that adults with mental retardation were not more distractible than adults without mental retardation. They suggested that some forms of distraction may have no effect or even a facilitative effect upon performance in a learning situation because they act as general arousers, resulting in greater alertness and concomitant improvements in attention.

Although there appears to be some inconsistency between studies, a particular pattern emerges that may help to explain these differences. Specifically, it may be that in tasks in which distractors are similar to the central task stimuli (i.e., the task requires more effortful processing) individuals with mental retardation show decrements in performance, whereas in tasks in which the distractors are easily distinguished from the central task stimuli, no such performance decrements are produced. Altogether, these data suggest that in some instances, individuals with mental retardation have enhanced difficulty in comparison with their peers without mental retardation in attending selectively to relevant cues (Pearson, Norton, and Farwell, 1997). The challenges facing researchers, therefore, are to identify the circumstances in which individuals with mental retardation do and do not demonstrate the ability to limit attention to task-irrelevant distractions and to develop methods and/or presentation formats that facilitate adaptive attending behavior. Additionally, the extent to which the results of laboratory-based studies of attention predict retarded individuals' behavior in educational and training settings remains to be elucidated. It is valuable, then, to determine whether it is possible to facilitate the use of mechanisms of selective attention by persons with mild mental retardation across a range of cognitive tasks.

A characteristic activity that is heavily relied on selective attention is the safe pedestrian behaviour, since one has to focus attention on the traffic environment and ignore irrelevant stimuli. Tabibi and Pfeffer (2003) indicated that attention is required for identifying road-crossing sites quickly and accurately, especially for young typically developing children. Dunbar, Lewis, and Hill (1999) found that 4- to 10-year-old typically developing children who were better at attention switching were more likely to show awareness of traffic when crossing a road, and children who maintained concentration when challenged by a distracting event, crossed the road in a "less reckless" manner. Furthermore, Hill, Lewis, and Dunbar (2000) found that 4- to 9-year-old typically developing children have difficulty paying attention to the features that make a road-crossing situation dangerous; namely, they have difficulty paying attention to relevant information and ignoring irrelevant. Unfortunately, little attention has been paid to the relationship between pedestrian skills and attention for children and adults with mental retardation. A limited number of studies have demonstrated that individuals with mild mental retardation show difficulties to find a safe place to cross the street and supported the need for pedestrian skill instruction (Matson, 1980; Page, Iwata, and Neef, 1976). There has been only one study, which shows that there is a significant relationship between attention and identification of safe and dangerous road-crossing sites in adults with mild mental retardation (Alevriadou, Angelou, and Tsakiridou, 2006).

The aim of the present study was to explore the suppression of irrelevant information of children with and without mental retardation in a non-laboratory task. For the problem at hand, a road-crossing paradigm was adopted. The task was presented by means of a table-top simulation displaying a selection of road-crossing sites varying in complexity in order to investigate the variables influencing children's ability with and without mental retardation to select safe road-crossing sites.

METHOD

Participants

The sample of the study consisted of 104 young individuals. To test their ability to select safe road-crossing sites, the 104 participants were further subdivided into four groups (n=26 per group) matched on mean mental age, using the Raven's Colored Progressive Matrices (Raven, 1965): two groups with mentally retarded children (Group A and Group B) and two groups with typically developing children (Group C and Group D). Group A and Group C were matched on mental age at 5.6 yr.; Group B and Group D were matched on mental age at 8.6 yr. Each pair of groups differed significantly in mean chronological age [Group A (M=7.8 yrs) and Group C (M=5.3 yrs) t=45.99, p<0.01), Group B and Group D (M=10.9 yrs) and Group C (M=8.2 yrs) t=51.19, p<0.01)]. All children with mild mental retardation were receiving special education in the nearest school in their community (inclusive education) and none were living in institutional settings. They were living in the broader area in the city of Kozani, Greece and were referred for diagnosis to the Counseling Centre for children with special needs. None of the children received any specific pedestrian skills instruction.

Group A composed of 26 children (13 boys and 13 girls) with organic mild mental retardation ranging in chronological age from 7.5 to 8.3 yrs (M=7.8 yrs, SD=0.2). Ten of the participants were premature and had anoxia at birth, two had postnatal head trauma, five had encephalitis, two were infected by the rubella in the mother, while the other seven had epilepsy. Group C consisted of 26 typically developing children (13 boys and 13 girls) with chronological ages from 5 to 5.6 yrs (M=5.3 yrs, SD=0.2). All preschoolers recruited from kindergartens. Mean mental age for the typically developing children in this group was 5.4 yrs (SD=0.3).

Group B consisted of 26 children with organic mild mental retardation (13 boys and 13 girls) ranging in chronological age from 10.5 to 11.3 years (M=10.9 yrs, SD=0.2). Ten of the participants were premature and had anoxia at birth, four had postnatal head trauma, five had encephalitis, while the other seven had epilepsy. Group D consisted of 26 typically developing children (13 boys and 13 girls) with chronological ages from 8 to 8.6 yrs (M=8.3 yrs, SD=0.2). All children were recruited from primary schools. The mean mental age for this group was 8.6 yrs (SD=0.2).

Materials

The method involved the use of a large traffic mat measuring approximately 120X100 cm. It comprised a street layout on which a range of trees, buses, and toy cars were placed to create situations similar to those individuals might encounter in the real traffic environment. The task was based on previous research on pedestrian skills (Ampofo-Boateng and Thomson, 1991; Tabibi and Pfeffer, 2002).

The recognition task featured the toy pedestrian standing at the edge of a road facing towards the road. Twenty-five road-crossing sites were represented separately, including one practice trial. Two tasks were designed using the 24 road-crossing sites: a) recognition task without irrelevant information constituted of 12 road-crossing sites in which 6 tasks represented "safe" situations (Condition 1) and 6 tasks served as "unsafe" (dangerous) situations (Condition 2) and b) recognition task with irrelevant information made up of 12 road-crossing sites in which 6 tasks represented "safe" situations (Condition 3) and 6 tasks served as "unsafe" (dangerous) situations (Condition 4). For the recognition task without irrelevant information, distracting visual information was removed from the scene (such as cats, dogs, children playing) allowing the participant to focus on the road site. Concerning the recognition task with irrelevant information, 6 unanimated distractions were included (fixed landscape) (Condition 5) as well as 6 animated distractions (Condition 6). Table 1 outlines the irrelevant information incorporated into specific road-crossing sites.

The situations were all matched as far as possible for complexity and surrounding layout. The sites included junctions, bends, parked cars or other obstructions. In constructing the sites, care was taken that each was rendered dangerous by the presence of only one of these features. Selection of the sites in both tasks was done with the aid of the Hellenic Ministry of Education (Road Safety Educational Programs). A range of possible situations was presented to independent judges who evaluated them. Only situations that showed 100 per cent agreement as to their manifest safety or danger were selected for use.

Road-crossing sites were presented in random order with a 1-min interval between trials. Trials were not time limited. Every individual was tested individually by a certified psychologist. Road-crossing sites information was recorded on a standard data collection form. Correct identification of a safe road-crossing site in each Condition was given 1 point. No point was given for identification of a safe road-crossing site.

**Table 1. Road-crossing sites with irrelevant information
presented in random order to participants**

Crossing site	Irrelevant information added	Safe/Dangerous identification
Straight road	Fixed landscape (unanimated)	Safe
Zebra crossing	Fixed landscape (unanimated)	Dangerous
Blind bend	Children playing in park with a ball (animated)	Dangerous
Pelican crossing (with green man)	Cat waking in a park (animated)	Safe
Roundabout	Fixed landscape (unanimated)	Dangerous
Traffic island	Fixed landscape (unanimated)	Safe
Traffic lights on red	Fixed landscape (unanimated)	Safe
Parked cars	Road construction (animated)	Safe
Road-crossing patrol	A gardener working at a flower-bed near the road (animated)	Dangerous
Brow of a hill	Fixed landscape (unanimated)	Dangerous
Junction	Cyclist (animated)	Safe
Traffic lights on green	A street cleaner with a push broom (animated)	Dangerous

Procedure

Informed consent was obtained before the investigation from the parents of all included children. According to our national and institutional guidelines for ethical review, institutional review board approval was not necessary. All children with mild mental retardation were examined in the Counseling Center, while typically developing children at school. The pedestrian task conditions were presented randomly to the participants. The examination was performed on individual basis. The pedestrian toy was positioned near to each of the road-crossing locations and each child was asked to judge whether should ("safe") or should not ("dangerous") cross the road. Depending on the participant's speed of performance, the task took 15 minutes to complete for groups C and D and around 25 minutes for groups A and B.

STATISTICAL ANALYSIS

The collected data were analyzed statistically. "Student's" t-test for independent samples was used to compare mean performance scores in task conditions between a) Group A and Group C and b) Group B and Group D. For the said purpose, statistical software package (SPSS/PC+ version 13.0, SPSS Inc., Chicago, Illinois) was used. A P-value less than 5% ($P < 0.05$) was taken as statistically significant.

RESULTS

The comparison of the mean performance scores in task conditions between mentally retarded children (Group A) and typically developing children (Group C) are shown in table 2.

Table 2. Mean performance scores in task conditions between Group A and Group C

Task Condition	Group A	Group C	t	p
Condition 1	M=3.19	M=3.50	t=1.73	ns
Condition 2	M=3.15	M=3.42	t=1.73	ns
Condition 3	M=2.15	M=2.50	t=2.56	p<0.05
Condition 4	M=2.12	M=2.54	t=2.77	p<0.01
Condition 5	M=2.96	M=3.31	t=3.02	p<0.01
Condition 6	M=1.31	M=1.73	t=2.88	p<0.01

The comparison of the mean performance scores in task conditions between mentally retarded children (Group B) and typically developing children (Group D) are illustrated in table 3.

Table 3. Mean performance scores in task conditions between Group B and Group D

Task Condition	Group B	Group D	t	p
Condition 1	M=4.81	M=4.96	t=0.75	ns
Condition 2	M=4.54	M=4.92	t=2.07	p<0.05
Condition 3	M=2.54	M=4.04	t=9.16	p<0.01
Condition 4	M=2.50	M=4.04	t=9.38	p<0.01
Condition 5	M=3.19	M=5.04	t=10.79	p<0.01
Condition 6	M=1.85	M=3.04	t=7.097	p<0.01

CONCLUSION

This investigation was undertaken with the purpose of exploring the suppression of irrelevant information of children with and without mental retardation in a non-laboratory task. The present data demonstrated significant differences between the mean performance scores of the Group A and Group C in Conditions 3, 4, 5 and 6. The score of the Group A was lower than that of the Group C. This finding, in accordance with previous evidence (Cha and Merrill, 1994; Merrill and Taube, 1996) seems to suggest that individuals with mental retardation have enhanced difficulty in comparison with their typically developing mental age controls in attending selectively via the visual mode to road-crossing sites, especially when irrelevant information stimuli are involved. In other words, mentally retarded individuals are more distracted by the presence of irrelevant information stimuli than are typically developing individuals. The selection of one stimulus over another is likely to involve not only facilitatory or excitatory processes directed toward the selected target, but also inhibition or suppression processes that operate to minimize responding to non-target stimuli (Tipper, 1985). Mentally retarded participants are, thus, less efficient in suppressing non-target information than typically developing participants (Cha and Merrill, 1994). Hence, this may result in performance decrements across a variety of tasks. Research data demonstrates that 5 years old typically developing children are particularly poor at distinguishing safe and unsafe traffic locations, especially when they involve irrelevant stimuli (Ampofo-Boateng and Thomson, 1991). The absence of significant differences between the mean performance scores of the Group A and Group C in Conditions 1 and 2, may be attributed to the fact that these tasks did not involve irrelevant information. It seems that these conditions are easy for both groups A and C, although they demand judging safe and unsafe traffic sites. Additionally, both groups A and C responded more efficiently to a road-crossing target without irrelevant information as compared to one with distractors, following the same developmental pattern (Group A: Condition 1 and 2=3.19 and 3.15 vs Condition 3 and 4= 2.15 and 2.12 respectively, Group C: Condition 1 and 2=3.50 and 3.42 vs Condition 3and 4= 2.50 and 2.54 respectively).

Our findings also illustrated significant differences between the mean performance scores of the Group B and Group D in Conditions 2, 3, 4, 5 and 6. The score of the Group B was lower compared with that of the Group D. This result is in line with earlier claims that individuals with organic mental retardation (Down syndrome) have difficulties filtering irrelevant auditory (Miezejeski, 1974) or visual (Merrill and O' Dekirk, 1994) stimuli. The observed difference may be ascribed to the incapability of the individuals with mental retardation to utilize inhibitory mechanisms of selective attention (see also Houghton, Tipper, Weaver, and Shore, 1996). It seems that mentally retarded individuals exhibit poorer selection skills and smaller suppression effects than do typically developing individuals (Hagen and Huntsman, 1971), showing some kind of cognitive inertia (Ellis and Dulaney, 1991; Dulaney and Ellis, 1997). Hasher and Zacks (1988) suggested that these suppression processes may be important components of attention. If irrelevant stimuli are not effectively suppressed, they continue to demand processing resources associated with limited capacity working memory. This would reduce the functional capacity of working memory for the processing of relevant stimuli, and, as a consequence, the efficiency of processing relevant information would be reduced. Hence, inefficient stimulus suppression processes may result in performance decrements for individuals with mental retardation across a variety of tasks (Tomporowski and Tinsley, 1997).

The absence of significant differences between the mean performance scores of the Group B and Group D in Condition 1 may be assigned to the fact that this is the easiest task for both groups. Several studies have shown that typically developing children differentiate better safe than dangerous crossing sites, especially when there aren't any distractors involved (Ampofo-Boateng and Thomson, 1991; Young and Lee, 1987). The same pattern seems to exist in mentally retarded individuals.

Irrelevant information affected the ability of the individuals with, as well as without, mental retardation. This is consistent with published results on attention (Tabibi and Pfeffer, 2003), which suggest that the animated distractions (adding more visual information) may have been sufficiently demanding for all the participants (Groups A and C, B and D). An increase in irrelevant information may highlight the vulnerability of all participants to interference more. On the other hand, mentally retarded individuals experience enhanced difficulty inhibiting the influence of distractors (i.e. Condition 6 –animated irrelevant information) than typically developing individuals. This explains the fact that the performance of all groups in Condition 6 is the lowest compared with all the other

Conditions. On the other hand, there are statistically significant differences between mentally retarded and typically developing individuals in both mental age groups (Group A =1.31 vs Group C=1.73, Group B=1.85 vs Group D=3.04).

As an alternative to this view, a metacognitive explanation might be supposed that the mentally retarded retardation did not judge right if the road-crossing condition was safe or dangerous. But metacognitive factors themselves cannot fully explain the whole findings. Additionally, motivational factors can also partially explain the differences found between Group B and Group D. One key factor hypothesized to affect the observed behavior in mental retardation is the history of failure in independent problem solving (Weisz, 1979). The greater history of failure that children with mental retardation experience in applying their own solutions to problems, the greater the amount of outer-directedness (reliance mainly on external cues rather than on their internal cognitive abilities to solve a task or problem) they show compared to typically developing children (Bybee and Zigler, 1998). Researchers generally report declines in outer-directedness among typically developing children at higher mental ages (Yando and Zigler, 1971; MacMillan and Wright, 1974). As typically developing children get older, they become more inner-directed, trusting their own solutions to problems. On the contrary, declines in outer-directedness are found much less consistently in older mentally retarded children (Bybee and Zigler, 1998). Again, motivational factors cannot fully explain the difference, especially between groups A and C.

In summary, our results indicate that selective attention is, at least, partially required for identifying road-crossing sites accurately. Although there are statistical significant differences in both mental age groups in favor of the typically developing participants, the differences are quantitative in nature. It seems that there are some qualitative similar patterns between participants with and without mental retardation. For example, the crossing sites that produced the most errors for all groups were the junction, the blind bend and the brow of a hill (especially when they were escorted by distractors) (this is a typical finding for typically developing children, see also Ampofo-Boateng and Thomson, 1991). Similarly, all groups, both at higher and lower mental age, had better performance in conditions involving unanimated than animated distractors. Another interesting finding is that the crossing site of the parked cars was judged automatically dangerous on the basis of the cars for both mentally retarded and typically developing individuals, especially at the lower mental age.

The present research findings highlight the need to design road-safety training programs for children with mental retardation. Presenting participants with a large traffic mat under controlled conditions facilitates the focusing of attention to the task in hand. This type of technique may have potential as a simple and attractive training device that might be used in the classroom to improve at least some aspects of mentally retarded children's road knowledge and skill. Whilst in the end there can be no substitute for training in realistic situations, it is possible that preliminary training using models might provide a basis on which in situ training might build. On the other side, the real pedestrian environment is even more demanding than the traffic mat used. It is more likely to provide interfering and distracting stimuli.

Standen, Brown, and Cromby (2001) stated that virtual environments appear to be a fruitful method of teaching skills for independent living to people with mental retardation. Standen and Brown (2005) stated that virtual reality can provide a safe setting in which to practice road safety skills that might carry too many risks in the real world especially for individuals with mental retardation. Similarly, Foot, Tolmie, Thomson, McLaren, and

Whelan (1999) suggested that computer-based tasks may be useful for training in pedestrian skills. Relevant attention skills may also be trained in this way. The advantages of such tasks are that they allow control of variables, can be used to develop specific skills and are attractive to children and adults with intellectual disabilities. Alevriadou et al. (2006) conducted preliminary studies on using computer animations to teach children with intellectual disabilities how to identify safe and dangerous road-crossing sites with encouraging results. Many of these studies showed some transfer of learning from the virtual to the real world for individuals with intellectual disabilities (see also the "virtual city" by Brown, Neale, and Cobb, 1999).

Further research is needed to determine which aspects of attention are most important for safe pedestrian behavior and the type of distractions that are most deleterious for child pedestrians with and without mental retardation. Additionally, the operation of distractor interferences, which is higher in some conditions than others, indicates that one important area for future research may be to analyze the precise conditions under which group differences in selective attention processes can and cannot be obtained.

REFERENCES

Alevriadou, A., Angelou, I., and Tsakiridou, E. (2006). The relationship between attention and identification of safe and dangerous road crossing sites in adults with mild ID. *Journal of Applied Research in Intellectual Disabilities*, 19(3), 239.

Ampofo-Boateng, K., and Thomson, J. (1991). Children's perception of safety and danger on the road. *British Journal of Psychology*, 82, 487-505.

Belmont, J.M., and Ellis, N.R. (1968). Effects of extraneous stimulation upon discrimination learning in normals and retardates. *American Journal of Mental Deficiency*, 72, 525-532.

Bergen, A-M. E., and Mosley, J.L. (1994). Attention and attentional shift efficiency in individuals with and without mental retardation. *American Journal on Mental Retardation*, 98, 688-743.

Broadbent, D.E. (1982). Task combination and selective intake of information. *Acta Psychologica*, 50, 253-290.

Brown, D.J. Neale, H., and Cobb, S.V. (1999). The development and evaluation of the virtual city. *International Journal of Virtual Reality*, 4, 28-41.

Bybee, J., and Zigler, E. (1998) Outer-directedness in individuals with and without mental retardation: A review. In J. Burack, R. Hodapp, and E. Zigler (Eds.), *Handbook of mental retardation and development* (pp. 434-461). Cambridge, UK: Cambridge University Press.

Cha, K-H. (1992). The effect of flanking context and its time course in focused attention processes of mentally retarded and nonretarded persons. *Dissertation Abstracts International*, 53, 2087.

Cha, K-H., and Merrill, E.C. (1994). Facilitation and inhibition effects in visual selective attention processes of persons with and without mental retardation. *American Journal on Mental Retardation*, 98, 594-600.

Crosby, K.G. (1972). Attention and distractibility in mentally retarded children. *American Journal of Mental Deficiency*, 77, 46-53.

Dulaney, C., and Ellis, N. (1997). Rigidity in the behavior of mentally retarded persons. In W. E. MacLean (Ed.), *Ellis' Handbook of mental deficiency, psychological theory and research* (pp. 175-195). Mahwah, NJ: Erlbaum.

Dunbar, G., Lewis, V., and Hill, R. (1999). Control processes and road-crossing skills. *Psychologist*, 12, 398-399.

Ellis, N.R., and Dulaney, C.L. (1991). Further evidence for cognitive inertia of persons with mental retardation. *American Journal on Mental Retardation*, 95, 613-621.

Ellis, N.R., Woodley-Zanthos, P., Dulaney, C.L., and Palmer, R.L. (1989). Automatic-effortful processing and cognitive inertia in persons with mental retardation. *American Journal on Mental Retardation*, 93, 412-423.

Foot, H., Tolmie, A., Thomson, J., McLaren, B., and Whelan K. (1999). *Recognizing the hazards. Psychologist*, 12, 400-402.

Hagen, J.W., and Huntsman, N. (1971). Selective attention and mental retardation. *Developmental Psychology*, 5, 151-160.

Hasher, L., and Zacks, R.T. (1988). Working memory, comprehension, and aging: A review and a new view. In G.H. Bower (Ed.), *The psychology of learning and motivation* (Vol. 22, pp. 193-225). San Diego: Academic Press.

Hill, R., Lewis, V., and Dunbar, G. (2000). Young children's concepts of danger. *British Journal of Developmental Psychology*, 18, 103-120.

Holowinsky, I.V., and Farrelly, J. (1988). Intentional and incidental visual memory as a function of cognitive level and color of the stimulus. *Perceptual and Motor Skills*, 66, 775-779.

Houghton, G., Tipper, S.P., Weaver, B., and Shore, D.I. (1996). Inhibition and interference in selective attention: Some tests of a neural network model. Visual Cognition, 3, 119-164.

MacMillan, D., and Wright, D. (1974). Outer-directedness in children of three ages as a function of experimentally induced success and failure. *Journal of Experimental Psychology*, 66, 919-925.

Matson, J.L. (1980). A controlled group study of pedestrian-skill training for the mentally retarded. *Behavior Research and Therapy*, 18, 99-106.

Merill, E.C. (1990). Resources allocation and mental retardation. In N.W. Bray (Ed.), *International Review of Research in Mental Retardation* (Vol. 16, pp. 51-88). Hillsdale, NJ: Erlbaum.

Merill, E.C. (2006). Interference and inhibition in tasks of selective attention by persons with and without mental retardation. *American Journal on Mental Retardation*, 111, 216-226.

Merrill, E.C., Cha, K-H., and Moore, A.L. (1994). The inhibition of location information by persons with and without mental retardation. *American Journal on Mental Retardation*, 99, 207-214.

Merrill, E.C., and O' Dekirk, J.M. (1994). Selective attention and mental retardation. *Cognitive Neuropsychology*, 10, 117-132.

Merrill, E.C., and Taube, M. (1996). Negative priming and mental retardation: The processing of distractor information. *American Journal on Mental Retardation*, 101, 63-71.

Miezejeski, C.M. (1974). Effect of white noise on the reaction time of mentally retarded subjects. *American Journal of Mental Deficiency*, 79, 39-43.

Neil. W.T. (1977). Inhibitory and facilitory processes in selective attention. *Journal of Experimental Psychology: Human Perception and Performance*, 3, 444-450.

Neil. W.T., and Westberry, R.L. (1987). Selective attention and the suppression of cognitive noise. *Journal of Experimental Psychology:Learning, Memory, and Cognition*, 13, 327-334.

Nugent, P.M., and Mosley, J.L. (1987). Mentally retarded and nonretarded individuals' attention allocation and capacity. *American Journal of Mental Deficiency*, 91, 598-605.

Page, T.J., Iwata, B.A., and Neef, N.A. (1976). Teaching pedestrian skills to retarded persons: Generalization from the classroom to the natural environment. *Journal of Applied Behavior Analysis*, 9, 433-444.

Parasuraman, R., and Davies, D.R. (Eds.). (1984). *Varieties of attention*. New York: Academic Press.

Pearson, D.A., Norton, A.N., and Farwell, E.C. (1997). Attention-deficit/hyperactivity in mental retardation: Nature of attention deficits. In J.A. Burack and J.T. Enns (Eds.), Attention, *development, and psychopathology* (pp. 205-231). New York, NY: Guilford Press.

Raven, J.C. (1965). *Guide to using the Colored Progressive Matrices*. London: Lewis.

Sen, A., and Clarke, A.M. (1968). Some factors affecting distractibility in the mental retardate. *American Journal of Mental Deficiency*, 73, 50-60.

Standen, P.J., and Brown, D.J. (2005). Virtual reality in the rehabilitation of people with intellectual disabilities. *Review. Cyber Psychology and Behavior*, 8(3), 272-282.

Standen, P.J., Brown, D.J., and Cromby, J.J. (2001). The effective use of virtual environments in the education and rehabilitation of students with intellectual disabilities. *British Journal of Educational Technology*, 32(3), 289-299.

Tabibi, Z., and Pfeffer, K. (2003). Choosing a safe place to cross the road: The relationship between attention and identification of safe and dangerous road-crossing sites. *Child: Care, Health and Development*, 29, 237-244.

Terdal, L.G. (1967). Stimulus satiation and mental retardation. *American Journal of Mental Deficiency*, 71, 881-885.

Tipper, S.P. (1985). The negative priming effect: Inhibitory effect of ignored primes. *Quarterly Journal of Experimental Psychology*, 37A, 571-590.

Tomporowski, P.D., and Tinsley, V. (1997). Attention in mentally retarded persons. In W.E. MacLean (Ed.), Ellis' *handbook of mental deficiency, psychological theory and research* (3rd ed., pp. 219-241). Hillsdale, NJ: Erlbaum.

Weisz, J. (1979) Perceived control and learned helplessness among mentally retarded and nonretarded children: A developmental analysis. *Developmental Psychology*, 15, 311-319.

Yando, R., and Zigler, E. (1971). Outer-directedness in the problem-solving of institutionalized and nonistitutionalized normally developing and retarded children. *Developmental Psychology*, 4, 277-288.

Young, D.S., and Lee, D.N. (1987). Training children in road crossing skills using a roadside simulation. *Accident Analysis and Prevention*, 19, 327-341.

INDEX

B

C

D

F

G

N

S

W

Y